Jail and Prison

Opportunity of a Lifetime

Victor Johnson

Jail and Prison

 www.heartsup.org

Cover design by Bell Media. Colorado Springs, CO

ISBN: 978-0-9822295-7-6

Printed in the United States of America

Heartsup!

CONTENTS

FOREWORD

I asked my dad if I could write a foreword for this book. That might seem a pretentious or presumptuous request, but reading through the lenses of those outside the prison system, I felt compelled to plug this book for "the rest of us." Unlike those who are incarcerated or in transition to the outside world, many of us have "got our stuff together": we have college degrees, spouses to come home to, two cars in the garage, two kids, a dog and a decent paycheck. We read science journals, invest in stock, and coach soccer. Some of us even go to church; others of us are even active in church, and we're pretty proud of ourselves. Or because we're "spiritual but not religious," we won't read a book packed with Bible references. This is the book we might give to "those who need it." Not ourselves.

That is because this book (or parts of it) will likely be offensive to those who haven't hit the proverbial brick wall. While inmates may receive its words as life-saving gulps of water, others of us might hear the voice of an "old fogey" at times in the following pages. It's the same voice I remember well from all those mornings as a teenager sitting at the snack bar in the kitchen where I grew up; Dad would sit across from me with his big honkin' Bible open, basically using the scriptures to tell me how to live my life. I don't remember, but I imagine I must have sat there looking like my teens sometimes do now when I'm "having devotions" with them – *Are they even listening to a word I'm saying?* I wonder, as I curse the day Snapchat was invented. The fact that Dad's words sunk in and took root gives me hope that I may be getting through to my own kids, despite the "fogey factor" I perceive in their distant eyeballs at times.

I say "offensive" because, while the stories in this book are at times wildly entertaining, other parts of these pages are hard to read. You won't hear this stuff on the lips of most televangelists or find it in the self-improvement section at Barnes & Noble. Truth be told, I've never heard much of this from many church pulpits. Yet it's straight out of the Bible, plain as day, and the references are here to prove it. Dad highlights the parts of scripture we've largely ignored in the modern western church. The parts that make us uncomfortable, disturbed, or even angry. The parts that poke and prod at our private lives, wherein we've convinced ourselves God isn't all that concerned. We hide our secret and not-so-secret sins behind our backs while we ask God to keep blessing and providing, to keep healing and delivering, and then wonder why He never comes through.

As a pastor I've had the opportunity to counsel people suffering with PTSD, anger, depression and anxiety. I'm always honest about the fact that I'm not credentialed as a therapist, but often my "clients" have exhausted those resources and are coming to me as a last resort. I simply apply the wisdom in this book, that which brought Dad out of twenty years of suicidal depression. And I have seen amazing results.

Christians are called to be a "light" in this dark world; I like to think of Dad as a laser beam cutting away at cancerous flesh. Those who recognize they are spiritually terminal (even as they live the American Dream) will run to the words of this book and gratefully receive them as from one who skillfully detects and removes that which is silently devouring them from the inside out. If you become daringly humble, I promise you'll hear, not the cutting remarks of a strict moralist (he is far from that, as you'll learn), but the hope-filled words of a sage.

Biblical scholars and the biblically illiterate alike will find the words in this book shockingly profound as Dad gets to the heart of our relationship issues with God and with people, and sheds light on the value of suffering. The wisdom in these pages is truly rare; savor it. You'll want to mark it up and make notes, so get an extra copy for a friend – inside or outside of prison. Truth be told, we've all "done time" in some kind of "prison" and, deep down, long for the freedom and authenticity that only Christ can give us. This book will help unlock that door.

Faith

ACKNOWLEDGMENTS

I wish to thank and express my deep appreciation to the chaplains at Brevard Correctional Institution (now closed), Brevard County Jail (Cocoa, FL), and Central Florida Reception Center (Orlando), as well as many of the officers there and at the Department of Juvenile Justice and Work Release Center, all of whom guided and inspired me, as well as my pastors who "covered" me since 1993. But I have two people I especially want to mention by name, without whom there would be no book.

Actually, I don't remember the name of the first person, an African-American nurse at Brevard County Jail. One evening as I started off to one of my Bible classes, she handed me five or six books she had written specifically for jail inmates. Each printed book cost her two dollars, and every time she saved two hundred dollars from her work as a nurse, she'd have another one hundred copies printed and then distribute them to the inmates. Her example humbled, shamed, and alerted me to my responsibility as a steward of what God had taught me over the years.

I read her books, returned them to the jail for the inmates, and pulled out of my computer files an article I'd written describing my theological journey from legalism to faith, ending a twenty-year period of severe suicidal depression. I began distributing the article – "How to Escape the Guilt Trap and Walk in the Spirit" – at the prisons and jail in 2003.

The print was so small (8 point) that Joe Hurston, missionary-aviator and owner of Cartridge Source of America, joked about it, then volunteered his son, Chris, to reset it in 12 point type, double the pages from four to eight, and gave me 800 hand-folded copies free! Plus *gave* me my first laser printer! (Thank you, my brother Joe – and Chris!)

I've since rewritten, shortened, and simplified the story, now available as the first chapter in this book. My nurse friend had all her books printed in LARGE print for the benefit of the many inmates who need reading glasses. I can't wait to meet her by her "new name" in heaven some day (Rv 2:17; 3:12).

The second person's name I do remember – a lifetime friend and fellow-pastor in the late 1970s. Jerry Charles, owner of Peak Vista Press. He started his own printing and publishing company back in those days in North Carolina and urged me to give him something to publish. I didn't take him seriously, nor did I think I had anything worthy of publishing. Then a few years ago he again began pestering me about publishing my articles. Again I put him off for the same two reasons, but told him to look at my website where I have most of them. End of discussion, I thought.

Imagine my surprise, then, when in the mail I find four copies of my book, composed of every article on my website, plus the last (2011) Christmas letter I'd sent him. That's when I decided to take him seriously and began editing, rewriting, and writing more for *our* first book.

But he had no idea he was working with someone with OCD, who would put him through *years* of tribulation and testing as I've re-written, changed, and added things, trying to get it *perfect*. And *no charge for his work!* Because he has seen the need, as I have, of ministering to our friends locked away by their issues and backgrounds, and waiting for "the spirit of wisdom and revelation in the knowledge of Him" – Jesus! (Eph 1:17).

Oh yes, I can't forget the many inmates over the years who have profoundly influenced me, taught me, encouraged me, corrected me, forgiven me when I'd gotten dogmatic or offensive, endured me when I was dry and windy, and *prayed for me*. You may not be aware of how much you meant to me, but I owe you my deepest, heartfelt gratitude. Thank you, thank you, and I say this through tears. Your reward awaits you in heaven. Because God has not forgotten you.

And finally, my wife and my daughter, a published author. My wife found scores of typos, spellings, and other mistakes I'd somehow missed, and my daughter still more. Between the two of them I ended up rewriting, rearranging, adding, and omitting chapters, which I plan to include in book two, or this book would have been much longer.

Truly we believers are all part of the same Body of Christ and need one another. Someday we may know how little any of us did on our own through God's grace, and how intricately connected we were to many unknown and unnamed members of that same Body.

PREFACE

One of the most well-known of Jesus' parables is that of "the Prodigal Son" (Lu 15:11–32). For years I've enjoyed painting a verbal picture of this paradox before a class of jail inmates:

A father has two sons. His youngest is an immature kid who wants his inheritance *now*, then leaves home and blows the whole thing on wild living – booze and prostitutes. If they'd had drugs back then, it would certainly have included them also. When he runs out of money and friends and ends up working in a hog-pen with nothing to eat except what he fed the pigs, he comes to his senses and returns home, willing to work as one of his dad's hired servants.

Meanwhile his older brother has taken *responsibility* for his inheritance, possibly invested it back into the family business, and continues faithfully working with his dad in virtual, if not actual, partnership with him. He's a perfect role model for every value Jesus and the Bible taught about faithfulness and integrity. He should be the one his dad throws a party for when this wasted kid returns looking for a better job than living with pigs (Mt 25:14–30; Lk 12:42–44; 19:12–26; 2 Tim 3:10).

Instead, his dad treats this no-good deserter who threw his inheritance away, like royalty, putting a ring on his finger, a robe in place of his hog-pen-stinking rags, and kills an expensive "fatted calf" for a huge banquet in his honor! No wonder the older brother is quite upset. It does seem as though Jesus is undoing everything He'd taught about faithfulness, endurance, honesty, and honoring one's parents (Mt 25:21; Lk 16:10–12; 18:20).

But of course, the deeper lesson is that of the heart. It's "a broken and contrite heart" God is after, even if it takes ruining your whole life to get there. "For God has committed them all to disobedience, that He might have mercy on all. Oh, the depth of the riches both of the wisdom and knowledge of God! How unsearchable are His judgments and His ways past finding out!" (Rom 11:32–33; Ps 51:17).

For if the older brother really is an example of what God is looking for, he should be right there helping with the banquet and embracing his long lost brother, hardly able to contain himself for joy at seeing a brother with a whole new attitude (Lk 15:10; Rom 12:15; 1 Cor 12:26).

This parable sets the scene for jail and prison. Or at least I thought it did until I got a little closer to these men and realized many of them struggle with the same attitude the *older* brother had: anger, jealousy, a feeling of betrayal, disgust with the system, a sense of entitlement, and blaming instead of forgiving those who did them wrong (Num 21:5–7; Phil 2:14–16; 1 Thes 5:18; Heb 7:15; 12:15).

They *could* be enjoying a heavenly banquet, feasting on the riches of God's grace abounding "where sin abounds." But instead they are "killing time" getting "institutionalized" and becoming more like the criminals around them instead of the saints God created them to be (Rom 5:20; Prv 13:20; 1 Cor 15:33; Eph 2:10; Col 1:27–29; 1 Pet 2:9; 2 Pet 2:18–20).

But thankfully, not all. I've also observed some of the finest men in the world, the top-of-the-line in most every field, from a world-class weight lifter, to millionaires in business, to doctorates in medicine, science, even theology. Ministers, pastors, military men and officers, artists, and musicians (Lk 20:21; Rom 2:11; Gal 3:28; Col 2:11).

And best of all, men who've been so mellowed and humbled by their failures and the chastening of the Lord, and who've grown in grace and wisdom, I feel honored to know and fellowship with them, and sometimes wonder what I'm doing teaching them, when they should be teaching me. And sometimes they do, in class rap-sessions, one-on-one fellowship, and when they share their testimony before the group (Mt 5:16; Eph 6:21; Col 4:9–14).

One prison inmate was the pianist for a well-known contemporary Christian recording artist. I asked him to lead worship from the chapel piano. We had some of the most awesome, glorious worship services I'd ever experienced in prison while he was there (Ps 33:3).

One of my friends there is an orthopedic surgeon who gives

me medical advice frequently, and got my wife through a frightening experience with a damaged ankle. Another gave me a full-page hand-written warning from the Lord, and it was right on! (1 Cor 12:1–27; Col 4:14; 2 Tim 4:11).

Inmates have given me advice for the work I do on my job (home-rental property maintenance): everything from air conditioning to automotive – skilled, experienced experts. This is the gold mine! I love every minute of it, and consider it the most precious experience in my whole life, and for which all my previous years of affliction and depression prepared me (1 Cor 12:21–23).

Sure, there are plenty of phonies. Like the guy growing a long beard so he could plead insanity. At least he was open enough to ask my advice. When I told him this charade was a mockery to the God he claimed to love so much, his beard was stylishly short the next time I saw him (Rom 12:9; 1 Pet 2:1).

And interestingly, God uses that wicked jail-environment as the *best* background to test and develop those whose attention He's gotten. It's like weight training or body-building. The stress of the weights breaks down muscle tissue, placing a high-protein demand to rebuild stronger muscle (Ps 66:10–12; Jer 15:16; Heb 5:13–14; 1 Pet 1:7).

That's where we chaplain volunteers come in, to aid the chaplain in providing a high-protein *spiritual* diet in hopes of watching these God-seekers put on supernatural strength for battles they face in jail and will face with satanic ferocity when they get out (Dt 8:3; Ps 78:24-25; Prv 24:10; Jer 12:5).

This book is actually a collection of many of the articles I've been writing and passing out to jail and prison inmates. I've purposely listed multiple scripture references throughout to give greater clarity to those who, to my joy, actually do take the time to look each reference up, making it quality devotional time (1 Cor 2:13; Col 3:16; 2 Tim 3:15–17; Jas 1:18; 1 Pet 2:2; 2 Pet 1:2–4, 23; 1 Jn 3:9).

"Be diligent to present yourself approved to God, a worker who does not need to be ashamed, rightly dividing the word of truth" (2 Tim 2:15; 3:15; Acts 17:11).

What scares me is when I see some of them walking these

principles out better than I am. It thrills me but also frightens me to think that while I teach others these awesome truths, I myself could be "disqualified" – "benched" on the sidelines, out of the game – for lack of personal diligence of my own, as Paul clearly warns (1 Cor 9:27).

So in fear and trembling, I offer what God has "freely given me" to my brothers and sisters, in hopes it will help them grow with me, "till we all come to the unity of the faith and of the knowledge of the Son of God, to a perfect man, to the measure of the stature of the fullness of Christ" (Eph 4:13; 1 Cor 2:12; Lk 8:15).

Note: Unless otherwise noted, all italics are mine throughout the book.

INTRODUCTION

A Web search on "fatherlessness and crime" brought up thousands of sites linking fatherlessness with "virtually every major social pathology," including "violent crime, drug and alcohol abuse, truancy, teen pregnancy, suicide. . . . The majority of prisoners, juvenile detention inmates, high school dropouts, pregnant teenagers, adolescent murderers, and rapists all come from fatherless homes."[1]

However, as already indicated, a dysfunctional, fatherless family may also provide a greater opportunity to know God than a normal, happy family. *It could well be the single greatest lost opportunity in the world.* Every "chapter" in this collection of articles is designed to give insight and understanding of how to turn your past "if onlys" into sheer glory.

Dysfunctional families produce spiritual giants, and a hostile environment is the perfect ingredient for spiritual greatness. Think of having Adam and Eve for parents; what stories they would have told of how they walked with God in the Garden of Eden, how they sinned by eating of the Tree of Knowledge, and of the lessons they learned as God restored them back to fellowship with Him. Yet their first child, in a fit of jealousy, murdered his younger brother (Gen 3–4).

Enoch is one of three of the greatest men of God (with Moses and Elijah) in the Old Testament. He stayed so close to God he walked right into heaven without dying. What a privilege to have had him for a father. But of all his "sons and daughters," we know of only one who followed in his footsteps – Methuselah (Gen 5:21–25; Heb 11:5).

Methuselah's children took the same road to disaster, apparently, except for Lamech, and so did Lamech's kids! With one exception again – Noah. When Lamech finally died at 777 years old, Noah and his family were the only godly people left in a world filled with total violence, including hundreds of children, grandchildren, and close relatives of the above great men of God. So God sent the Flood and started over with Noah and his three sons. That covers the first 10 generations from Adam, recorded in Genesis 5 and 6.

Ten generations later, and again almost all of Noah's descendants have "gone astray," so God starts over with Abraham, whose father and siblings were all idol-worshipers! But Abraham, through an unwise decision, caused major turmoil and a split in his home between Ishmael and Isaac (Gen chaps 12, 16–17, 21; Is 53:6).

Then Isaac saw the same tragic division between his twin boys – Jacob and Esau – that lasted many generations as war between Israel (of Jacob) and Edom (of Esau). And the wicked Herod-kings during the time of Christ and the apostles were Idumeans – descendants of Esau! (Gen 25:21–34; 27:1–46; Num 20:20; 1 Kgs 11:14; 2 Kgs 8:20–2; 2 Chr 25:20; Is 34:5–6; Jer 49:17–22; Ez 25:12–14; Ob 1:1ff (ff means "following" verses); Mt 2:1–19; Lk 23:7–15; Acts 12:1–21).

Isaac's godly son Jacob produced one of the most dysfunctional families ever: incest, treachery, jealousy, false imprisonment, deception, and mass murder. God disqualified his first three sons, one after the other, as unfit for the leadership role of the family (Gen 34:13–31; 35:22; 37:11–35; 49:1–7).

Judah, the fourth of Jacob's sons, was no better, and in some ways worse. The only one of Jacob's sons who married an ungodly Canaanite, God destroyed his two oldest sons for their wickedness, and then he, Judah, nearly burned his daughter-in-law to death for getting pregnant, not realizing it was his *own* baby – twins, as it turned out!

Yet Judah and Joseph, the half-brother Judah had sold into slavery, ended up as two of the most important role models for godliness in the Bible – *especially Judah!* (Gen 37:26–28; 38:1–26; 43:8–9; 44:16–34; 49:8–12; 1 Chr 5:1–2; Rv 5:5).

Aaron, brother of Moses and appointed by God as the first high priest of the new nation, Israel, had four sons, who had also been appointed priests. But God slew his two oldest for their disobedience not long after "they saw the God of Israel" and "the very heavens in its clarity," and "did eat and drink" there with Him (Ex 24:9–11; Lev 10:1–2; Eccl 7:8).

The father of Gideon, one of Israel's godly rulers, was a Baal worshiper, and Gideon's son Abimelech was one of the most wicked men in the entire Bible. Jephthah was kicked out of the family by his brothers because he was born through his dad's sex with a prostitute. But he led Israel in victory over her enemies and became one of her godly rulers (Lev 10; Jgs 6, 9, 11; Heb 11:32).

The prophet Samuel was raised away from his father, and his surrogate dad was Eli the priest, who's horrible failure as a father cost him and his biological sons their lives. Yet Samuel's "sons did not walk in his ways; they turned aside after dishonest gain, took bribes, and perverted justice" (Sam 1, 3-4; 8:3).

King Saul turned out to be almost another Hitler, but his son Jonathan was one of the most godly and humble men in the Bible (1 Sam chap 14, 18–22).

David, a "man after God's own heart," was one of the worst father-role-models in the Bible, failing to discipline his sons, losing three of them through murder, and execution, and another through death in consequence of his adulterous affair with Bathsheba and his murder of her husband, Uriah. Yet out of that relationship (he had at least seven other wives) came the wisest and greatest king ever – Solomon (2 Sam 11–19; 1 Kgs 1, 3, 10–11; 1 Chr 3:1–9; Mt 12:42).

But despite all Solomon's wisdom about fathering and disciplining children, his son Rehoboam "forsook the law of the Lord, and all Israel along with him" (2 Chr 12:1; Prv 22:6, 15; 23:13, 24; 29:15).

When you read Kings and Chronicles, you'll notice that some of the worst kings came from the most godly fathers and some of the best kings came from the most wicked fathers. Yet out of all the mix and mess came the men who gave us the faith we live by today. For tragic or painful family circumstances that drove others *away* from God, brought these deeper *into* God (Prv 15:31–33; Heb 11).

Every *disadvantage* you have is a *stewardship* like your gifts and advantages. A stewardship is something entrusted to a steward for his care of it, his responsibility regarding it, like money, abilities, children, a wife, a job, a home, an inheritance, a vehicle, *time,* etc. This is how God both tests and develops us in preparation for eternity, where we'll have responsibilities according to our faithfulness in the "little things" we were entrusted with on earth (Gen 18:17–19; Mt 25:14–30; Lk 16:10–12; 1 Tim 3:5).

While we think of *assets* and *gifts* as stewardships, we'll also be held accountable for how we handled our *liabilities* and *disabilities.* Some disabled people wither away in self-pity, while others with worse disabilities go on to become Paralympic athletes or role-modeling servant-leaders. I love to hear the testimonies of ex-convicts and ex-addicts, for they teach us *anything is possible with God* (Gen 18:14; Jer 32:17, 27; Lk 1:37; 18:27).

The most hopeless situations give God a chance to demonstrate His grace, and the "survival of the fittest" is the one who decides to take full advantage of that grace. They come to God and don't give up. Those who nurse their grudge or pain fall into *dis*-grace! (Prv 24:16).

God is so merciful and gracious, it's tempting to assume he "forgives" even while we go on sinning. On a Youtube.com site a man discovered that a black hole he'd just copied on his copier created an opening wherever he placed it. He held it against a candy-bar machine, reached through the hole and got himself a free candy bar. Then he held it against a locked door, reached through the hole, and opened the door from the other side. Inside the room was a safe. He taped his magic hole on the door of the safe, reached in, and pulled out wads of cash.

Then he crawled through the hole all the way into the safe. But the paper with its black hole fell off the door. Now he was trapped inside the locked safe with no way to get out (Ps 52:7; 62:10; 1 Tim 6:6–10).[2]

Like Midas, who turned everything he touched to gold until he turned his food to gold and almost died of starvation, I watch men and women who've discovered the "magic" power of *grace* to turn their sins into "gold" slowly destroy themselves through using God's mercy and love to go on sinning. But grace has only one purpose: to reveal God's love and power to redeem our foolishness and draw us to Him in intimate fellowship. And then to empower us to a life of obedience and fruitfulness and generously impart that grace to others (Acts 4:33; Rom 6:1–14; Jude 1:4; Eph 4:29; 2 Tim 2:2).

Most people in the world are anything but pain-free. They are hurting and need people who *understand* them. Who better to understand them than those who've lived through the pain of fatherlessness until they found the peace, comfort, and joy from the only perfect "Father in heaven," whose Spirit in us calls Him affectionately, "Abba" – Hebrew for Daddy! It doesn't get any better than that! (Mt 6:9; Mk 14:36; Rom 8:15; Gal 4:6).

1. The Politics of Fatherhood.http://www.fathersforlife.org/articles/Baskerville/politics_fatherhood.htm (accessed June 4, 2014).
2. "The Black Hole." https://www.youtube.com/watch?v=P5_Msrdg3Hk (Accessed June 4, 2014).

SECTION ONE

ROOTS OF TRANSFORMATION

(The Change)

But we all, with unveiled face beholding as in a mirror the glory of the Lord, are being transformed into the same image from glory to glory, just as from the Lord, the Spirit.
2 Corinthians 3:18 NASB

Wait!

I hope you read the *Preface* and *Introduction*
(if you haven't already)
They are two very important articles
essential to the whole book

CHAPTER 1

Get Up! How to Use the Romans Seven Reset Button

The godly may trip seven times, but they will ***get up*** *again. But one disaster is enough to overthrow the wicked.*
Proverbs 24:16 NLT

Danger ahead

Peter warns that Paul speaks of "some things hard to understand, which untaught and unstable people twist to their own destruction, as they do also the rest of the Scriptures." The following truth is liberating to those who truly "delight in the law of God according to the inward man," but deadly to those who are looking for a license to "continue in sin that grace may abound" (Rom 6:1; 7:22, 2 Pet 3:16; Jude 1:4).

It compares to OxyContin, a powerful painkiller, but extremely addictive and dangerous when misused for pleasure. *Read at your own risk and only if you are dead-serious about walking in obedience with God!*

The guilt trap

How did I ever get back in this mess? you ask. You *knew* you were going to make it this time, especially after God used your testimony in jail and you helped so many others.

Now here you are, totally wasted again. What started out like another normal day (what's *normal* anymore?) turned into the worst day since you've been home.

It all started over a comment you made. Your wife took it the wrong way and you both ended in a big blowup. She screamed, "I knew you hadn't changed; I knew all you had was jailhouse religion!" On and on she went, cursing and screaming.

You "could've killed her," but you really wanted to kill

yourself because you knew every word she shouted was true. So you walked out, at least this time without hitting her. Then the bottom fell out. The booze, the partying, the gambling (you tried to salvage your losses). And finally . . . the woman.

Somehow you made it back home after 4:00 AM, but can hardly remember. Your stumbling around woke up your wife, who got up screaming again, the kids crying, terrified. You should have stayed away, at least till the kids went to school. Now *they* know their dad is *still* nothing but a piece of garbage. All that "time" for nothing!

Your wife is begging you to leave, or *she* will. She's had it with you for the last time!

How did it ever come back to this after such a dramatic change? You felt so good in jail, so clean; you knew you were a new creature in Christ, that old things had passed away according to 2 Corinthians 5:17. You knew you'd never go back to your old life. You thought you could forget the past and reach ahead. And you preached it to others (Phil 3:13).

Now it's over. Maybe jail is where you belong. Your wife and kids deserve someone else, and maybe she's already found someone, which is why she's begging you to leave.

Your situation may not be this drastic, or it may be worse – not one night, but weeks or months! But for many it still boils down to that feeling of total failure, of hating yourself, of giving up completely, and wondering why others can change but you cannot.

So I want to tell you what happened and how to get back up and start over. In fact, with a thing called *understanding,* you can actually turn your disasters into the very thing God and your wife and kids are looking for and need desperately – humility and brokenness (Ps 51:17).

What happened is, you got a little over-confident you could make it on short rations – starving your inner man, your spirit, and feeding your flesh. Too much Internet, social media, or TV, working too many hours or not enough, meeting up with your old homeboys, or just wasting time instead of taking that time for God as you did in jail. And thinking you only needed one church service a week. Or, God forbid, none at all! (Phil 3:3; Eph

4; 1 Cor 12; Rom 12).

And maybe an old addiction came back. Drugs. Alcohol. Pornography. Just moderate at first, but you thought you could *handle it*, riding the fence (Mt 6:21–24; Gal 5:17).

You lost the feeling of desperation you had in jail that kept you serious about God. You had others around you and chapel services that kept you on your toes. And more time. Then you got free and slowly (or quickly) began to relax. Too many other things competed for your time. Besides, things weren't that bad anyway.

A lifestyle doesn't change overnight. Even people radically transformed can easily slip back into the old life if they're not careful. The Bible is the Owner's Manual that comes with our New Birth in Christ. If we learn how to use it wisely, it will transform us through God's power and light.

Some manuals are easy to follow; they need little explanation. I'm not a mechanic, but I've done most of the mechanical maintenance on the vehicles I've owned for the past 30 years, including engine overhauls.

But I could never have done it without the constant help of manuals and mechanic friends who coached me and would come over and help me. My repair manuals are greasy and worn from use. Plus, I used manuals from different publishing companies for the same vehicle the way I read different translations of the Bible to get a better picture and catch something I may have missed.

I've made serious, expensive mistakes when I didn't pay close enough attention to the manual or thought I didn't need advice. Two times I learned the hard way how important the coolant sensor is to the starting of an engine, something the manuals pointed out, but I underestimated.

Yet I've done the same thing with God's Manual, the Bible, and not stayed in close fellowship with His family, His Body, the church, for guidance and strength. And the lessons cost me, *and others*, far more than a ruined engine (2 Tim 3:14–17).

Learning to listen

I was raised in a pastor's home, graduated from Bible college, was at the end of my seventh year of pastoring, and had a godly wife, two kids, and soon one on the way. But I was slowly going insane with depression and rage.

I knew something must have gone wrong in my childhood and had spent years studying psychology to find it, including appointments for psychological diagnosis, without success. Before my problem completely destroyed me, I decided to give God a last-ditch effort and seek Him "with all my heart," according to Jeremiah 29:13.

After six months of doing everything I knew – praying almost around the clock for thirty days, a ten-day fast, and waiting in agony for the God who "will never leave or forsake" us, He finally spoke two words: s*top reading*. It's the hardest thing I've ever done, like a lifetime heroin addict quitting cold-turkey. Because reading was my *substitute* for God, my drug of choice. It gave me an identity as a man of godly knowledge, but I didn't *know God* (Heb 13:5; Jn 14:17; 1 Jn 2:3–5; 5:20).

It took about ten days of silence for my mind to get quiet enough to *listen* to the Holy Spirit. But He led me back to His Word and began to slowly – "precept upon precept . . . line upon line . . . here a little, there a little" – *reveal* truth to me from scriptures I'd known only superficially. It revolutionized my life and turned the bad news of my failure into the Good News of *how* to walk in victory through a clearer understanding of faith and grace (1 Kgs 19:12; Is 28:10; 1 Cor 2:9–11; Eph 1:17–18).

Then I began a series of mistakes in the name of "grace." Some of those mistakes have cost me dearly and I'm still paying for them. But learning the hard way again has brought me back to see what I missed in God's Instruction Book, which says *grace will lead me to intimacy with God Himself*, giving me *victory* over sin, not merely "forgiven" and still in *bondage* to it. "For sin shall not have dominion over you, for you are not under law but under grace" (Rom. 6:14; Gal 4:3, 9).

Unconditional love

The most important principle of this new walk is God's unconditional love. It's the way we're supposed to love our wife and kids and the way our parents should have loved us. My parents loved me that way, but they made the mistake of bragging on me. Praise is what children need, the books say, and it's true.

But it backfired on me because I thought they loved me for my hard work. So I became an obsessive-compulsive workaholic, and eventually began to hate myself because I knew I always fell short of perfection in obedience to God.

To ease my internal rage I carried an imaginary sawed-off shotgun and blew my head off constantly while I dreamed up ways of killing myself painlessly and imagined a noose lying on my shoulder; it comforted me to think escape from this hell could be that close. Yet I knew I'd never take my life, because I feared God – the cause of my self-hatred, so I thought.

Friends had tried to explain that I should forgive and love myself, and "let go and let God." But I knew that if God couldn't forgive and love me, who was I to by-pass God? If I could ever be convinced God loved me unconditionally, my problems would be history and I'd be the happiest man alive. But how could He love me when I knew I'd mess up again before the day was out?

Yet hidden in two books of the Bible was a simple formula I'd never found in psychology or all the spiritual books about Christian living I'd read.

The Romans cure

The first thing God brought me to in Romans was chapter four and then Galatians three. It was like I'd never noticed these chapters before, although I'd written a term paper in college on "justification by faith," based on them (and others) and had memorized all of Galatians as a teen in Youth For Christ Bible quiz competition.

Only now I desperately needed them, like a drowning man reaching for a life-preserver. Romans four became my "antidepressant." It's about how Abraham's *faith* in God made him righteous, not his good works, because *faith* brings us into *relationship* and *fellowship* with God, who changes our hearts and gives us power over sin (Rom 8:1–14; Heb 8:10).

But Romans four left me with a much bigger problem: I'd

been trying to live by faith for many years, but somehow it wasn't working. And if I simply *believed* and didn't worry about my weakness any more, I might *really* get careless and mess up big-time, and *suffer the consequences!* (Gal 6:7–8).

If I had not learned to listen to God, I would have missed His further instructions. He next led me to chapter seven and two verses in chapter three. There I found the answer I'd been searching for. I saw how God's holy law was never intended as a set of rules, but rather to *reveal* the horrible condition of our *hearts – where the problem lies!*

"Now we know that whatever the law says, it says to those who are under the law, that every mouth may be stopped, and all the world may become guilty before God. Therefore by the deeds of the law no flesh will be justified in His sight, for by the law is the knowledge of sin" (Rom 3:19–20).

Rules can't change our *hearts*, but if they can reveal God's high standards and show us how far we have come short of them, we will begin to cry out for His power and grace through knowing Him personally (2 Cor 3:18; Gal 3:23–29; Eph 1:17ff; Col 1:9–11).

That's really what God's after. He can change our hearts *only* through *relationship* and *fellowship* with Him and His family, His "Body, the Church." But there's something in us that "can't handle" the *vulnerability* and *transparency* this kind of relationship demands – *until* we come to the end of our *selves* and crave relief. That's where God had finally brought me (Jn 15:1ff; Eph 4:1ff; Col 1:18).

It wasn't the Old Testament law and Ten Commandments that revealed the awful condition of my heart. Like the "rich young ruler" in Mark 10, I'd "kept [them] from my youth," at least the last six Jesus quoted to him (Ex 20; Mk 10:19–20).

It was the much higher standards of "the kingdom of God" in the New Testament that exposed my phoniness. This deals with our *motives*, the secret intents of our *heart*, where to look at a woman lustfully was equal to adultery, and to hate someone is like murder (Mt 5:21-22, 27–28).

What really convicted me is that we should not fear being misused, abused, and taken advantage of, but rather bless, give to, love, and pray for those who so hate and mistreat us (Mt 5:11–12, 38–48; Rom 12:17–21; Cor 4:9–13; 13:4–7; 2 Cor 6:1–10; 11:22–28).

My attempt to live up to that standard is what brought me to the end. Trying so hard to be giving, loving, and kind to the people who took advantage of me and cared less about God or served Him insincerely or were careless in their spending habits and expected me to bail them out ate away at my sense of "fairness" and "justice" until I couldn't take it anymore.

The harder I tried, the more depressed I got, until it finally led to insane rages in private – screaming, cursing, hair-pulling, fist-pounding temper tantrums nobody knew about, even as I pastored a congregation and lived a more or less perfect life before them. That's why I can understand the problem of the ex-con in the story I opened with.

That's also why Jesus quoted only the last six commandments to that wealthy young man: the *first four* were his problem, as well as mine. They're about making God number one, for without Him we can't do anything right, at least with the right *motive* (Ex 20:1–11; Jn 5:19; 15:1–5; Rv 3:1).

Romans Seven

This chapter was always fun to teach because everybody gets trapped between the *desire* to do good and the lack of *ability or heart* to do it. I remember teaching it in a Youth for Christ Bible Club at my high school in the late 1950s. But I obviously never really understood it. Now my life depended on it.

The first twelve verses establish the value of the law, that it is eternal, "holy, and just, and good." It can *never* be "done away with," as many sincere believers have done. Our relationship with God is like being married to the Perfect Law-keeper. His demands are *impossible* to keep, but there's no way out of the marriage. Either He dies or I die. But He will never die; He (the Law) is *eternal!* Alas, it is *I* who must die! But *how* can I die?

My dad raised us kids with this holy precept: you must *die to self!* That was my whole problem: I had read many books about how to walk the Christian walk, but they always concluded with a certain amount of self-discipline, agreeing with Dad about *dying to self* and with Jesus about *denying* oneself. But self-discipline was my whole problem, my obsession, the thing I never could do *enough* of (Lk 9:23).

The Normal Christian Life (1957), by Chinese writer Watchman Nee, came closest to answering this problem as he explained Romans 6–8. But I was incapable of grasping it until my endless attempts to keep God's holy (New Testament) law finally "killed me" (Rom 7:11–13; Eph 2:1; Col 2:13).

As a drowning man going down for the last time finally gives up in hopelessness and quits fighting for his life, I came to the end of my self-discipline when I could finally say with Paul, "O wretched man that I am! Who will deliver me from this body of death?" (Rom 7:24).

The "dead to sin" of Romans six could only be theory until I actually *experienced* my inability (death) to overcome sin. And when I did, God handed me the Romans seven solution. I soaked in the chapter like a dry sponge, meditating on each verse for hours, days, weeks, and months.

Gradually I began to see myself in two parts: my "old man," my "body of death" totally *incapable* of obeying God, and my "new man" totally incapable of *disobeying* Him. Because it's no less than *Christ* in me, "the hope of *glory*" (Eph 4:22–24; Col 1:27–28; Heb 4:12).

This corresponds with 1 John 3:6 and 9, "Whoever abides in Him does not sin. . . . Whoever has been born of God does not sin, for His seed remains in him; and he cannot sin, because he has been born of God" (also Jn 15:1–5; 1 Jn 5:18–21).

Romans 7:16–17, repeated in verse 20, are the verses that actually set me free. "If, then, I do what I will not to do, I agree with the law that it is good. But now, it is no longer I who do it, but sin that dwells me." It actually took months of searching and quiet "waiting on God" so my *heart* could understand how it could be true in the light of God's holiness and my fear of blowing it really bad if I were to relax and take these verses literally (Ps 40:1).

Eventually I realized this chapter depends on Romans six and eight as our body parts depend on one another. Romans six establishes our legal *standing* of being *dead to self* through the death and resurrection of Christ. And Romans eight tells us to *walk* in that mind-set, to be *spiritually minded* . It's the *fight* of faith. That's what John's "abide in Him" means – "walking in the Spirit," in His resurrection life, so we don't "fulfill the lust of the flesh" (Gal 5:16; 1 Tim 6:12; 2 Tim 4:7).

If I "will" to do right but can't, the problem is the *mind*.

I grew up with the idea that "walking in the Spirit" meant living in a state of "holiness," not messing up. But as hard as I "willed" to do right, I couldn't do it consistently. The seven verses in Romans 7:15–21 contain the word "will" seven times in the context of this intense struggle. (Count the *I, me, my, mine, myself* pronouns in Job 29 and the same words in Romans 7 and you'll see Job had the same struggle; then compare Job 40:4–5 and 42:5–6 with Romans 7:24.)

In the context of these three chapters (6–8), backed by Galatians 2:19–5:26, I began to see it meant *standing in my mind on who I am in Christ, even when my flesh messes up.* "For to *will* is present with me, but how to perform that which is good I do not find. . . . For I delight in the law of God according to the inward man. But I see another law in my members, warring against the law of my *mind*. . . (Rom 7:18b, 22-23).

Personal failure too easily draws me into a vicious cycle of fear, self-hatred, despair, anger, blame, denial, and so on, making it impossible to recover spiritually or hear God's remedy or wisdom. "For those who live according to the flesh *set their minds* on the things of the flesh, but those who live according to the Spirit, the things of the Spirit. For to be carnally *minded* is death, but to be spiritually *minded* is life and peace" (Rom 8:6; see 2 Cor 5:17; Col 1:27–28).

The "mind" here is far more than just the brain; it's the mind renovated by the Spirit-breathed Word in our hearts. "Be transformed by the renewing of your mind." That God "may give to you the spirit of wisdom and revelation in the knowledge of Him, the eyes of your understanding being enlightened . . . " (Rom 12:2; Eph 1:17–18).

It's a deliberate – or desperate! – act of faith: "That you put off, concerning your former conduct, the old man which grows corrupt according to the deceitful lusts, and *be renewed in the spirit of your mind*, and that you put on the new man which was created according to God, in true righteousness and holiness" (Eph 4:22–24).

Holiness, holy, sanctify, sacred, sanctuary, and *saint* all come from the Greek word *hagios* (#G40),[1] meaning "separated to God," which begins with my heart (my will, my "delight") and continues with my mind (Acts 26:18; Rom 6:19; 1 Thes 5:23).

Lapsing into carnal, fleshly, and sinful activities can be a strong indication of where my mind and heart are and what I've been feeding my mind on. Romans 7:17 is not an excuse to "continue in sin that grace may abound," but God's invitation to come humbly and with a "whole heart" to Him in our weakness for a cleansed and renewed mind, and strength to *overcome* sin (Ps 119:2, 10, 34, 58, 69, 145; Jer 3:10; 24:7; Mt 11:28; 22:37; Jn 15:1–5; Rom 6:1, 12–19; Eph 2:8; 1 Jn 2:15–17; 3:2–8).

Otherwise obedience can take a huge amount of *self*-effort, which isn't obedience at all, but "dead works." God wants our "works" to come from *resting* in Him, letting Him work in us by His Spirit. That's why it's called "the fruit of the Spirit"; it's God working in and through us (Rom 8:9–14; Gal 5:18–25; Heb 4:11–13; 6:1; 9:14).

Obedience is a love affair!

For it's only through *enjoying* His love without trying to *earn it* that we then find it easy to love others spontaneously and unconditionally through *His love in us*. That's why Jesus said loving God and others fulfills the whole law, which includes the first four (God) and the last six (others) of the Ten Commandments, as well as the other 603 commandments in the *Torah*, the "Law of Moses," Genesis through Deuteronomy. And in Matthew 7:12 He included "the prophets." Wow! (Mt 19:18–19; Jn 14:21; 15:12; Gal 5:13; Jas 2:8).

In September, 1976, when the full impact of this truth finally dawned on me, I went wild with joy. The church members who had "given me a hard time," I wanted to be around them all the time, loving them in some way, listening to their needs so I could help them. I couldn't get enough of people because they were the *sole objects* of God's unconditional, bubbling love that had resurrected me from suicidal insanity (Mk 2:17; 15:7).

Romans 7:24–25 is the pivot on which all this hinges: "O wretched man that I am! Who will deliver me from this body of death? I thank God – through Jesus Christ our Lord! *So then, with the mind I myself serve the law of God, but with the flesh the law of sin.*"

My walk with God, including my behavior, is simply the product of where I keep my mind, whether *serving the flesh*, where sin gets its power through "the law of sin and death," or "with the mind" serving "the law of God," where grace gets its power, through "the law of the Spirit of Life in Christ Jesus" (Rom 8:2–6).

"Set your mind on things above, not on things on the earth. For you died, and your life is hidden with Christ in God." It's the "inner man," the "mind of Christ," not the thinking of the "natural man," but your mind and human spirit in tune with the Holy Spirit. It's what "salvation" is based on – believing with the heart until it transforms our speaking, our mouth-confession (Rom 10:8–10; 12:2; 1 Cor 2:9–16; 2 Cor 4:13; Eph 1:17–18; 3:16; 4:22–24; Col 3:2–3, 10).

This may take only a moment, or hours, or even years for a major breakthrough, as in my case, until I learned (and keep learning) how to yield to the Holy Spirit and stay in tune with Him. It may come through waiting on God in silence, through meditating in the Word, through worship and prayer, as we minister to others, or through coming to the "end of ourselves" and "looking to Jesus" (Ps 1, 38–40, 119; Is 40:28–31; 42:16; Lk 11:1–13; 18:1–14; Acts 7:54–56; Heb 12:1–2; 13:2–3, 12–16).

And sometimes for no apparent reason, God suddenly gives us an "epiphany," a revelation-breakthrough that lifts us out of ourselves, as it were, and into the glory! It's these occasions, mainly the ones I experience in the middle of my greatest trials, that make me willing to go through whatever it takes and not give up. Probably the way an addict anticipates his next high and will take any risk to get it (Ps 1:1–2; 37:3–7; 40:1–8; 119:9–12; Is 40:31; 42:14–16; Lam 3:19–32; Mt 24:46–47; Lk 11:5–13;

18:1–8; 1 Cor 14:15; 3:16; Eph 6:11–18; 1 Thes 5:16–18).

Our failure to enjoy this awesome "walk in the Spirit," if we truly "fear the Lord" and "delight in His law," comes from our lack of understanding, weak faith, or too many distractions – "the cares, riches, and pleasures of life," including *cyber-distractions* – social media, smart phones, etc.

And that is where the *striving, pressing, wrestling, labor, and diligence* should be applied. Not *self*-discipline, but in seeking to *know Him intimately* through *time* with Him and His Word, like getting to know the most awesome wife or husband you could "only imagine" (Mt 11:12; Lk 8:14; 13:24; 16:16; Rom 7:22; 9:16; Eph 6:12; Phil 3:10, 14; Heb 4:11; 11:6).

Look up and get up!

Now back to our opening scene. Your family has again turned against you. You feel hopeless and helpless; you now realize you'll *never* change.

But the Manual! What did it say? It said I have two parts – one who hates God and cannot possibly change, and one who loves God and can't possible disobey. It says that if I *set my mind* on Christ, in Whom I am a "new man," and *abide* (remain, live) there, I can immediately *reckon*, count it as fact, my "old man" to be "*dead to sin*." My sin now, instead of condemning me, actually *confirms* that I'm hopelessly dead, yet *liberates* me to stand in Christ, who took my death in Himself and paid the price of sin that caused death (Rom 6:11; 7:13; 8:9–11; Eph 2:1; 4:22–24).

As proof that the price was adequate, "God raised Him from the dead." My position "in Christ" includes me in His death and resurrection by *faith*. Faith is deep-level *substance*, the invisible underlying reality behind everything that exists (Rom 4:25; Heb 11:1, 3; Col 1:17).

This is why the prayer of salvation ("sinner's prayer") covers two simple facts: confessing (speaking) with my mouth the Lord Jesus, and believing *with my heart* "that God has raised Him from the dead." This heart and mouth faith-confession, if *genuine*, "births" my spirit-man into reality and now provides a "wireless connection" between Christ and me, rebooting my conscience, opening my spiritual ears, and tying my destiny to His! (Acts 13:30; Rom 7:4; 10:9–10; 2 Cor 5:17; Col 3:3).

So to finish my story: You're seriously getting ready to do something stupid because of the self-hatred, despair, anger, and bitterness. You *deserve* to punish yourself and those who hurt you by going back out and throwing off all restraint – booze, drugs, women, anything goes now! What the h. . . . Nobody else cares. Why should you?

That kind of thinking is the reasoning of the "carnal mind," which leads to death. It's what God designed all these scriptural "antibodies" for, from Romans through Colossians (Rom 8:5–8).

Everything now hinges on your next move. Think this way: *God, please forgive me for not accepting Your love, the love You suffered so terribly for, as Mel Gibson portrayed in* The Passion of the Christ. *Forgive me for insulting You after the price You paid and the gift You would love to give me if I could only learn to receive it in this awful pit of failure* (Gal 2:19–21).

Forgive me, Father, for thinking this is the end, that there's no remedy, when Your Son died to cover every possible thing that could go wrong – even my failure again and again. If You expect me to forgive others 70 times 7, help me believe You can forgive me that much so I can get closer to You, not farther (Mt 18:22; Lk 17:4).

God, I know You love a broken and contrite spirit. I'm so broken now I can hardly muster the strength to believe You could ever change me. But I must believe, because You are the only hope I have left (Ps 34:18; 51:17; Is 57:15; 66:2).

Daddy, help my unbelief like You helped the man who admitted his unbelief and You delivered his son from demonic torment. Teach me how to live and abide in You and not cave in to fear and the horror of my own wretchedness (Mk 9:24).

You will most probably have to stay there for a while, maybe hours or days (taking time off work, even), the same length of time you would go out and wreck somebody else's life with your anger and crazy attempt to get even with those who can't stand you. Or drown your troubles in booze, pills, drugs, sex, or whatever (Gen 32:24–30; Eph 6:11ff).

But stay there, alone with God, and "be renewed in the spirit of your mind," allowing His Spirit to replace your fear with faith. This quiet time of humbling down after such failure will not only revitalize your walk with God, but "after you have returned" to Jesus, as He told Peter before he denied Him, you'll be able to *strengthen your brethren,* as you once did in jail (Lk 22:32; Rom 12:2; Eph 4:23).

You also need this time of quiet humbling to hear God's wisdom in how to face your family and the people you disappointed or hurt. Sometimes the things we do in our fleshly mind-set carry long range consequences, and *it takes a lot more faith to walk them out than if we could have maintained our faith in God to begin with* (Gal 6:7–8).

That's why it's far easier to learn to be "spiritually minded" *before* rather than after we've had a fleshly fling with its long-range consequences. How many men have I seen come back to jail and end up with a long prison sentence – sometimes for murder – through what started out as a little carelessness and lack of "the fear of the Lord" (Prv 8:13; 9:10; Gal 6:7–8).

This is why these times of "waiting on God" must become a lifestyle. It's about abiding, living in Christ, the true Vine (Lam 3:22–32; Jn 15:1ff). Selah – stop and meditate on it.

The Romans 7 family plan

Romans seven became a powerful tool in my relationships with others, especially my family. I found I could instantly transform a huge family disagreement and quarrel I had started by suddenly telling them, "Hey, did you hear that old man talking? I can't believe what he said."

At first they blamed me for using this as a cop-out. But when they saw how it humbled me and gave me time to collect myself and think *responsibly* instead of *reacting* in the flesh, they discovered something had changed in me.

Here's one of my more serious examples: I was working at an apartment near my home (my job – property maintenance). My teenage son had come over to talk to me about something; his mother (my wife) came with him. I began lecturing him about surfing too much at the beach and a few other things. But I could see he was getting angry (Eph 6:4; Col 3:21).

Suddenly, without saying a word, he smashed the window (he didn't know I was about to replace) with the back of his fist and walked home, bleeding. Instantly my wife shouted at me, "You're sending your son to hell, you're so hard on him!" She went on and on, and I felt angry, but ashamed, knowing she was right.

I dropped my tools, walked home, sat down, and with my face in my hands, felt like one of the worst fathers alive. I'd taken a course in child psychology in college, weeping through one of the text books as I read of dysfunctional homes and the hearts of children and teens torn apart by them.

As a teen going through suicidal depression I dreamed of what a loving and wise father I'd be if I ever made it that far. Now here I was with four kids, three of them teenagers, and failing this one miserably. How could I ever undo the damage I'd just caused?

I tried to remind myself of the truths God had taught me that had set me free. His Word says Christ is in me, my "new man," and I cannot sin. When I sin, it's not the *real* me, but my "old man," my "body of death" hidden in Christ's death. When God sees me, He sees me through the "finished work" of His Son, clean and righteous, holy and without a single blemish (Rom 6:5–11; Col 1:22).

On the other hand my failure loomed before me like an untamable monster. I knew my son would never buy my "it was my old man" line at this critical moment. He was in pain, and I was the cause. How could I so easily tell myself and him, "It is no longer I who do it, but sin that dwells in me"? (Rom 7:17).

The battle raged in my mind for five or ten long minutes: what should I believe – the evidence of my failure or the eternal truth of God's Word? It was hard, like fighting everything inside me screaming *no, no!* (Rom 4:17–22).

Finally I stood, walked into my son's room, and sat down on his bed behind him as he sat at his desk, staring out the window. I had no idea what to say at first, but then spoke two words softly: *I'm sorry.*

He turned around and faced me and together we stood, embraced in a father and son bond that went deeper than our failures. God's "grace and truth" had overcome Satan's lies – again (Jn 1:14–17).

Many years later, this son has his own family. He's actually a far better father than I was, seriously, having learned through my mistakes, through his own reading and experiences, and by understanding Romans 7.

And it's the reason I see jail and prison as the number one place where this truth has the most potential to turn hopeless situations into glory. Like the people who sinned worst, but who in response to Jesus' love, loved him more than normally "good" people (Lk 7:47; 15:32).

I'm aware many will abuse the *freedom* aspect of Romans 7, as I have often done. We fail to take enough time to let God speak or change our hearts, and then we pay the consequences. This is obviously why Peter warned those who twist Paul's difficult writings to their own destruction. I too, have to resist discouragement over the thought of *where I could be now if only* I had taken more time to listen to God and avoided major life-altering bad decisions, misusing "grace" (Gal 5:13; Jude 1:4).

But for all my abuse of the liberty I've found through this chapter, I wouldn't trade it for anything in the world. And for those who truly want to walk with God and *take time* to get to know Him intimately, your days ahead can be filled with "joy inexpressible and full of glory" (1 Pet 1:8).

Trust me. *Trust Him!*

1. *Strong's Exhaustive Concordance*: Hebrew/Greek Dictionary. (as with all other Greek word numbers in this book).

CHAPTER 2

Jail and Prison Should Produce More Men and Women of God in America Than Bible College or Seminary: Why Don't they?

It is my opinion that a prison experience is among the most powerful character building events in the universe. . . . If you've experienced prison, then you have an advantage over many people. You have already tasted devastation. Now it's time to learn recovery.[1]

Part One

What is "success" from God's view?

At seventeen our oldest granddaughter secretly decided to join the Marines. Her mother, our oldest daughter, cried for two weeks, but finally turned it over to God, which released Him to work it all out for His purpose, according to Romans 8:28 ("And we know that all things work together for good of those who love God, to those who are the called according to His purpose.")

In the process, the Marines, noticing her potential for leadership, chose to send her to college when she finished high school, then receive her in four years as a Lieutenant instead of a "grunt." So now she's in college and ROTC.

The other day I got this email from her mother: "For the longest time Anna was convinced her drill instructor hated her. He seemed to be always picking on her unfairly, over tiny little things, even things she couldn't help. I kept telling her he's just acting like a drill instructor, and not to take it personally.

Anyway, she has toughed it out and refused to be discouraged by his treatment of her and others.

"Recently someone happened to catch this [video] clip with their phone during one of her drill practices. Ten seconds in, if you listen carefully, you can hear this same drill instructor suddenly say something random but highly significant for Anna: 'You're going to be unit leader next year.' That is a huge honor. He's [obviously] been watching the way she responds to him!!! She said it was one of the happiest moments for her."

Maybe you don't or didn't have a mother or dad to encourage you by telling you what's going on behind the scenes and that God's gonna' work it all out for good if you'll just hang in there and trust Him. But because I did, and their encouragment helped me make it this far, I owe it to you and will "pay it forward" what I learned, even as our children have learned from Mom and me and are teaching their kids the principles that will get them through everything life's "drill instructors" can throw at them (Gen 18:19; Dt 4:9–10; 6:6–7; 11:19–21; 32:46; Ps 78:2–9; Prv 6:20–22; 22:6; 2 Tim 1:5; 3:15).

Because our short earthly life is not about convenience, comfort, and what the world calls "success," and before you know it, it's over, and then we're reaping the results of the time we spent here. Rather it's all about training our spirit-man for an eternal dominion, beginning with authority over demonic rulers of darkness in order to reclaim this planet – and all of creation – back to God. If that sounds far out, look up the following scriptures, which barely scratch the surface: Gen 1:26, 28; Ex 19:5–6; Ps 2:8-9; 8:4–6; 115:16; 149:5–9; Dan 7:22, 27; Rom 8:17–22; Eph 6:10–12; 2 Tim 2:11–12; Heb 2:5–7; 1 Pet 5:8–9; Rv 2:26–27; 3:21; 5:10; 20:4.

In other words, getting an education is good, but it pales in comparison to the training of our attitudes, our character, our "inner man." And a *harsh* drill instructor may give our granddaughter far more than what she'll learn from books and lectures by "kind and considerate" professors (Prv 19:18; 2 Cor 6:3–10; Eph 3:16; 2 Tim 2:3; Heb 6:15; 12:1–11).

That's why jail and prison can be more valuable than even Bible college. Because while college trains the mind, it is unfair treatment, emotional abuse, trials, and difficult or impossible circumstances that train the spirit, giving us a strong "wireless" connection to God. And if Jesus could do "nothing of Himself but what He sees the Father do," *how much less can we without that vital spiritual connection?* (Jn 5:19, 30; 8:28; 9:4; 12:49; 14:10; 15:5; 2 Cor 12:9–10).

Unless you don't mind being a "grunt" in the coming eternal Kingdom – if you make it! And that term, which indicates the beginning level of service in the army or marines, is a good biblical analogy, because while we're saved by faith, we'll be judged and rewarded with various levels of responsibility and authority by the kind of *works* our faith, faithfulness, and character produce! (Prv 24:12; Jer 32:19; Mt 16:27; 25:14–30; Lk 16:10–12; 19:12–26; Rom 2:4–10; 1 Cor 3:11–15; 2Cor 5:10; Eph 6:8; Jas 2:17–26; 1 Pet 1:17; Rv 2:23; 22:12–15).

The Bible is a source-book of endless encouragement and wisdom, but it comes from people who were tested and tried by fire – and much of it as a result of *their own mistakes and downright sins!* That's why it's so comforting: if they not only made it, but saw God turn their worst nightmares into sheer glory and wisdom, anybody can make it! All you need is the correct *viewpoint!* (Dt 8:2–3; 8:16; Ps 66:10–12; Prv 17:3; 29:18; Is 48:10; Zec 13:9; 2 Cor 3:18; 1 Pet 1:6–7).

Just in case you are or have been an enlisted military person starting out at the bottom and feel put down, consider the experience of David Terry, whom this same daughter of ours had taught when he was a youth in Sunday School. In 1998 he enlisted in the U. S. Navy. He always did his very best with the integrity his church background had instilled in him, *plus way more than what was required of him.*

And because he applied for law-enforcement certification, as an E-2 he actually did the work of an E-6. He advanced to E-3, then passed an exam for E-4.

When his superiors noticed his diligent and honest work ethic, they hand-picked him for advancement to E-5 as an administrative clerk. There he gained the experience and reputation that caught the eye of his admiral, who suddenly picked him out of a long list to be his secretary. Which meant every action decided by the admiral had to be processed and implemented (carried out) with authority and in writing by this formerly unknown sailor to the envy of many of those whose "rank" they assumed entitled *them* to this high status.[2]

A *faithful* and *honest* work-ethic are the two building blocks of true success, regardless of background. In 1980 David Koch (pronounced cook) emerged from his five-year prison sentence with *nothing* . . . but a determination to tell the truth, and to apply himself at any assigned job with the best of his ability. After a month of closed doors (he told the truth about his prison time), he finally landed a job mowing lawns and cleaning airplanes and their hangers. Armed with this "high road" approach to life, he eventually became a professional pilot with his own flight training school, and owned and operated several other companies. The quote at the beginning of this article is taken from his book, *Slaying the Dragon* (the dragon being all the reasons for failure).[1]

Jesus said it like this: "If you are faithful in little things, you will be faithful in large ones. But if you are dishonest in little things, you won't be honest with greater responsibilities. And if you are untrustworthy about worldly wealth, who will trust you with the true riches of heaven? And if you are not faithful with other people's things, why should you be trusted with things of your own?" (Lk 16:10–12 NLT; see Lk 22:25–27).

Three major advantages

I see three reasons why jail and especially the longer term of prison are one of the best instruments of training for a man or woman of God in the making, and could well be more effective and natural than the more artificial classroom setting of Bible college or seminary.

(Seminary, by the way, is similar to Bible college, but it generally follows a four-year college degree, which means the courses may be more intense academically and without the secular [non-biblical] courses required in Bible college for a bachelor's degree.)

(1) The best opportunity for God to demonstrate His grace and show Himself strong is among those who *need* Him.

"Those who are well have no need of a physician, but those who are sick. I did not come to call the righteous, but sinners, to repentance" (Mk 2:17b).

The Bible has more answers than any of us have problems for, but those who have more problems get to enjoy more solutions and will spend more time with our Counselor, Comforter, and Helper – the Holy Spirit (Is 9:6; Ps 16:11; Jn 14:16, 26; 15:26; 16:7; Rom 15:5; 2 Cor 1:3–4; Heb 13:6).

(2) The most valuable treasure on earth is *time*, for it is the one thing working people never have enough of no matter how much of everything else we have. Lack of it causes stress, keeps relationships shallow, frustrates completion of projects and goals, and, most tragically, hinders or stagnates spiritual growth, prayer, and intimacy with God. No matter how hard we try to make room for more time, we rarely succeed at getting enough. Yet ironically an inmate gets this extremely valuable gift in lavish abundance as a "reward" for his crimes! (Ps 39:4–11; 90:9–12; Lk 16:15–16; Jas 4:14).

(3) The most important goal, in fact the only goal of any permanent value, is *wisdom*. Wisdom guides relationships as the helmsman guides his ship (Prv 3:15; 4:5–9; 7:4–5; 8:14–16; 16:16; 24:3; Eccl 8:5–6; 9:14–16; Dan 5:11–14; Lk 1:17; 2:52; 21:15; Acts 6:3; Rom 11:33; 1 Cor 2:6–7; Eph 1:8, 17; 3:10; Col 1:9, 28; 2:3; 3:16; 4:5; Jas 3:17).

We were created for fellowship, the main activity of relationship. God gave us the responsibility of taking dominion over this planet, but dominion (rulership and authority) is only the *means to restore, maintain, and maximize fellowship*.

This is the other irony about jail, that as a consequence for breaking the law, inmates are handed on a silver platter some of life's greatest challenges in relationships, like athletes supplied with the very best equipment for their training (Jer 12:5; Prv 24:10; Heb 12:3–4, 11).

I see these three areas as God's gifts graciously handed to those we think deserve them least, but whom God knows need them most! That's why I see jail and prison as potentially more effective for the making of spiritual giants than Bible college and seminary, and I've seen many inmates make use of these three areas to great advantage in their spiritual development.

But sadly, something happens in the spiritual birth canal as they transition from jail to the outside. This article is a wake-up call for those with *heart* to "apprehend" that for which Christ Jesus has "apprehended" them, and see their incarceration for what it really is – the opportunity of a lifetime! (Phil 3:12 KJV).

The problem is that we tend to see life as a means to be comfortable and happy instead of an opportunity for training comparable to military training.

Reason # 1: learn under His yoke, not yours.

To those who "labor and are heavy laden" with sin, Jesus said to come to Him, take his yoke, and *learn of Him*. "For I am gentle and lowly in heart, and you will find rest for your souls. For My yoke is easy and My burden is light" (Mt 11:28–30; see p. 123, third paragraph, for definition of "yoke").

It's the perfect prescription for the prison inmate, bogged down with the heavy weight of his sin, and then the "yoke" of his sentence and the rejection, mistrust, or disappointment of his family and others. "Good and upright is the Lord; therefore He teaches *sinners* in the way. The *humble* He guides in justice, and the *humble* He teaches His way" (Ps 25:8–9).

The student, however, enters Bible college usually with support from family, friends, and the whole social framework. He doesn't feel that gnawing hunger and need the inmate might feel. Furthermore, what he learns from books and professors feeds his intellectual desires more than his spiritual needs. And the more he learns, the more confidence he feels in *himself* and in his future, and the more respect he gains from people and leaders.

While this may well be the blessing of God, it could also be a serious hindrance to spiritual growth, as Bible history proves (Dt 8:10ff; 2 Chr 16:7ff; 18:1; 19:2; 26:16; 2 Kgs 20:12–18; Lk 8:14).

We know that faith comes from hearing the *revealed word* "from the mouth of God." *But this word is best revealed in an atmosphere of humility, not "confidence in the flesh"* (Mt 4:4; Rom 10:17; Lk 10:21; Phil 3:3; also Ps 10:17; Prv 15:33).

When the disciples asked Jesus to increase their faith, He told them of the power of even a tiny mustard seed of faith. And then He illustrated the kind of *attitude* this faith thrives in – that of a slave (Greek, *doulos,* #1401) who after working all day and before feeding himself, humbly and dutifully prepares his (probably rich and maybe arrogant and abusive) master's supper without complaining or expecting even a "thank you" (Lk 17:5–10).

God told Habakkuk, "Behold the proud, his soul is not upright in him; but the just shall live by his faith" (2:4). Pride will eventually destroy faith (Ps 138:6; Prv 16:5, 18; 29:23; Eccl 7:8; Is 2:12).

Our daily "cross" (His yoke) is *God's remedy for our pride,* like Paul's "thorn in the flesh" that kept him teachable and humble. Jesus continually connected being His disciple, which means one who is taught by Him, with taking up one's cross and denying himself (2 Cor 12:7; Lk 9:23–24; 14:26–33; 17:33; Mt 10:38–39; 16:24–25; Mk 10:21–29; Jn 12:25).

Knowing what is *His* yoke, *when* to "bear the cross," and *how* to deny ourselves can be confusing, because it can be "an appearance of wisdom in self-imposed religion, false humility, and neglect of the body, but . . . of no value against the indulgence of the flesh" (Col 2:23).

But jail and prison are (usually) the natural consequence of disobedience. "For he who sows to his flesh will of the flesh reap corruption" (Gal. 6:8a). There is no question of legalism here, for it is not "self-imposed religion" but God's judgment against sin and rebellion. For the justice system "is God's minister, an avenger to execute wrath on him who practices evil. Therefore you must be subject [submissive]" (Rom 13:4–5; Titus 3:1; 1 Pet 2:13–14; 2 Pet 2:10; Jude 1:8).

Here is a ready-made yoke, furnished by the Department of Corrections and *ordained* and *authorized by God* to disciple (teach) us and bring us to Him. The fact that the "system" might be riddled with corruption, hypocrisy, greed, and inconsistency is no problem to God, for when Paul wrote the above, the head of the Roman government was Nero (called by the title Augustus in Acts 25:21, 25), probably the most perverted, wicked, and "sick" leader in history, and Paul wrote his best epistles while his prisoner, and finally met his end under Nero's order to take off his head.

All through Bible history God used the most *wicked* to correct His own people, from Pharaoh and Nebuchadnezzar to the Herods and Roman emperors. Those who *resisted these wicked rulers resisted God!* Only when their laws went against God's law was it right to refuse (Prv 3:11; 15:10; 22:15; 23:13; Jer 2:30; 5:3; 7:28; 22:25; 24:4–7; 25:8–11; 27:6-8; 28:14; Hab 1:12; Zeph 3:2; Acts 4:19; 5:29; Ex 1:17; Rom 9:17).

How pointless and self-defeating it is to spend one's jail time complaining about the abuses, disadvantages, and hypocrisy in the system, undoing and reversing God's awesome process of correction and restoration to *true freedom and glory!* Take *His yoke and learn from Him,* "and you will find *rest"* (Num 11–14; Heb 3–4).

Reason #2: heart-revelation verses head knowledge.

From almost his first day in college, the student begins to fill his mind with knowledge from several subjects at once, stuffing and cramming it in at a rate far exceeding his ability to absorb it. He has no choice and it will take decades – actually a lifetime – to digest and assimilate hundreds of books and articles, and thousands of lectures compacted into four years just for a bachelor's degree.

In the meantime he *thinks* he *knows* this material simply because he has passed his exams and courses. He may know it with his mind, but does he *understand* it with his heart and have the *wisdom* to apply it in the right way, at the right time, and with the right *attitude?* (Eccl 8:5–7; Prv 8–9).

When I graduated with a bachelor's degree in "ministerial studies," I thought I was ready to change the world, the church, and even my fellow ministers. But after a few months of pastoring I began to painfully realize my spiritual poverty, and that while my head was full, my heart was pitifully empty (1 Cor 8:1–2; 13:2).

I had taken courses for all the books of the Bible, but it was as though I knew almost nothing about it when it came to converting these truths into heart-ministry or practical living. I had to start over, "precept upon precept . . . line upon line . . . here a little, there a little," as God revealed it to me "from faith to faith," "grace for [more] grace," as I grew "from glory to glory," and "strength to strength" (Is 28:10, 13; Jn 1:16; Rom 1:17; 2 Cor 3:18; Ps 84:7).

I remember in college *longing* for the day I could finally have enough *time* to *meditate* and *soak* in the words of the Bible itself and try to find rest from my inner pain and suicidal depression (Ps 1; 119:10–11).

Inmates don't realize the high value of the *time* they have to deal with the mountain of issues that brought them there, combined with new ones in jail. Some inmates don't know whom their wives are sleeping with, or do know. Many of them have been forsaken by their children or have court-orders not to communicate with them or with their wives.

They know that when they get out they may fall into the same traps all over again and be back with a longer sentence, or classified as "habitualized" – *uncorrectable!* Their minds may be filled with anxiety, fear, self-hatred, rage, resentment, bitterness. And tormented in an inferno of unsatisfied lust for sex, money, drugs, booze, or just plain *freedom*.

But they have two things that can change all that and bring deep rest so glorious that even in jail their lives can be as though in heaven. They have the Word and *time* to *absorb* it and apply it to their problems! (Dt 11:18–21).

That is what cured my depression many years ago (1976). In my utter desperation, I finally took enough *time* to spend daily with God and His Word until the Holy Spirit, my Teacher, led me to the answers to my problem (Jn 14:26).

But it took a year and a half, during which time I battled daily with the fear and guilt of neglecting so many other important things in order to choose the "one thing" that was "needed." Hardly a day went by that our closest friends didn't condemn me for "wasting" all this time, and warning my wife, getting her upset almost to the breaking point (Mk 14:4; Lk 10:42).

That's why it hurts to see inmates so anxious about the jail time they have instead of the *many unresolved issues they have* and still know so little about God's awesome *answers* to those problems (Phil 3:10).

But I also hurt when I see them doing what I did in college and for years afterward – cramming more head-knowledge of the Word into their minds than they can absorb in their hearts. It makes us Bible know-it-alls with little understanding of those around us, turning the Bible into the "tree of the knowledge of good and evil" – the *cause* of the fall, instead of the "tree of life." For the Bible is *spiritual food*, not *information* for the intellect.

Yet they have enough *time* not only to know and fully absorb and rest in those glorious answers, but to know Jesus personally and intimately. Consequently our prisons should be like Bible training centers pouring out men of God by the thousands.

And there's still one more factor that contributes to this potential for such amazing grace.

Reason #3: people-stress is vital for spiritual growth

Not everybody in jail seeks God. I've found only about ten percent bother to attend church services, and about ten percent of those are *really* serious about God – only a handful in a thousand inmates. And when they get out, it may boil down to only *one* in a thousand, as Solomon estimated (Eccl 7:28).

But that's precisely *the way God forms His spiritual giants.* Noah and his immediate family were the *only ones* walking with God in a world so filled with violence that God had to destroy it in the Flood (Gen 6:5–8; Heb 11:7).

Moses stood faithful among two or three million "stubborn and rebellious" Israelites who, when they didn't get their needs or wants met, complained, rebelled, and even threatened to kill him. Yet this is exactly the reason for all the revelation God gave Moses, providing us with the foundation for the Bible – Genesis through Deuteronomy (Num 11–16, 20–21).

Elijah felt he was the only one standing against Israel's Baal worship under King Ahab and his wife Jezebel, famous only for their utter wickedness. And Jezebel had killed all the prophets she could find not hiding in caves (there were schools that trained prophets). God told him there were 7,000 others who "had not bowed to Baal," but they no doubt kept it secret. Yet it took these extremely hostile circumstances to produce one of the greatest prophets in the Bible (besides Moses and Enoch), and who, like Enoch, went straight to heaven without dying (Gen 5:24; 1 Kgs 17–19; 2 Kgs 2; Heb 11:5–6; Jas 5:17–18).

Without difficult, hard-headed people, there would be no need for these solutions, nor would there be opportunity to try them out and witness their amazing power to bring victory and restoration (1 Sam 17:37; 1 Jn 4:4; 5:4; 6:33; Rom 8:35–37; 1 Cor 15:57; Rv 2:7, 11, 17, 26; 3:5, 12, 21; 12:11).

The pressures of ministry in the New Testament were even more severe, but they produced men of *much greater strength* and able to endure far worse afflictions while *rejoicing instead* of *complaining* (Num 11:10–15; 20:1–13; 1 Kgs 19:1–4; Job 3; Jer 20:14–18; Mt 11:11–12; Acts 4–5; 14:19; 16:16ff; 1 Cor 4; 2 Cor 6:3–10; 11:22–30).

Modern prisons are no exception. Probably the two most dangerous prisons in the West – Los Olmos in Argentina and Bellavista in Brazil – became the most godly prisons: Bible training centers for inmates. The transformation at Los Olmos took place through the prayer and ministry of one inmate and one staff employee. The change at Bellavista occurred through one ex-convict whom God called to go back as a volunteer to where he'd been incarcerated. (*The Lord of Bellavista*, by David Miller, 1998, available on Amazon.com; Los Olmos Revival – http://www.courtofheaven.com/pdfs/books/5-OlmosPrison-16.pdf (accessed June 20, 2014).

Spiritual growth is impossible without learning to interact with and take responsibility for the people around us, beginning with His family, His Body, the Church. The Bible is a manual on this subject, and *the more difficult the people around us, the more use we get out of the Manual*, and the more experience we enjoy watching God stand behind those "exceedingly great and precious promises." What a challenge! (2 Pet 1:4).

In Bible college most of the students are normal and fairly well-behaved. At worst, they might stay up late making noise and keep you awake for awhile. In jail, your food may be stolen from your locker, your back may be stabbed (literally), your cell-mate might fill your cell with cigarette smoke in defiance of your "religion" and the no smoking rule, and an officer might confiscate your books and Bibles, slander you ruthlessly, violate your rights, or hurt you physically.

The pressure to retaliate against an inmate rather than be known as a wimp might be more than you can handle. And happening to see another inmate commit a crime or sexually abuse a weaker inmate could make *you* the victim of his next crime, especially if he suspects you might "snitch."

But the Bible was written for real men facing these kinds of problems and far worse. Daniel found himself in a den of lions just for praying. Three young Jews ended up *inside* a super-heated furnace for refusing to bow to the king's golden image. The prophets Micaiah and Hanani ended up in prison because each fearlessly told his king the truth he didn't want to hear, and Zechariah (not the biblical writer) was stoned to death for the same reason (Dan 3, 6; 1 Kgs 22; 2 Chr 16:7–10; 24:20–22; Mt 23:35; Heb 11:32–38).

All the apostles, except John, were assassinated for their bold witness – some by crucifixion. John was exiled to an island prison camp to work in the mines and stone quarries. But these pressures produced the New Testament and John's slave-labor imprisonment gave us the book of Revelation.

The New Testament churches had hypocrites, baby believers who acted like spoiled children, sexually immoral "believers," and members who under today's laws would be in jail. But through them the more mature and sincere learned wisdom, patience, boldness, forbearance, and through Paul's letters to them, more understanding of God's ways (1 Cor 1:1–4; 5:1ff; 6:16ff; Eph 4:28, 8–14; Col 3:8–17; 1 Tim 1:20; 2:17; 3 Jn 1:9–10).

Learning wisdom when it's too late to apply it

I always felt it's sadly ironic that we parents don't learn the wisdom we need to properly raise our children until it's too late to use it on them, and now they're damaged by our immaturity during our child-rearing years. And it's too late to re-train them by what we've learned since, though, thankfully, they've learned a lot by our mistakes and have already applied it to their own children. But it's still pretty humbling to see how far we missed it in so many areas.

But because yesterday was my wife's and my fiftieth anniversary, I'd been pondering this apparent "mutation" in God's human engineering after spending a couple days with three of our children and most of their children, amazed at how well they adjusted in spite of our blunders. Then about an hour ago, the answer suddenly came into focus. From our earthly, success-driven viewpoint, it seems like a waste of the most valuable asset in God's economy, for He tells us wisdom is worth more than rubies, and "all the things you may desire cannot be compared with her" (Prv 3:15; 8:11).

But God's wisdom goes beyond our understanding, for He often gets more use out of our dysfunctional, damaged personalities than He does from our "goodness," especially if it doesn't come from His Spirit in us (Is 64:6; Mt 5:6; 9:12–13; Mk 2:17; Lk 5:31–32; 15:11–32; 16:15; Jn 15).

Here is some of that wisdom you might need to use now: If one or both of your parents have messed you up, the best thing you can do to repay them is first, forgive them, second, pray for them, and third, ask God how He might use you in their restoration and healing. That way your own wounds will heal, you'll stop the "generational curse" from passing through you to your children, and God could use you to minister the love and acceptance *their* parents probably didn't give them.

And if you have messed your kids up by a bad example and rotten relationship, ask God for wisdom to become a part of their healing. It's why wisdom is so valuable – it's all about restoring and redeeming relationships. And it's the kind of prayer God is seriously listening for and will answer, if *you* listen! (1Kgs 3:7–12; Job 28:12–28; Prv 8–9; Jas 1:5–7).

One of King David's biggest failures was lack of wisdom in dealing with the horrendous problems among his own children in the wake of his tragic moral failure. Sin always has consequences, and how we deal with them can either bring redemptive healing, or create a vicious cycle of many more problems. Read the whole long story beginning in 2 Samuel 11 to the end of the book (Ps 22, 32, 38–40, 51, 69).

It all goes back to why God left Satan in the Garden of Eden to tempt His new masterpieces – Adam and Eve. And will let him loose again after the "millennium," a thousand-year reign of Christ and His Bride, the Church. He wants the very *highest quality* our God-created character is capable of producing. And that takes constant testing under heat and pressure (Jas 1:2–4, 12; 1 Pet 1:6–7; Heb 12; Rv 20:1–10).

Modern technology has learned how to make high quality oil from garbage of all kinds. First, it's ground to fine powder, then with water added it's subjected to heat and pressure in two stages. A past life of "garbage in" can be "oil out" if you can stand the heat and pressure![3]

My favorite devotional is the one for October 24 from *Streams in the Desert* (Mrs. Chas. E. Cowman, 1925): "A bar of steel worth $5, when wrought into horseshoes, is worth $10. If [made] into needles, it is worth $350; if made into penknife blades, it is worth $32,000; if [made] into springs for watches it is worth $250,000 [1925 values]. What a drilling the poor bar must undergo to be worth this! But the more it is manipulated, the more it is hammered, and passed through the fire, and beaten and pounded and polished, the greater the value.

"May this parable help us to be silent, still, and longsuffering. Those who suffer most are capable of yielding most; and it is through pain that God is getting the most out of us, for His glory and the blessing of others."

1. David Koch, *Slaying the Dragon.* (Los Angeles: Imacaulae Media, 2009), 43
2. Conversations with my daughter, and verification by phone with David Terry. July 9, 2016
3. https://en.wikipedia.org/wiki/Thermal_depolymerization

Jail and Prison Should Produce More Men and Women of God in America Than Bible College or Seminary: Why Don't they?

Part Two

A spiritual education, paid for by the state!

Using hardship as training

In one of my jail classes I asked the guys how Derrick's trial went (name changed), since he wasn't in class. They said he got twenty years, was upset over it, and that's why he wasn't here. So after class I had him pulled out so we could talk one-on-one.

He told me he'd been trusting God and faithfully serving Him in jail, leading Bible studies and the prayer group, encouraging and mentoring the men, helping them out with their needs; he'd had faith God would give him victory in his trial and he'd go home. (I've heard this often, and sometimes they're right on.) He might have even fasted (going without food), as they sometimes do before their trial. But now God had let him down, apparently. I could see he was really discouraged, on the verge of giving up on God, as though serving and trusting Him was all in vain.

But at least he had come out of hiding to see me, so I knew there was hope. He listened carefully as I told him real faith does not consider the negative circumstances, but sees things from God's viewpoint. And in order to purify our faith and wean us from depending on the visible, outward realm, He often hides Himself, even seeming to abandon us (Job 9:11; 23:8–10; Ps 22:1; 88:1ff; Is 47:15; Jer 20:14–8; Lam 3:1–42; 1 Cor 4:8–13; Rom 8:36).

"It is the glory of God to conceal a matter, but the glory of kings is to search out a matter." It's like military training, especially the training of Navy Seals, where you can ring the bell any time you can't take it and want out. How do the ones who make it persevere against what seems like sheer torture, physically and mentally? They see the goal in their *mind* (Prv 25:2–3; Rom 8:24–25; 2 Cor 4:18; Heb 11:1–3, 25–27).

The biblical definition of faith is Hebrews 11:1, "Now faith is the *substance* of things hoped for, the evidence of things not seen," because it's seen spiritually, which is more real – substance, substantial – than the visible, physical world. "Where there is no revelation [vision or spiritual insight], the people cast off restraint [no motivation to take responsibility for doing the right thing]" (Prv 29:18a).

Viktor Frankl, a Jewish psychiatrist among those incarcerated in Hitler's concentration camps, watched fellow inmates die, not from physical illness, but a failure to understand the meaning of life. He developed a school of psychotherapy based on his observations, called *Logotherapy* (Frankl, Viktor. *Man's Search for Meaning.* 1959).

So I told Derrick the fact that he'd given up over the loss of his trial showed he didn't have *real* faith. Instead, he was trusting in his own works, which is why Paul so strongly and frequently wrote that we're not saved by works, and the works we do must originate in faith rooted in the work of Christ, not our own performance (Rom ch 3–6; 8:1–14; Gal 2:19–21; ch 3–5; Eph 2:1–8, Heb 4:9–10; Jas 2:14–26).

Real faith would come away from that trial still trusting that God was working and had something else in mind – more important than physical freedom. I've seen many inmates (okay, *not* many) return from a lost case and facing fifteen years to life, but still rejoicing in the Lord. I have friends in prison who've developed strong faith and deep understanding of God's ways, don't worry about their life sentence, and trust that when God knows they are ready and need to be out, it will happen! (Gen 18:14; Jer 32:17; Lk 1:37; Eph 3:20).

The story of virtually every man or woman of God in the Bible is one of training that would make Navy Seal "hell week" look like kindergarten by comparison. Here's a short description from Hebrews 11, the "faith chapter":

"Others were tortured, not accepting deliverance, that they might obtain a better resurrection. Still others had trial of mockings and scourgings, yes, and of chains and imprisonment. They were stoned, they were sawn in two, were tempted, were slain with the sword. They wandered about in sheepskins and goatskins, being destitute, afflicted, tormented – of whom the world was not worthy. They wandered in deserts and mountains, in dens and caves of the earth" (Heb11:35b–38).

There were no officers or a doctor to oversee and monitor their training, nor a bell to ring if they wanted to quit. But "through faith" they "subdued kingdoms, worked righteousness, obtained promises, stopped the mouths of lions, quenched the violence of fire, escaped the edge of the sword, out of weakness were made strong, became valiant in battle, turned to flight the armies of the aliens. Women received their dead raised to life again" (Heb 11:33–35a).

What's so interesting is that when you read the Old Testament history of these saints in the "hall of faith" (Hebrews 11), it seems their faith failed at times. I was going to list them with their human failures, from Genesis (Noah, Abraham, Sarah, Jacob), Exodus (Moses), Joshua (Joshua, Rahab, a harlot), Judges (Gideon, Barak, Samson, Jephthah), and 1 & 2 Samuel (Samuel and David), but I'm too embarrassed about it.

It would take a whole book to show the balance of how God uses us as a "Treasure" (Christ) in an "earthen vessel," a clay pot! And how God uses our weakness to strip us of pride and "confidence in the flesh," in order to use us more effectively and with purer, stronger faith that perseveres in the face of our failures! (Ps 32, 38, 51; 2 Cor 4:7; 13:4; Heb 6:11–12).

By the way, to my surprise, Derrick lifted up his head, began to smile, and the light came on again in his eyes. He realized God was still in charge. This is why understanding God's ways is so important ("search for meaning"). Because then you know that His silence may not be His abandonment or disapproval, but that He's working something of critical importance behind the scenes (Ps 103:7; Is 30:18–19; 50:10–11).

Rip off the masks!

So life is a series of challenges – learning and training opportunities, but God gives us freedom to avoid them if we choose to. While we learn these great truths in Bible college, we don't have the time or the hardships to *experience* and absorb them to the same depth a typical prison inmate has.

We get better at performing, more creative in writing, more clever in speaking, and more ignorant at how "wretched, miserable, poor, blind, and naked" we are behind all this outward display of our intellectual "riches." Then we wonder why we have difficulty understanding common people with their weakness, sins, addictions, stubbornness, and rebellion (1 Cor 1:17; 2:1–5; Rv 3:17; Ex 4:10; Is 6:1–5; Jer 1:6–7; 17:9–10; Ez 3:15; 2 Cor 11:29; Heb 2:17–18; 5:2).

Some can handle education without letting it go to their heads, and the old saying holds true for them: *the more you know, the more you know how much you don't know.* To learn from these educated but humble teachers is truly a privilege (1 Cor 8:2).

Much, if not most, of our attempt to look good is like the fig leaves Adam and Eve hid behind – a false identity. It takes a lot of work to polish and wax these fig leaves so people will love and approve of us. Deep inside we long to be free, to really be ourselves, but because we fear *rejection,* some of us will do almost anything to avoid being cut off from our friends.

I used to joke about men wearing their pants below their buttocks, having to hold them up to walk in order to be accepted by their friends. At the beginning of one prison service I walked behind the pulpit with my own pants pulled down that far. The inmates cracked up and so did I – because they knew it was not normal for a preacher. I used it to get them to see how abnormal and uncomfortable it was.

Boy, was I in for a surprise! They not only defended themselves loudly, telling me their pants were made to wear that way and it *was* comfortable, but they turned it around and pointed to preachers' styles and why we have to wear a coat and tie (though I never did, even as a pastor). At that point I had to admit they were right. There's hardly anybody who does not feel self-conscious if he or she is not in sync with the current styles. My wife gets rid of her clothes – and mine! – as soon as she notices they are out of style. And that covers hair styles, shoes, purses, and even glasses.

So while those guys cured me of my judgmentalism, they didn't convince me we're not all deeply entrenched in some form of approval addiction. As one man of God said, "Public opinion is enemy number one."

I must add, however, that a mature and biblical understanding is style that's *appropriate*, *sensible*, and *respectable*. These are various translations of the New King James rendering of "modest" in 1 Tim 2:9, which Paul applies to women. While there's no reference to men's clothing styles in the New Testament, it's obvious these adjectives would apply to us also. A "sensible" Christian view is clothing that doesn't draw attention to itself or the sexuality of the body: because our calling is to reflect the glory and fragrance of Christ (2 Cor 2:14–16; 3:18; 10:17; 4:6, 17; Eph 1:12, 18 5:2; Phil 3:19–20; Col 1:27; 1 Thes 2:12, 14, 20; 1 Pet 1:24; 4:11–14; 5:10).

God wants to open the eyes of our inner man to the world of reality, past the superficial. Waiting in darkness can increase our pain until we begin to see our little world of illusions and the *stress, expense, cheating, crime, or craziness* involved in "keeping up appearances" – the name of a "typically English" TV program which exaggerates the problem so we can all see what we're really like behind the masks we wear (1 Jn 2:15–17).

If we can *endure patiently*, we'll begin to see both the horror of our sickness, and then the glory of an intensely *personal* God who *loves* to transform us through *revealing Himself* (Ps 25:14–15; Ex 20:21; 1 Kgs 8:12; Ps 139; Is 1:6; 6:5; 1 Pet 1:7).

"But we all, with unveiled face, beholding as in a mirror the glory of the Lord, are being transformed into the same image from glory to glory, just as by the Spirit of the Lord" (2 Cor 3:18). *When we keep "looking to Jesus" in our darkness, "the Spirit of the Lord" transforms us* little by little (Job 19:7ff; Ps 16:8–11; 22:1ff; 40:1ff; Is 30:18–19; 42:16; 50:10; Lam 3:1–42; Heb 12:2).

Paul compares it to looking into a mirror, which shows us first what's in ourselves that needs changing, and then what's in *Christ-in-us* through faith in Him. It's the perfect balance between humility and faith that Habakkuk saw when he patiently waited in darkness for God's answer (Hab 2:1–4).

The N.T. Greek word for *transformed* is (almost) the word *metamorphosis*.[1] When a caterpillar has faithfully nourished itself on its vegetable diet (the revealed Word), there's a time when it "hangs it up" and dies, like a seed planted (Gen 15:12; Rom 4:19; Ps 22:1f; 38:9–15; 40:1ff; 68:20; 88:5; Jn 12:24).

Not only does it completely die, but most of its body turns to liquid inside its cocoon (moth) or chrysalis (butterfly). All the molecules of its old body are there, but the DNA now re-arranges them to form a brand new creature, specially designed for flight and reproduction.

It all took place in the quiet waiting period inside the darkness, which allowed those mysterious genes to do their work. However, the final stage is vitally important to the survival of these awesome "lapidoptera": the struggle to emerge from the grave of their cocoon/chrysalis. Anyone watching might think it will never make it and be tempted to slit the opening wider to let it out (Eccl 11:5; Is 50:11; 1 Cor 10:12–14).

But these beautiful insects will be deformed and unable to fly *unless each one goes through the intense struggle*, during which its wings develop through the circulation of the fluids in the process (Gen 32:22–32; Hos 12:3–6; Mt 11:12; Lk 16:16; Rom 4:19–22; 1 Tim 6:12).

Wisdom is found in deep darkness (Job 28).

The dark waiting time is one's best opportunity to *hear* "the rebukes of life," to "take inventory," to gain *understanding*, to find humility and "the fear of the Lord," and to experience "the instruction of wisdom" (Ps 119:71, 75; Prv 15:31–33; Is 30:18ff; Heb 12:1–17).

It's seeing the death of the "old man" in God's mirror, where the purifying, cleansing, enlightenment of the Word, the *Logos* (#3056), separates soul from spirit so we can see the hidden motives of our *soul*, how it *copies* (fakes) spiritual things, trying to look good (religious). That Word strips us "naked and open to the eyes of Him to whom we must give account" (Heb 4:12–13).

As the masks of superficiality that deprived the inmate of *rest* in his attempt to win love and approval by looking good get ripped off in the darkness, pain grips him. In the past he deadened his pain with drugs or alcohol or sex or partying or "doing something stupid."

But in jail he has *time* to think and reflect, to allow the Spirit through many sources to speak to him about his need. He speaks through other inmates, correctional officers, volunteers, and through chaplains. Whether these people are kind or not is not important. His willingness to *receive correction* even from hard-headed people like himself is (Ps 141:5; Prv 1:25, 30; 9:7–10; 10:17; 12:1; 13:1; 15:10, 12, 31; 23:35; Jer 8:9; Jn 3:19–21).

He could have learned the same thing through church or family. Both are God's *normal* means of breaking us down and building us up (plan A). Through their weaknesses, problems, dysfunction, and many, many failures, churches and families provide a balance of darkness and light necessary for spiritual growth. Even plants need a balance of darkness and light (photoperiodism).

But when one is not emotionally equipped to navigate these turbulent rivers, jail and prison are God's plan B for the same purpose until he's ready to go back and face the challenge of church and family, and "put his mouth in the dust," blind and deaf to fear, accusation, and suspicion, but watching and waiting for grace to be "exalted [lifted up] in due time" (1 Pet 5:6; Job 42:1–6; Ps 38; Prv 8:32–36; Lam 3:29; Is 42:18–20).

That is, *if* he will *listen* in the darkness instead of repeating the same pattern of "lighting his own fire" through trying to *manipulate the system and those around him in order to avoid exposure and pain. This is truly what makes prison* prison *instead of a learning center for transformation.*

A court appeal is justified when the convict is innocent; I've seen the Holy Spirit provide miraculously as the inmate works on his case. But an inmate trying to find errors and loopholes in his trial in order to *cover* his guilt might well *undo* what God has carefully planned for his emptying, refining, perfecting, and *true* freedom (Ps 18:26; 78:18–31; Prv 12:22; 19:5, 19).

Messed-up people may not need *programs* as much as they need these three things: time, the Word, and the pressures of messed-up people around them. If only they can be taught how to manage these three areas for their spiritual growth, they can end up some of the most valuable ministers to others in need, far better than I'm doing with the limitations of my "education" (1 Cor 1:26–31).

But what happens when they get out?

With the weight of grace overwhelmingly in favor of the weak and humble rather than the "wise and prudent," I hurt to see so few inmates tap into this vast potential for the power and glory of God. And instead, I must admit from what I've observed, there are far more college and seminary-trained men and women of God laying down their lives than ex-convicts, at least here in the U.S. (Mt 11:25; Lk 10:21).

While I was teaching a class at the county jail and pointing out this dilemma, it suddenly dawned on me why this tragic loss of potential exists. I saw in my mind and from my own experience in Bible college the seemingly endless years of hard work and travail it takes to plow through day after day, night after night, semester after semester, with little sleep, working a job on second or third shift, studying into the wee hours of the morning for exams or term papers, weary beyond endurance, yet still hanging on, hoping against hope that it will eventually end. And finally we're free to begin putting into practice what we've learned.

But after graduation, instead of being God's mighty man of faith and power, we're filled with more head-knowledge than wisdom, and we have yet to pay for all that education, gained through a few scholarships, grants, and much more in loans and credit-card debt. But we've hung on this far, and the overwhelming sense of responsibility drives us on through interviews and rejections until finally we land our first ministry opportunity (1 Tim 4:12–16; 2 Tim 2:1–7, 15).

The pressures during those first few years of ministry can be overwhelming. Many leave the ministry in discouragement or burnout and choose secular work rather than suffer financial and personal humiliation, frustration, condemnation, and stagnation at the hands of controlling board officials, hard-headed church members, or high maintenance baby believers still in "diapers" (1 Cor 1:10ff; 3:1ff; Heb 5:12–14).

Even so a sizeable number continues on through every hardship, gaining more strength in God through affliction and tribulation. And over the years their head-knowledge trickles down into heart-revelation, wisdom, and compassion. I recently heard the pastor of one of the largest churches in Florida say on TV that during the first years of his ministry, he'd lock himself in his office to hide from facing anybody after preaching and cower in fear and agony because his sermons were so bad. (Mine still are, which is why I'd rather *write* – to your benefit, I hope!)

Yet with all the failures and money, sex, and power-ruined ministers, our Bible colleges and seminaries remain the basis for thousands of genuine men of God preaching the Gospel today, forming the backbone of "the church of the living God, the pillar and ground of truth" (1 Tim 3:15).

This is true in America but not in most foreign countries, where for years God has been raising up powerful spiritual leaders from among common men and women without formal Bible training, especially in Asia, Africa, and South America, and now in the Middle East, many from among Muslims and even *terrorists!*

I love natural things like natural food, natural healing remedies, natural wood. And I've come to appreciate the most important natural in God's Kingdom – being 100 percent who you *really* are, the *transparency* of 2 Corinthians 3:18 and Hebrews 4:13. It's the Bible's greatest challenge and one of the secrets to knowing God intimately (Ps 39; Is 6; Hab 2; Phil 3:3–10; Heb 4:12–13; Rv 2:2–5).

That's why I believe jail and prison present this world with one of the most *natural* means of producing genuine men and women of God. Many I've come to know are submitting to dehumanization and humiliation with grace and patience. I've watched them grow strong through the Word and faith into men God is using effectively in these institutions as spiritual leaders, counselors, intercessors, and Bible teachers. Some of the most powerful preachers I've heard there make me feel out of place when I get up to speak after them.

But when they get out, far too many of these spiritual-giants-in-the-making eventually fall by the wayside, many of them back into their old lifestyle. Like the seed sown into stony ground, "he receives it with joy . . . but endures only for a while. For when tribulation or persecution arises because of the word, immediately he stumbles." Or like the seed sown among thorns, "the cares of this world and the deceitfulness of riches choke the word, and he becomes unfruitful" or brings "no fruit to maturity" (Mt 13:20–22; Lk 8:14).

What happened to all this potential? As I continued to talk to these inmates, I could feel their eagerness as they looked forward to getting out. Then suddenly it hit me: to even the most "spiritual," *freedom* was their number one goal, whereas for the college grad, *responsibility* was the goal.

When the inmate is released, he is so relieved to be free that his focus is more on that and making up for the lost time! He forgets that God has used this opportunity, "where sin abounded," to reveal Himself and His super-abounding grace in a unique way because of the humbling and confinement. *His carnal longing to be free overpowers the inner call of God* (Rom 5:20; Jn 12:24–26; 1 Cor 9:19).

His goal is no longer caring for others or in knowing God intimately, but in "staying straight" *in order to stay free.* When he finds he can, in fact, stay out of trouble and resist temptation, church and his time with God become less important (1 Cor 12; Eph 3-4; Heb 10:25).

He doesn't realize how essential the *fellowship* he had in jail was to his stability and strength. And even with all his deep knowledge of the Word, he is unable to patiently make the transition from friends who've "been there and done that" to believers who may never understand where he's been and coming from . . . and *might always suspect him.*

Instead of seeing this as a challenge to exercise more faith and dig deeper for more humility and brokenness – an opportunity regular church believers rarely have – he is gradually (or suddenly) offended, discouraged, or distracted by "the cares, riches, and pleasures of life" (Lk 8:14; 10:41; Mk 4:15–20; 10:24; 1 Tim 6:10).

Soon, this would-be mighty man of God, with all the potential for *grace* to work through his humble background, slips back into the old mode. Far too many end up back in jail or prison, where I hear their stories (1 Cor 10:12–14).

Great challenges are great opportunities for grace!

But there are yet more factors that compound the problem. A college graduate has one of the most valuable pieces of paper in a lifetime: a *college degree*.

This little document speaks volumes to employers and church leaders: Here is one who has endured the lengthy process of getting an education. His past speaks for his future – he may well serve them as faithfully as he served his teachers. And experience has proven this is generally true (Lk 16:10–12).

An ex-convict has nothing to show but a history of *felonies*, the extreme opposite of *faithfulness*. His "degree" is a rap sheet that tells employers and church leaders there's a very good chance he will again fail, like the millions before him – once a criminal, always a criminal!

If he mentions his conversion experience and his faithful Christian service in jail, he is accused of having "jailhouse religion." Add wrist to neck tattoos, lack of marketable skills, and ignorance about job interviews and resumes, and the ex-inmate may go through months of unsuccessful attempts to find a decent job or one adequate to support the family he is trying to take responsibility for (1 Thes 3:10–12).

And family brings up still another problem – perhaps the biggest yet. Many of the hardest years are behind the college grad. The future will bring him acceptance and encouragement from family and friends, enabling him to keep his identity intact and his eyes on the goal, even through many failures.

But if jail and prison were hard, the worst is yet to come for the ex-con. From the day he sets his foot on free soil his family and friends greet him with a friendly smile that may hide a mountain of suspicion and conditional love. "You've betrayed us before. How long will you last this time," is the hidden, or not so hidden, message. Often all it takes is one failure and an avalanche of accusation and condemnation from others, himself, the Accuser of the Brethren – Satan, and even from God, it *seems*, drive him back into the horror of his past (Rv 12:10; Lam 3:1–18).

On the surface these disadvantages looming like huge mountains look *impossible* to overcome. I can easily understand the despair and hopelessness these men (and women) face, and I'm sure it accounts for the high failure rate, especially considering their past background of repeat failure and the endless problems of their family environments (Prv 24:16).

But again, when I look at it from God's viewpoint I see a *great advantage* and a speedy *shortcut* to the glory of what "many prophets and kings [and seminary graduates] have desired to see and have not seen." These ex-convicts may have had a hopeless beginning, but God has more than made it up to them in those three blessings this article is about: time, the Word, and the relationships. *If they fail to utilize this huge advantage almost nobody in the free world has, what else can God do?* (Lk 10:24; 19:11–27).

Furthermore if God reveals Himself to "babes" and "gives grace to the humble," then what might take the "wise and prudent" many years to finally understand is readily available to this humble ex-criminal who has reaped brokenness and travail, and now *stands on the threshold of divine favor* (Mt 11:25; Lk 10:21; Jas 4:6; 1 Pet 5:5).

For it is precisely these kinds of impossibilities that God's Word and mustard-seed-mountain-moving-faith in it and in Him are designed for. David was the last and least among eight sons of Jessie, and was given the least significant job – watching sheep, living with them day and night (1 Sam 16:11; 17:34–37).

But he used "doing time" to great advantage. He fine-tuned his heart to God's ways through Moses, Joshua, Gideon, Samson, Samuel, and the endurance of Abraham, Jacob, Joseph, and Job. And God developed his faith on lions, bears, and Goliath in preparation for bigger faith-battles: King Saul's jealousy and treachery, the "wicked and worthless" among his own small army, the insubordination of his leaders, and hordes of enemy armies (1 Sam 16–28; 2 Sam 3, 10).

Then faith to recover from his own horrendous crimes of adultery and murder and the terrible, unending divine chastening that followed him to his death bed, not to mention another act of disobedience that cost the lives of 70,000 of his own people (2 Sam 11–24; Ps 32, 38, 51).

The story of Joseph is even closer to home for inmates and ex-cons. He never had the chance for a formal education or a job interview, for he was sold as a slave at seventeen, and a few years later thrown into prison on a false rape charge because he refused to cave in to the lustful desires of his master's wife. For his obedience he was locked away in a dungeon, probably for the rest of his life without parole. Betrayed, forsaken, and forgotten by family members and those whose trust he'd patiently earned, his future was beyond hopeless (Ps 88; Lam 3).

But his humble faith, his forgiving heart, and his willingness to learn the lessons God was teaching him in these agonizing tribulations were *precisely the training that prepared him* to be second in command under Pharaoh as governor of Egypt – and (can you believe?) teacher of *wisdom* to *Pharaoh's elders!* And . . . restorer of his Father's lost sons (Gen 37–45; Ps 105:17–22).

These are *Old Testament* examples – men who "desired to see" and "hear" what we have in the New Testament. We have the teachings of Jesus, the insights of Paul and others on *how* to apply them through the power of the Spirit. And we have the Revelation of Jesus to John about how the gates (strategy) of Hell and Death are destroyed by the hosts of heaven through the faith and obedience of believers (Rv 12:11; Mt 16:18).

"For we walk by faith, not by sight." It doesn't take nearly the faith to present a college transcript with a degree to an employer than it does a rap-sheet and probation papers. The first might well be trust in man and the arm of flesh. But the ex-con with no hope but in *God* has all the advantages of heaven behind him, with a host of angels and a "great cloud of witnesses" to cheer him on (2 Cor 5:7; Jer 17:5; Heb 12:1).

"For you see your calling, brethren, that not many wise according to the flesh, not many mighty, not many noble, are called. But God has chosen the *foolish* things of the world to put to shame the wise, and God has chosen the *weak* things of the world to put to shame the things which are mighty, and the *base* things of the world and the things which are *despised* God has chosen, and the things which *are not*, to bring to nothing the things that are, that *no flesh should glory in His presence*" (1 Cor 1:26–29).

It all depends on which set of facts he sets his heart on – how he utilizes what he learned in prison. For "we do not look at the things which are seen, but at the things which are not seen. For the things which are seen are temporary, but the things which are not seen are eternal" (2 Cor 4:18).

It's about time we see what God can do with this vast untapped potential – men and women "taught of God" in what may rightly be "among the most powerful character building events in the universe" – our jails and prisons.

1. #G3339, *metamorpho-o*

CHAPTER 3

The Fear of the Lord

The fear of the Lord is to hate evil.
By the fear of the Lord one departs from evil.
Proverbs 8:13a; 16:6b

No Pain, No Gain

Drug and alcohol addictions are the best thing that ever happened to many people. Why? Because addictions are the outward symptoms of a deeper problem inside, like a blemish on the surface of the skin connected to a cancer underneath. Programs that deal only with the addiction are like covering the cancerous sore with a band-aid. No wonder some popular government drug-treatment programs can't even control drug use within the program!

Why are we so eager to get rid of our addiction without dealing with the cause? Because the addiction, more than the cause of it, is what destroys our finances, our families, our health, our minds, and may land us in jail again and again.

What then is the cause? It's a deadly mixture of freedom and pleasure. It's the illusion that life is all about satisfying my immediate need to feel good and eliminate any kind of physical and emotional pain as quickly and conveniently as possible.

Imagine that: the idea that these awesome bodies of ours which contain an indestructible soul created by in infinitely wise God who designed us in His image to communicate and fellowship with Him for eternity . . . and these awesomely complex beings exist for only one reason – to feel good!

And if feeling good and escaping pain are all that matter, then whoever interferes with my quest for pleasure becomes my enemy – someone I must manipulate, run or hide from, fight against either verbally or physically . . . or maybe even eliminate. Then if I end up in jail, instead of owning up to my self-centeredness so I can "hear the rebukes [corrections] of life," I continue the same path of blame, manipulation, and bad-mouthing others (Prv 15:31).

"If you reject discipline, you only harm yourself; but if you listen to correction, you grow in understanding" (Prv 15:32 NLT).

Buying Pleasure on Credit

A friend of mine had been a borderline alcoholic most of his life. Raised in a Christian home, he made countless attempts to quit, but his friends always lured him back. Yet when the doctor gave him an ultimatum regarding his health and *life*, suddenly alcohol was no problem. He quit cold turkey.

But due to his past irresponsibility with alcohol, his offspring, to the third generation so far, are reaping the consequences of his lifestyle – alcoholism, drug addiction, crime, and prison. And one of his sons and a young adult grandson have already died from causes related to this kind of living.

If this grandfather had feared God as he feared losing his health, he could have quit decades ago and set the right example for his family. And now he'd be enjoying not only improved health, but happy family relationships instead of conflict, stress, and no end to legal expenses or those related to the upkeep of his *codependent middle-aged* children!

When Moses asked God to show him His glory, God revealed Himself as "merciful and gracious, longsuffering, and abounding in goodness and truth, keeping mercy for thousands, forgiving iniquity and transgression and sin."

That's one side of His glory, the one many, especially teens, use to excuse an ungodly lifestyle. But the rest of it reads: "By no means clearing the guilty, visiting the iniquity of the fathers upon the children and the children's children to the third and the fourth generation." In other words, our sin affects not only ourselves, but our descendants also, exposing them to the heat of judgment (Ex 34:6–7).

But the fear of the Lord is more than fear of consequences; it is reverence and awe of a holy God whose "consuming fire" burns with intense love and passion to purify us until we too burn with that same passion to shine forth His glory that others also may know Him (Song 8:6–7; Is 6:1–7; Eph 1:4; 2 Cor 11:2; Col 1:22, 28; Heb 12:29; Jas 4:5).

God's holiness is like the beneficial, life-giving glory of the sun, whose rays purify on contact. But the sun would also destroy our planet if it weren't for the protective atmosphere and the magnetic shield around it – a picture of our protection in Christ through His atoning blood (Num 18:5; Ps 84:11; 1 Cor 3:12–15; 1 Pet 1:7; Rv 3:18).

Who are you deep down?

When we fear man's law more than God's, we'll do whatever we can get away with, like drugs, smoking weed, shoplifting, lying, cheating on exams, lying on applications, and more – a *lifestyle* that *seems* normal until it grows into the bondage of addiction and co-dependency. "Because the sentence against an evil work is not executed speedily, therefore the heart of the sons of men is fully set in them to do evil" (Eccl 8:11; see Ps 52:3; Prv 28:9; 30:12; Is 5:20).

Some years ago I casually asked my juvenile class of girls and boys how many of them would rob a bank if they knew they could get away with it. Before they answered they wanted assurance that they could really get away with it. When I assured them, almost all of them raised their hands. It took me completely by surprise.

I figured it was a teenage attitude, and almost as a joke decided to ask my adult men in prison and jail, many of whom I thought were strong believers because of how well they knew the Bible. But to my amazement, more than half raised their hands, especially when I assured them, as with juveniles, they would never be caught and could have all that money, tax free.

I call this test a self-diagnostic mini-MRI because it gives them a spiritual picture of their own hearts. It tells them they fear man, not God, and temporary punishment in jail rather than eternal punishment in hell. And that if they will rob a bank, they will do anything else if they "know" they can get away with it. For the true test of integrity is what a person does when no one sees or will ever know.

But most heart-breaking, it tells me these men who study the Bible, attend church services in jail, and claim to have a relationship with Jesus through the new birth, are completely willing – if only temporarily – to turn their backs on Him who died for them, who loves them passionately, and whose plans for them are beyond their wildest dreams.

No doubt this "MRI" also reveals that while they may know enough *about* God to receive His forgiveness and mercy, they really don't "know the love of Christ which passes knowledge" that they "may be filled with all the fullness of God." They have not yet learned His ways or become intimate with Him to the point of feeling His pain or His anger when they disobey Him (Ps 32; 38; Eph 3:19; 4:30; Heb 3:7–11).

Some of the men felt justified if it meant stealing to provide for their families, or as long as nobody got hurt, or if it was a bank and not a person. It's like God was still a far-off idea, rather than their Provider, Care-giver, "Shepherd and Overseer," their Daddy, their *Spouse* who created them for intimate fellowship with Him for eternity (Gen 22:14; Hos 2:16; Mt 6:9; Jn 17:21; Rom 8:15; Eph 2:5–7; Phil 3:10; 1 Pet 2:25; 5:7).

They may understand a little about His mercy, but they do not comprehend the magnitude of the price Jesus paid to grant that mercy. Or if they've watched Mel Gibson's *The Passion of the Christ*, they know only a little of the *physical* suffering, but not the horror He went through *spiritually* – an eternity of Hell compressed into a few hours of time on the cross as our Sin-bearer (Lev 4, 16; Ps 22; Is 53; Mt 27:46; 2 Cor 5:21).

Why change?

When the consequences of breaking the law, whether God's or man's law, are delayed or don't seem to outweigh the pleasure or benefit gained, it's simply natural to do what our "fleshly desires" want to do (Eccl 8:11).

One inmate was shocked when I mentioned that sex before marriage was sin. He knew "adultery" was wrong, that it's stealing another man's wife or cheating on yours. But he thought sex with girlfriends was an expression of love, part of a normal date. He wanted proof. When I read one of the many verses on "fornication," he wanted the definition of the word. I thought he was really looking for a way to prove me wrong (2 Cor 12:21; Gal 5:19; Eph 5:3; Col 3:5).

The following week each of us came with the dictionary definition: "sexual intercourse between people who are not married to each other."[1] He was awed and amazed and told us he would faithfully keep this command. I was totally surprised to see a man in jail that serious about obeying God. It's rare!

Jacob's son Reuben fully expected to receive the special inheritance of the firstborn when his aged father brought his twelve sons before him for their final blessing. But he was *disqualified* as "unstable," *unfit* for the heavy *leadership responsibility* of the firstborn. Because many years earlier he'd had sex – just once – with Jacob's concubine (a secondary wife). His act was more than sexual sin. It was disrespect of his father's authority. Like many who take God's command to "abstain from sexual immorality" lightly, he had *no fear of God* (Gen 35:22; 49:3–4; Lev 18:8; 20:11; 1 Thes 4:3).

The reason it's so easy to take it lightly is that it seems to be all about love and relationship, which is what Jesus taught – love your neighbor as yourself, do to others as you'd have them do you. If it's "mutual consent," how can it be wrong? It's so beautiful, natural, and love-ly! (Mt 7:12; 22:39).

Yet the breakdown of the family, with sexual unfaithfulness at its root, is the *number one cause of crime* because *uncommitted* love is *irresponsible – not love at all!* For it produces single-parent and dysfunctional families, robbing people of what they need most – unconditional love: the love that forgives, protects, and commits "for better, for worse, for richer or poorer, in sickness and in health, till death do us part." That's the heart of the traditional marriage vow, by the way. A Web search on "breakdown of the family" with "crime" will easily confirm this conclusion (Mal 2:13–15; Eph 5:25–33; 1 Pet 3:7).

Many times when I would casually mention to a class of boys and girls in detention center that sex outside of marriage is sin, they'd start laughing and joking with each other, slapping high-fives, as though it's the funniest thing they'd ever heard. When I'd finally get their attention I'd ask, "How many of you have both your biological mom and dad to go home to when you get out?"

And suddenly they'd get quiet, when only about one in six or more raised a hand. Then I'd tell them, "In about fifteen years, I'll be talking to your kids in this same place because you are playing the same game with sex your parents did, and producing babies with no commitment to provide the love they need from both a faithful mother and father who claim them as their own."

And then I realized I may already be talking to children of boys I taught in the state correctional facilities since the time I started in Florida in 1993.

Which again is why if God's love is not enough to stop this drive of "hormones" and passion, and we've changed man's law so it's okay, the only thing left to show us something is drastically wrong with us are the *addictions*. Because if they don't kill us first, at least it gives those "hated police" a *lawful* reason to round us up and "detain" us so God can get a *Word* in edgeways (Is 10:5; Prv 23:13).

One inmate said, "I've got everything right – no more drugs [well, he's in jail]. But I can't let go of sex." I answered, "That's why drugs are not your *real* problem." Another who'd been heavily involved in the sex industry told me, "It sucked the life right out of me, leaving me empty and destitute. I'm here trying to recover."

A friend, an alcoholic, has phoned me for prayer occasionally, pleading with me in tears to pray that God will deliver him of this addiction, which has virtually ruined him. *But he can't see the connection between his addiction and his total disregard of God's law regarding sex – no fear of God* (Prv 15:31–33).

And so addictions have done one good thing: They've shown us (the hard way) that "the law of the Lord is perfect, converting the soul. . . . The fear of the Lord is clean, enduring forever; the judgments of the Lord are true and righteous altogether. More to be desired are they than gold, yea, than much fine gold. . . .

Moreover by them Your servant is warned, and in keeping them there is great reward" (Ps 19:7–11). Wow – *Great reward!*

Feeding the fire

However, there are two areas that if you don't deal with them, will constantly frustrate or destroy every attempt you may make to come clean and go with God: it's what you do with your mind and your heart.

First is music, rap, TV, movies, Internet, social media, reading material, and video games. They are the *food* for your mind and spirit, making you either week or strong, carnally (fleshly) minded or spiritually minded (Gal 5:16–25; Col 3:1–6).

"For those who live according to the flesh *set their minds* on the things of the flesh, but those who live according to the Spirit, the things of the Spirit. For to be carnally minded is *death*, but to be spiritually minded is life and peace" (Rom 8:5–6; see Prv 4:23; Phil 4:8).

"Your eye is a lamp that provides light for your body. When your eye is good, your whole body is filled with light. But when it is bad, your body is filled with darkness. Make sure that the light you think you have is not actually darkness. If you are filled with light, with no dark corners, then your whole life will be radiant, as though a floodlight were filling you with light" (Lk 11:34–36 NLT).

From the "lamp" of our hearts, "come evil thoughts, sexual immorality, theft, murder, adultery, greed, wickedness, deceit, lustful desires, envy, slander, pride, and foolishness. All these vile things [darkness] come from within; they are what defile you" (Mt 7:21–23 NLT).

In third-world countries when people involved in witchcraft come to Christ and truly repent, they bring their satanic paraphernalia and burn it, as they did in the book of Acts – several million dollars worth of books. I've heard of others in America who destroyed entire collections of CDs or music cassettes when they came humble and broken in true repentance before the Lord. An inmate told me his mother kept telling him to get rid of his bad music CDs that were "poisoning" his mind. *He* never did, but his dog Corey got to them and ruined *all* of them (Acts 19:19).

In 1996 God transformed Pond Inlet, a town in northern Canada that had been destroyed by alcoholism – families shattered by physical and sexual abuse, the economy ruined, a suicide rate 20 times the Canadian average, and even wildlife gone.

When revival came through the desperate praying of believers, sinners repented and completely filled the town dump with illegal drugs, bad music CDs, and pornographic magazines, all valued at 80 to 100 thousand dollars. The people cheered while the Royal Canadian Mounted Police burned the last overflow pile of them to ashes. The curse was broken and God brought prosperity and healing back to the community until even the wildlife returned in abundance.[2]

I understand the struggle, however. I played piano for a club or two while I was running from God in my youth. When I came back to Him I thought I could still play for a party here and there and make a little easy money. But one New Year's Eve party (1963–4) for a bunch of doctors, lawyers, and professionals who drank themselves drunk while I played broke the spell of "darkness" in me. When I got home, I cried my way to repentance until my "lamp" shined with heavenly light (Jn 3:20 –21).

Yet even then I didn't want to give up my "fake books," the expensive black-market music books with all those night-club songs I'd played. But to my shame, in God's corrective love, someone stole them. (I didn't have a dog!)

"Do not love this world nor the things it offers you, for when you love the world, you do not have the love of the Father in you. For the world offers only a craving for physical pleasure, a craving for everything we see, and pride in our achievements and possessions. These are not from the Father, but are from this world. And this world is fading away, along with everything that people crave. But anyone who does what pleases God will live forever" (1 Jn 2:15–17 NLT).

Light and fellowship

The second area is *friends*, because we all need fellowship. But friends are the environment that creates a lifestyle. "Don't fool yourselves. Bad friends will destroy you"; "associating with bad people will ruin decent people"; "wicked friends lead to evil ends" (1 Cor 15:33 *Contemporary English Version, God's Word, International Standard Version*, respectively – in that order).

How can we resist temptation unless we fear God more than we fear the disapproval of our friends? That's why we need the encouragement, fellowship, and support of a church family the way a baby needs a family to live and grow (Rom 12:4–5; 1 Cor 12:12; Eph 4:4, 11–16; Heb 10:25; Ps 26:8; 27:4–6).

"But if we walk in the light as He is in the light, we have fellowship with one another, and the blood of Jesus Christ His Son cleanses us from all sin." We all desperately want answers to prayer but often don't understand that prayer and *obedience* work together. We fear consequences and hardship more than we fear God and love His will (1 Jn 1:7; 5:14; Jn 15:7).

"You ask and do not receive, because you ask amiss, that you may spend it on your pleasures. Adulterers and adulteresses! Do you not know that *friendship with the world is enmity with God? Whoever therefore wants to be a friend of the world makes himself an enemy of God.* Or do you think that the Scripture says in vain, 'The Spirit who dwells in us yearns jealously?'" (Jas 4:3–5).

Considering how badly we need God, nobody wants to be His enemy. Furthermore, His Spirit "yearns jealously" to guard us for Himself, like a faithful Husband, and would draw us away from sin to Himself – if only we'll yield to Him. Yet our lifestyle often plants us smack in the center of His *judgment* instead of His mercy, and we wonder why things go from bad to worse. For there is no curse without a *cause!* (Rom 6:15–23; Col 3:1ff; Prv 26:2; Jgs 2:1–4; 3:1ff; Is 30:19).

My greatest moral temptation

At age twenty-four I faced one of the most serious temptations of my life. I'd grown up in a pastor's home but turned away from God. Even a year at a Christian college (Evangel U) hadn't changed me. Then in late 1963, through Dad's intense intercession (praying) for me (with the added prayers of my sister, Sharon, I found out later), I came back to God (another story), but after three more semesters of college and Bible school, I still had a lot of rebellion, questions, confusion, depression, and very little faith.

But in 1966 I gave in to my dad's request and enrolled in the Bible college of *his* choice in hopes of preparing for the ministry. I also had a job after classes, and a very nice, refined much older "Christian" woman, a fellow employee, made me an offer that in other circumstances might have been no temptation (Gen 3:5–6).

However, knowledge has always been my biggest temptation (Gen 3:5). This woman told me she could teach me things that would make me a "wonderful husband" to my future wife. That sounded appealing because I intended to be exactly that someday, as well as a good father to wonderful children.

She proposed that when I leave my shift at midnight, I should come to her house and she would teach me all I needed to know about sex. Since I'd never studied that subject I figured this could truly prepare me to be an awesome husband to some wonderful wife (Prv 5–7).

So this offer appealed to me – a free sex-education with a real experience "lab class." Nobody would pay attention to when I came home, since in those early years lights went out and students retired at 11:00 PM in the dorms where I stayed.

The only thing that stood in the way was a weakly-developed sense of *the fear of God* deep down in my conscience. It bothered me just enough to make me hesitate in my decision to take this tempting offer. After all, I was in Bible college, learning the Bible. And almost every book in the Bible clearly taught that sex outside of marriage was a major sin with serious spiritual and eternal consequences, though I was still not too certain about hell or whether the Bible was really *God's* Word.

But somehow the education aspect seemed almost to overrule the moral side. I made a list of pros and cons, and the list was equal on both sides. After two or three weeks of this inward battle, on the way to work one day, I cried out, *God, I'm too weak to pray about it anymore. Cause someone else to pray for me; I'm about to give in!*

It was either that night or the next, but when she called me on my shift to ask if I'd decided yet, in the dialogue she said something that suddenly jolted me out of my sleep of death. Instantly I recognized the trap of Satan and the pit to which he had almost lured me. I was free! (Prv 7:21–27).

Two weeks later a friend known on campus as "the prayer warrior" stopped me in the hall and asked, "Hey Vic, were you going through something about two weeks ago?"

"Yes," I replied, without revealing what it was. "Why?"

"God laid you on my heart and I prayed for you."

I was shocked and amazed that God truly did "know my sitting down and my rising up," and "understand my thought afar off." He really "knows how to deliver the godly out of temptations" (Ps 139:2; 2 Pet 2:9).

But the second half of this verse adds, "and to reserve the unjust under punishment for the day judgment" (2 Pet 2:9). If God knows how to deliver us from temptation and we don't allow Him, it only indicates the secret wickedness of our hearts, and that we really *want* to do it! *There is no fear of God before our eyes!* (Rom 3:18; Jas 1:13–14).

Obedience – how it works and its reward

God tells us more about *how* He delivers us from temptation in 1 Corinthians 10. Verse 13 says there is no temptation that is not "common to man, but God is faithful, who will not allow you to be tempted beyond what you are able, but with the temptation will also make the way of escape, that you may be able to bear it."

I used to feel that verse was not reliable because His people frequently do fail under temptation. I felt God was a little unrealistic about His claims and didn't really understand how much some of us are "in all points tempted as we are" (Heb 2:17–18; 4:15–16).

Then one day I noticed the verses on either side of verse 13. Verse 12 says, "Therefore let him who thinks he stands take heed lest he fall." This is exactly how I felt – so weak in myself that I *knew* I needed help. And God – true to His Word – spoke to someone else strong and alert enough to pray for me, even as Jesus prayed for Peter in his hour of temptation, "that your faith should not fail" (Lk 22:32).

And verse 14 says, "Therefore, my beloved, flee from idolatry." This means the "way of escape" may not be visible or apparent until we let go of our distractions (idols). "We do this by keeping our eyes on Jesus, the champion who initiates and perfects our faith." No wonder "the fear of the Lord is the beginning of [opens the door to] wisdom" (Heb 12:2 NLT; Prv 9:10).

But there's more to the story. A really "great reward" followed, for "He *rewards* those who *sincerely* seek Him." My pitiful, but desperate cry for God to speak to someone else on my behalf was, apparently, the "sincerity" God needed to hear (Heb 11:6a NLT; Gal 6:7–9).

A short time after this crisis passed, I hit one of the lowest points in my life. I knew I needed more than sex: I needed a wife – someone to draw me out of myself. God had delivered me from the most difficult moral temptation of my life, but I still felt hopelessly lonely and depressed.

On the way to work after class the day after I'd hit rock bottom, I suddenly blurted out, "God, I've got to have a wife in *one month*." Then I felt ashamed for such a foolish prayer and asked God to forgive me. It was May 5, 1966. The next day a friend asked me to find a girl to double-date with him and his girlfriend, for we "underclassmen" were not allowed to go out on a date without another couple.

I'd met a girl on campus a couple days earlier who seemed like a lot of fun – nothing serious, and I figured she'd oblige me. But in the process of trying to find her, another girl I'd known there walked by me, and on the spur of the moment I asked her. She agreed.

I would never have dated her again because I figured she was not "my type." But something she said in our conversation sent an arrow to my heart. We decided to get married as soon as the semester was out, and kept our relationship morally pure. It was truly *a God thing!* (Prv 18:21–22).

My minister father arranged the wedding, and together with another minister, married us. The date was June 5, 1966, unintentionally, but *exactly*, one month from the date of my "foolish" prayer. It was Psalm 139 all over again.

I'd gotten so desperate for a wife I'd told God I'd marry anybody, even a prostitute. I'd long given up my main desire in a wife, that she play the piano. But God had not forgotten. My wife was one of the college chapel organists. She ended up teaching our four children the piano, they all play or have played piano *and guitar* for church services, and one of them is a trained worship leader on piano and violin.

God did give me "wonderful children," a "wonderful wife," and I'm still working on the "wonderful husband" part. But I've long since learned that good sex has little to do with sex education and *everything* to do with knowing and obeying God, and loving my wife – *long before bedtime!* (1 Cor 7:4ff; Eph 5:25; Prv 5:15–19).

This God-picked wife is still with me, 50 years this June (2016), and is everything I never knew I needed so desperately in a wife. Only God could have done it, but *the fear of the Lord* was the means He used to deliver me from what would have certainly steered my life into a terribly different direction (read Deuteronomy 28).

But it's never too late if we're still alive. *Some of the worst sinners and most hopeless addicts have become the most awesome saints.* I see jail-ministry volunteers who've "been there and done that" as *more qualified by their past than I am*, but they've paid a bigger price in pain, broken relationships, and loss of families, homes, and material things. They learned the hard way, but they learned well (Gen 38, 44; 1 Cor 1:25–31; 15:9; 1 Tim 1:15).

For the wise will finally learn that everything hinges on the *kind* of pleasure we choose – intense "highs" which burn out like firecrackers, demand increasing, out-of-control doses, destroy relationships, cost more in this life than we can ever pay, and in the life to come, unending horror! (Rv 20:15).

Or with a little uncommon sense, we'll humbly take responsibility for the life God has given us, endure the testing and training of our faith, and begin to experience a pleasure far deeper, infinitely more meaningful, longer lasting, and with surprising benefits both in this life and the life to come. Like a "sparkler" that burns on and on and gets brighter and more beautiful as it burns (Ps 37:1–7; Prv 4:18; 2 Cor 4:14–18; Heb 12:1–17; Jas 1:2–4; 1 Pet 1:3–9).

Because our Source is God! (Heb 12:2; 1 Jn 5:11).

1. The most common Internet dictionary definition
2. Otis, George Jr. *Transformations II, The Glory Spreads*. The Sentinel Group, CA, 2001.Video.

CHAPTER 4

The Power of Forgiving

Resentment destroys more alcoholics than anything else. From it stem all forms of spiritual disease.
Alcoholics Anonymous Big Book, p. 64.

Don't destroy yourself: there's a better way
Unforgiveness is a normal part of life because we've all had people or friends who have failed us, double-crossed us, abused us, lied to us, betrayed us, cheated us, hurt us physically, or ruined us completely (Ps 41:9).

Jails, psychiatric wards, and hospitals house many people emotionally crippled, disabled, like lepers quarantined from relationships and feeding on a diet of blame, criticism, bitterness, and hatred. All because they don't know how to forgive. Or don't want to.

But broken families are the main culprit behind most of it. Malachi 4:6, the last verse in the Old Testament, pronounces a curse on the earth when the hearts of fathers and children do not turn to each other.

Robert Stearns in his book, *Prepare the Way* (*or Get Out of the Way*),[1] comments on this verse: "Our nation is bearing the fruit of fatherlessness in a myriad of ways. We all know it. We know the statistics, and inherently we know that the root of societal problems is the breakdown of the family. *And the breakdown of the family is largely due to the absent, abusive, or withdrawn father.*"

Josh McDowell, a popular writer, speaker, and researcher, said that a boy with a good to excellent relationship with his father is only six percent likely to go into drugs, alcohol, and violence compared with a 68% likelihood of one raised in even a two-parent biological home, but with a *fair to poor relationship with his father.*

McDowell found that teen killers like the one at Columbine High School in Denver had either a distant relationship with their fathers or none at all. And a thirty-year study at Johns Hopkins found "the probability of mental illness, hypertension, malignant tumor, coronary heart disease, and suicide had to do with lack of closeness to one's parents."

He mentioned the time Michael Jackson broke down during a talk at Oxford University and started to cry uncontrollably. When he finally regained his composure, he told how as a child during a rehearsal he turned to his dad and said, "Daddy . . ." His father answered, "I'm not your daddy, I'm your manager." He told the audience, "All I've ever wanted in life was for my father to call me and say, 'Michael, I love you.' And he never did."

McDowell began to share his heart as a daddy to audiences. He'd say, "I wish I could be your daddy, your father, and you could be my son or daughter." Guys all over started waving their hands; then they started yelling out, "I want to be your son, would you be my daddy." Once 100 guys stood up and shouted, "I want to be your son!"

At a high school assembly in Memphis there were fifteen hundred kids waiting to hear him. The principal had warned him there was a group of Gothics on campus that would break up the assembly and try to throw the speaker off campus, and that they do it every single assembly; they get kicked out, but they come back and do it again. When he started to speak, six Gothics came up, dressed in black and black makeup, wearing big dog collars and wrist and ankle bands with spikes, totally covered in tattoos and piercings, every kind of hair color, and big chains and one with a huge iron cross on his chest.

He suddenly switched his talk to the subject of intimacy. "Intimacy is the capacity to be real with another person and Christ can give you the confidence to be real through His forgiveness and indwelling presence." At the end of his speech the head of the Gothics suddenly leaped toward him and came up to within six inches of his nose and said very respectfully, "Mr. McDowell, would you give me a hug?"

The number one question he gets from kids all over the

world is, "Would you give me a hug?" When Josh said yes, the Gothic instantly clamped his arms around him, put his head on his right shoulder, and in front of 1500 kids cried like a baby. And when he finally stepped back, he said, "Mr. McDowell, my father never once ever hugged me or told me he loved me."

Hugh Hefner said he knew his mother loved him but she never showed it, so he had to learn about love from the movies. Josh believes that if he'd received "unfailing love" from his father, there never would have been *Playboy*.

When asked by President Bush's speech writer what was the greatest problem facing America, McDowell told her the greatest problem facing America is "the daddy," then emailed her 78 pages of research to prove it. When Bush got to that in his speech, he got the loudest standing ovation of the speech.

Mothers' love and attention are taken for granted; dads' are not. And when it's given, when they pray with them and cry with them, the impact is "totally out of proportion, because it's not expected." Josh said it's *never* too late to begin the reconciliation process. He added that his most important ministry is loving his wife and children.

I gathered the above information from a recorded speech McDowell gave to the chapel at *Focus on the Family* in 2006. At the end of his speech James Dobson, founder and then president of *Focus*, quoted the late Derek Prince (well-known man of God, international speaker, and writer) as saying the biggest problem in America is "renegade males" – men who are not doing their job.

How to change things

When in 1981 God suddenly spoke to me that my pastoring days were over, I was shocked, wondering what I would do, since I felt called to the ministry and had pastored twelve years. He led me to a couple local Bible schools, where I taught Bible subjects for a number of years. And in 1993 the door opened in Florida to begin teaching men in the local state prison, and later other detention and prison facilities.

It has become the passion of my life to encourage these men to use their time to allow God to transform them from victims of society's neglect and abuse, to men who will help restore others like them. But so much of it begins with a grasp of the power of forgiveness.

When I finished working on the above material from *Focus on the Family*, I came into my living room just as a young lady on a Christian TV channel told of how her abusive father had refused her many attempts to establish a father-daughter relationship with her that could have brought healing and reconciliation. Finally she turned to God and found what she'd been looking for all her life – *His* fatherly love! It restored her completely and her face glowed with God's glory and love as she related this experience.

I know it's difficult for many of the men I see in jail to hope for a restored relationship with their dads or children, if that's what's lacking. But if they find that relationship in God first, He will break the *curse* Malachi spoke of and release His guidance in the restoration process.

Our inability to forgive reveals our ignorance of God's ways. We want justice or revenge. What we don't realize is that God actually wants it more than we do and has the ability to do it without destroying Himself or us. Because our attempt to get even will destroy *us* rather than the one we're trying to repay (Rom 12:19).

One of the most gifted men I've ever met, and on his way to a brilliant career as a military officer, did just that. He felt so frustrated that the law would (or could) do nothing about a terrible situation, he took justice into his own hands. He did it within sight of a restaurant where I've taken my wife to eat more than once.

I met him in prison on a life sentence for murder. There I believe he will become in the Spirit what he looked forward to in the natural – a high ranking officer in *God's* army, right there on the front lines in prison!

All of us have one time or another done something "in the flesh" to "teach someone a lesson," only to short-circuit a far better plan using *spiritual* weapons instead of carnal (Prv 24:17–18; Mt 5:44; Rom 12:17–21; 2 Cor 10:3–6).

The civil rights movement in the late 1950s and early 60s

illustrates two opposite attempts to achieve racial reconciliation in America. One method used the "eye for an eye" method of returning evil for evil. It seemed like the only remedy against blind bigotry, oppression, and violence against other human beings created in God's image. But all it did was create a vicious cycle of anger and retaliation, like the tribal feuds of jungle warfare. Incidentally, the leader of this movement had a poor relationship with his father, who'd modeled a negative reaction to racial prejudice from whites.

The other method used the biblical response of forgiving and loving one's enemies. I recently read the biography of Martin Luther King, Jr. and was amazed to see how deeply rooted in the Bible was his refusal to retaliate against every extreme of violence against him and his people, including bloodshed and murder. *But it allowed God to get below the surface and deal with the heart of hatred and prejudice.* I also noticed the tight bond he had with his father and the positive role-model he saw in him in the racial area.

Spiritual laws are as non-violable as natural laws. You ignore the law of gravity, you pay, sometimes with your life. You break the law of love and mercy, and you pay also. When God says that by returning kindness for evil it will heap coals of fire (shame) on your enemy's head, He reveals the number one law in the spiritual world and *the secret of how He wins our love.* That's how the non-violent civil rights movement in America *sensitized the conscience of white Americans from the president on down until the change took place from inside out* (Rom 12:17–20).

Racial prejudice still exists, but God has given us the only remedy that works over time: "Do not be overcome by evil, but overcome evil with good" (Rom 12:21).

"The Conversion of a Cruel Master"

One of my favorite stories is a pamphlet by the above title, one my dad read to me years ago, by Rev. James B. Finley, from *Sketches of Western Methodism, 1857.* [2]

A plantation owner in Virginia owned a number of slaves, and through the preaching of visiting Methodist ministers, he, his family, and his slaves all accepted Jesus Christ as their Savior. Cuff was the most dedicated, intelligent, and loyal of his slaves, and his conversion made him that much more fervent and faithful in everything he did, and he became the spiritual leader among his brethren.

A church formed on the plantation and when other ministers were not available, Cuff would preach, bringing deep conviction and trembling hearts among the other plantation owners who attended the services. But his aged and kind master finally died, and the estate fell into the hands of his creditors who sold the slaves.

A young infidel (atheist) was told of Cuff's high integrity and purchased him, but was warned that he had only one fault: "He would pray and go to meeting." The infidel felt sure he could "soon whip that out of him."

At the end of his day's work, Cuff retired to a thicket of trees near the garden and, kneeling, began to pour out his heart to God in prayer. As he prayed, the young wife, walking in the garden, heard him calling on God to bless his new master and mistress, and she broke down in tears.

On Sunday Cuff attended the church meeting in the morning and at night. But on Monday morning when his master found out where he had been, he demanded that he quit praying. When Cuff answered that his Master in heaven commanded him to pray and he "can't quit praying," the infidel determined to change his mind by a brutal whipping.

After stripping him of his garments, he tied him to a tree and gave him twenty-five strokes with a strip of rawhide. When Cuff still refused to change his mind, he gave him another twenty-five lashes. Still Cuff would not change his mind.

"This so enraged the infuriate fiend, that he flew at him with all the rage of a tiger thirsting for blood, and plying the bloody weapon with all his remaining strength, he stopped not till he was obliged to give over from sheer exhaustion."

When again asked whether he would stop praying, Cuff answered, "No, Massa, you may kill me, but while I live I must pray." With that the master told Cuff he would whip him like that every time he prayed or went to the church meeting.

When his wife attempted to plead with her angry husband, he shouted that if she didn't shut up, he would whip her also. He went to bed cursing God and raving like a madman, but couldn't sleep all night, turning and groaning over the "horrid visions of his tempest-tossed mind."

As dawn drew near he cried out, "I feel that I shall be damned! O, God, have mercy on me!" and begged his wife to find someone who would pray for him. She told him she knew of only one – the poor slave he had whipped so mercilessly. But the infidel felt sure he wouldn't pray for him. "Yes," said the weeping wife, "I think he will."

When a servant brought Cuff in, he expected another whipping, for he'd been praying all night for his master. "What was his astonishment, when he entered, to find [him] prostrate on the floor, crying for mercy!"

Cuff fell on his knees beside the infidel and "with a fervor and a faith that opened heaven, he wrestled hard with God for the guilty man." With the morning light came the light of joy to burst the chains of sin inside the master's darkened heart. When he stood, he embraced his faithful servant, exclaiming, "Cuff, my dear brother in Christ, from this moment you are a free man." His wife also found the freedom of Christ's love.

His new master employed him as "chaplain at a good salary, and Cuff went everywhere among his scattered brethren preaching the Word. The master himself became a zealous and successful minister of the gospel, and lived many years to preach that Jesus whose name he had blasphemed, and whose disciple he had scourged."

Why God takes His time

The biggest problem with God's way of love is that it seems to take forever, as though He doesn't care about what I've had to go through. It's not that God's not concerned or doesn't love us, but because He loves us in a more *responsible* way than simply giving us what we want when we want it, like spoiled, whining babies.

How *ignorant*, how *short-sighted* it is to want revenge when this attitude shows a childish immaturity that drastically needs purging! I once lived with the same attitude, even committing murder in my mind or wishing God would do it. But it backfired on me in the form of depression, self-hatred, and a major anger problem – rage! I lived in my own little hell. But when God set me free (chapter one), my life became heaven-on-earth and I fell in love with everybody!

Occasionally I meet an inmate who has learned to use the power of forgiveness as a way to restore his enemies to God. One in particular put several of his own such experiences into writing and I often asked him to read some of his published articles to the chapel group. My favorite ones tell about how another inmate steals something of his – a radio, shaver, etc., and how at first he's angry and wants revenge as he used to do (he was a boxer).

Instead, he applies Romans 12:20–21, returning good for evil, which allows God to bring conviction – "coals of fire" (shame). Eventually the thief becomes his friend and gives his heart to Jesus. That's why I see jail and prison as the perfect *laboratory* to test the things one learns about love, mercy, and the *wisdom* to use it as he's led of the Spirit (Rom 8:14; 12:20).

You see, God's first and more *natural* choice to deal with *me* is to use my *enemy*, because *forgiveness* is the most obvious result of His *redemption of my sins!* In other words, if I can't forgive others no matter how badly they've hurt me, it reveals a huge crack in my own salvation. It shows I don't comprehend how much *I* have been forgiven.

When I do come short of God's expectations, as we all do, instead of feeling broken, humble, grateful for His mercy, and full of Joy as I bask in His grace, I'll struggle with guilt and self-condemnation, because my attitude toward those I won't forgive comes back at me: I can't believe God forgives me ("can't forgive myself")!

No wonder Jesus said that if we don't forgive others, God will not forgive us. We're cut off from His mercy and exposed to Satan, who goes around looking for someone to "devour," someone not protected by God's forgiveness. And that's scary! (Mk 11:26; 1 Pet 5:8; Prv 24:17–18).

What we may blame on "low self-esteem" is nothing less

than esteeming *others* low, which comes back on us. "What goes around comes around." Jesus said to love God with all your heart, soul, strength, and mind, and love your neighbor as yourself. The reason we can't love our neighbor is not that we don't love ourselves, because Paul says that "no one ever hated his own flesh, but nourishes and cherishes it" (Lk 10:27; Eph 5:29).

When we don't love others it's because we don't love *God* with all our heart and *abide* in *His* love; we can do *nothing* apart from God. "He who abides in love abides in God, and God in him" (Jn 15:5, 9; 1 Jn 4:16b; Gal 5:13–22).

"Beloved, let us love one another, for love is of God; and everyone who loves is born of God and knows God. *He who does not love does not know God,* for God is love." Jesus said to "love one another *as I have loved you.*" God delivered me from depression and rage when I finally took the time to *know* Him enough to "abide in *His* love" (Jn 13:34; 15:12; 1 Jn 4:7–8).

God's version of self esteem is found in Philippians 2:3, "Let nothing be done through selfish ambition or conceit, but in lowliness of mind let each esteem others better than himself." The New Living Translation reads, "Be humble, thinking of others as better than yourselves."

Judgment Day begins now

It's so tempting and natural to think that "someday" God will "deal with" so-and-so and bring justice! But in the meantime, what is *my* attitude storing up for *me* on Judgment Day? "There will be no mercy for those who have not shown mercy to others. But if you have been merciful, God will be merciful when He judges you" (Jas 2:13 NLT).

It's easy to judge others, yet expect God to forgive us for all kinds of irresponsible behavior and wicked thoughts, which Jesus taught are no different than committing the act, as far as one's personal guilt before God (Mt 5:21–28).

"Therefore be merciful, just as your Father also is merciful. Judge not, and you shall not be judged. Condemn not, and you shall not be condemned. Forgive, and you will be forgiven" (Lk 6:36–37).

As I write this, the murder trial of Casey Anthony airs on TV daily. I saw a half-hour of it as I ate lunch yesterday. The way the attorneys cross examined the witnesses and investigators reminds me of what it might be like when we stand before the judgment seat of Christ (Rom 14:10; 2 Cor 5:10).

"How near were you to churches and pastors where you could have received help with your problem? Did you have access to a Bible, Christian TV, or know of a friend, relative, or grandparent who knew God enough to help you?

"Do you remember when you did such and such, and excused yourself with the idea that I would forgive you because you knew My reputation for love, but you never listened to my teaching on holiness and judgment against sin, hearing only what you wanted to hear? (Eph 4:22–32; 1 Jn 3:4–10).

"You didn't take hell seriously or that you might go there, but did you bother to inquire any deeper into a subject as important as your eternal destiny? What time did you spend getting to know Me and My ways compared to the time you spent in pursuit of pleasure, entertainment, social media, Internet, and your "I" - phone? (Ps 37:4; Rom 12:2; Col 3:2).

"What did you do with your jail time? Did you see it as a punishment you didn't deserve, correction you didn't want or need, or as the chastening of your heavenly Father and the *gift of time* you needed to know Me?" (Heb 12).

What a weeping and wailing will erupt on that Day from people who took God's grace so lightly, and yet held grudges against others without seeking to understand that God wanted to heal and forgive their *enemies* also and could have used their influence and prayer for them instead of their criticism, resentment, and even hatred! (Prv 24:17-18; Mt 5:44; Lk 6:27, 35; Rom 12:18–21).

For we know that some of the greatest saints have come to Christ from the lowest depths of wickedness, and often through the love and forgiveness shown them by the people they hurt the most (Acts 7:55–8:1; 22:3–4; 1 Cor 15:9; Gal 1:13; Phil 3:6; 1Tim 1:13).

Jesus set the example when on the Cross in agony He

prayed, "Father, forgive them, for they don't know what they are doing," as the soldiers "gambled for His clothes" and the religious leaders and others mocked Him, including one of the criminals crucified with Him (Lk 23:34ff NLT).

Jesus gave a parable about a servant who owed the king millions of dollars, and the king forgave him the debt when he pleaded for mercy. But after his debt was forgiven, he went to one of his servants who owed him a few thousand dollars and commanded him to be imprisoned until he paid up.

When the king heard about it, he had him brought back and told him, "Should you not also have had compassion on your fellow servant, just as I had pity on you?" So he "delivered him to the torturers until he should pay all that was due to him. So My heavenly Father also will do to you if each of you, from his heart, does not forgive his brother his trespasses" (Mt 18:24–35).

Unforgiveness slowly destroys a person from inside out, spiritually, emotionally, and physically. It's the result of invisible "torturers," demons who feed on "slander" (*devil* means "slanderer"). It's the "torture" of one's conscience, poisoning *oneself* to hurt someone else. It's the fear and insecurity of one who doesn't know "the love of Christ which passes knowledge" (Eph 3:19; Heb 12:14–17).

Tortured people torture others with angry words, using the "f" word all the time instead of "g" words – *he's a great guy, it's a good day, God is good, he's got it together, going God's way,* and *gonna make it with God's help! I for-give you; will you for-give me?* (Prv 10:12; 15:18; 25:15; 29:22; Mk 11:25–26; Col 3:13).

No wonder unforgiving people are so often driven to drugs and crime. They don't understand the torture deep inside driving them to do the irrational ("stupid") things they do (Prv 5:22; 26:27; Gal 6:6–7).

My Dad

My dad was one of the most wonderful fathers a son could have. He brought us five kids up telling us stories from the Bible and a wide range of reading. He always made the story more interesting than the original as he impersonated the characters. While he'd tell them he'd massage our back, feet, and neck. It was sheer luxury! Even after I'd quit believing there was a God after high school and the death of my mother, I'd let him talk to me about God just for the pleasure of getting another foot massage, which he gladly did!

But somehow I developed a resentful attitude toward him because he was too laid back for me. Many years later I learned my problem was "obsessive compulsive disorder." I saw everything through the eyes of perfection, and it angered me to see him do things imperfectly, like giving money to con-artists and others who took advantage of his kindness.

I developed this same anger toward laid-back school teachers, like my chemistry teacher who ignored the kids in the back of the class conducting their own chemistry experiment until an explosion rocked the school and terminated this easy-going teacher. I deeply admired the strict no-nonsense, no-smile, stern teacher who took his place even though I only made a B in her class, and could easily have made an A with the other teacher.

My favorite teacher in eighth grade was Mr. Cushman, who with his drill-sergeant voice walked up and down the aisles between desks checking homework and any little sign of misbehavior. He executed punishment with a long 1x4 inch wood paddle and made the offender bend over his desk in front of us terrified students as we wondered who'd be next. I also had my turn over his desk, but I loved him because he kept order and I learned so much in his class. Plus he dramatized history the way Dad dramatized his stories.

But the price I paid for this attitude and anger was suicidal depression, which stalked me for 20 years like a demon from hell, and maybe it was. In 1965 I packed up everything I owned, including my library of books, and headed off to Wheaton College, the Harvard of Christian colleges. I told myself I'd never again set foot in Dad's house and have to deal with his imperfections.

But at Wheaton my mind locked; I couldn't concentrate; resentment was eating my heart out. I dreamed of suicide constantly and finally took a battery of tests at Chicago Counseling Clinic (now closed) which proved I was indeed messed up. They said I needed to be institutionalized or I'd kill myself once I saw inside myself (my heart – Jer 17:9).

I tried to commit myself to the Illinois State Mental Institution, but they refused me because I was not a resident of Illinois. Wheaton wouldn't admit me in the fall unless I took summer classes to make up for my sub-standard grade point average. Besides, I'd run out of money.

I went home totally humiliated. My dream – the perfect education, the perfect job (history professor), and the perfect wife (I had a long list of requirements for my future wife) – had ended in disgrace. Even the mental institution had rejected me!

Like the prodigal son's father, guess who accepted me with open, loving arms, strong hands skilled in the art of massage, and the best story teller in the world? Yes, my faithful, imperfect, but incredibly forgiving dad! (Lk 15:11–32).

It took another eleven years for God to set me free from my depression and anger, but the summer of 1965 was the first breakthrough. For I could no longer look down on Dad when I saw where my pride had led me. And it was the following December when I took his advice to attend Southeastern Bible College (now Southeastern University, Lakeland, FL) where he'd wanted me to go instead of Wheaton, and where he said I'd find a wife. I'd scoffed at him: Southeastern was too humble for me; I wanted the *best*.

How submitting to my dad brought me exactly what I needed (my wife) is told in the previous chapter, "The Fear of the Lord." Some of us have to learn the hard way, which is why I feel so at home with my *brothers* in jail, and long to see them set free of the wounds that have driven them to hurt themselves and others.

I know they need a lot of practical help, especially when they get out. I took a week off from my work years ago to look into getting involved in practical ways to help them, like a half-way house. But through it God helped me understand that I must stick with what He has called *me* to do: help them get to the root of their problem *spiritually* until they too bubble with God's love – even for the ones who hurt them most by their example or betrayal.

When they get truly free on the inside, heaven will begin to open up for them, and all that potential locked inside will find glorious expression as they discover the joy of walking in step with their Creator and Deliverer.

"For God has imprisoned everyone in disobedience so He could have mercy on everyone. Oh, how great are God's riches and wisdom and knowledge! How impossible it is for us to understand His decisions and His ways! . . . For everything comes from Him and exists by His power and is intended for His glory. All glory to Him forever! Amen" (Rom 11:32–33, 36 NLT).

1. Shippensburg, PA: Destiny Image Publications, Inc., 1999. Print. 89
2. https://books.google.com/books?id=S_OWGwXVWs4C (accessed Nov 15, 2014)

SECTION TWO

Grace Flows in Obedience

(The Commitment)

For I know whom I have believed and
I am convinced that He is able to guard
what I have entrusted to Him until that day.
2 Timothy 1:12b NASB

CHAPTER 5

Speaking the Truth

Bob Lupton wrote this first section in his "Urban Perspectives" and has granted me permission to use it.

There is a cancer quietly eating away at the lives of inner-city people. It is a more subtle disease than alcoholism, more hushed than venereal disease, less violent than rape but no less destructive. It seldom attracts media attention, but it is more pervasive than any disease on the epidemic list of the Center for Disease Control. This quiet killer is "the lie."

In the poverty culture of the inner city, the lie is a way of life. It is a tool the powerless use to get what they need (or want) from the powerful. It prevents courts from taking children, landlords from evicting families, caseworkers from cutting food stamps.

Perhaps the sickness would not be so severe if the poor used the lie only to manipulate and protect themselves from those outside their culture. But it does not stop there – the lie is highly contagious. Husbands and wives deceive each other with macho games and broken commitments. Mothers turn sons against absent fathers and manipulate them to become providers by whatever means the street affords.

Children, too, learn to lie to get what they want. By the time they are adolescents, the young men have learned how to deceive young women out of their virginity. Young women have learned to use their babies to manipulate young men. Both have learned to deny the truth of their own emotions. And when they have learned to live without trust or commitment, they are ready to face adulthood in a culture where only those strong enough to endure chronic paranoia and isolation survive.

Not long ago I was a member of a Bible study for young adults that met in a nearby public housing project. For a year we met weekly to read and discuss scripture, and share part of our lives together. Occasionally our prayer and sharing dipped below the surface into personal areas. But mostly we used cautious God-talk and politeness.

One week the dishonesty reached a level that disturbed the normally placid surface of our group. Richard, my co-leader, couldn't stand it any longer. "It's time to get real!" he declared.

In the following weeks that's exactly what we did. The surface boiled with deep emotions. Anger, distrust, jealousy, and fear mixed with tears and hollering and confessing and hugging. Admissions of illicit drug use and cheating on the housing authority came to light. Malicious gossip and slander were confronted. Anger at me for being "rich" and not helping more surfaced.

I was afraid the group would break apart under this intense pressure, but it did not. Instead its cohesiveness increased. Those on the fringes were drawn into the center. We sat for hours on cement floors and broken-down pieces of furniture, no one wanting to miss out on a moment. It was as if we had opened a gushing well of healing, life-giving waters in the middle of a parched, disease-ridden land.

Such simple truths – confessing faults to one another, speaking the truth in love, bearing one another's burdens. They are powerful medicine for those of us who suffer from the desperate disease of deceit. And strong medicine, too, for those of us whose deceit is neatly disguised behind spiritual facades.

(Read Bob Lupton's books for enlightened and essential understanding of *urban ministry* – Amazon.com)

Transparency

Jesus said, "Come to Me, all of you who are weary and carry heavy burdens, and I will give you rest" (Mt 11:28 NLT).

Much of the heavy burden that makes us so weary is our attempt to look good before our friends: peer pressure. Which explains why opening up to one another in that Bible study became such therapy. They discovered being real did not bring rejection, but acceptance, since they *all* had issues they were hiding (Rom 3:9–18).

It's risky to come out of hiding because rejection is the most painful emotion anyone can experience. How is it that we can have everything we need physically, even lavish wealth, power, and fame, yet want to end it all in suicide? Because God created us for one main purpose: fellowship with Him, through which we are "conformed to the image of His Son." This need is so profound that attempting to fill it any other way, whether by human relationships, sex, money, things, or chemical highs, only deepens our problem (Eccl 7:29; Rom 8:29; Phil 3:10).

There's a beautiful irony about jail: while the majority of inmates continue to maintain their "image" in jail, criticizing everybody and everything God uses to rip off their masks, a few discover the incredible blessing of *time* to search their own hearts and find the God who alone can fill that void (Heb 11:6).

Last week I sat around a table with about seven or eight guys, all of whom had come to jail with a drug problem, and all expressed concern they might relapse when they get out. Except one. He said he'd been an addict since he was eight, but this time in jail he'd finally found what had been missing all his life: God.

I asked him how he's any different than most everybody in my Bible studies who say they're "saved," yet still feel apprehensive and fear temptation when they get out? He said he began studying the Bible on his own and simply found his way to a genuine relationship with God through trusting what it said (1 Jn 2:3–4; 5:20).

This is precisely what Jesus meant when He said, "And you shall know the truth, and the truth shall make you free." Truth is liberating because God, who knows who we *really are* beyond our false fronts, loves us unconditionally and passionately. And patiently waits for us to finally come to Him with our *whole heart* (Jn 8:32; Mk 12:33).

But here's the irony: it often takes a major failure to bring us to that point. The Fall of Adam in the Garden was a great tragedy that plunged the world into a self-destruct mode. But consider how perfect this couple was in their sin-free pristine beauty, yet had no idea that lurking in their hearts was a secret desire to be "like God" and independent of His control. All it took was a little encouragement from one who'd already taken this bait, and both of them "fell" for it (Gen 3:5; Is 14:12–17; Ez 28:17).

Solomon, the wisest king who ever lived, who taught much about this subtle danger in Proverbs, also fell into the same trap. This is why he ended up writing Ecclesiastes, warning the rest of us (1 Kgs 10–11; Prv 3:1–8; 4:23, etc).

The Fall and Restoration of David

But most shocking is his father, David, the *man after God's own heart*, who wrote half of the Psalms, or more, who's example would model that of "the Son of David," Jesus. Who would have dreamed that in the peak of his success as king, he would end up stealing the wife of Uriah, one of his top army officers – and did it while this faithful soldier risked his life on the battlefield as David slept with her. And then had him intentionally killed under enemy fire so he – David – could have his wife for keeps! (Mt 1:1; 1 Sam 13:14; 2 Sam 11–12; 1 Chr 11:41; Acts 13:22).

If I'd been God, I might have forgiven him, but only after getting him off the throne, removing his eight or more wives, and exiling him on an island like Alcatraz, where he'd die alone and deserted (Dt 17:17; 1 Sam 18:27; 2 Sam 5:13; 1 Chr 3:1–9).

But God not only forgave David, but allowed him to keep his throne (eventually – another story – 2 Sam 15–18), his wives, and . . . Bathsheba (Uriah's former wife), the obvious *favorite* of them, two of whom were king's daughters. Furthermore, God included two of Bathsheba's sons *by David* in the ancestral lineage that led to Jesus: one through Mary (Solomon) and the other through Joseph (Nathan). And Matthew didn't hide David's sin recording it: "David the king begot Solomon by her who had been the wife of Uriah" (1 Chr 3:1–9; Mt 1:6; Lk 3:31).

How can God be so incredibly merciful? Because it often takes the most devastating failure on our part to bring us to *transparency*, to utter and complete *honesty* with ourselves and with God. Which demonstrates the tremendous *value* of being who we *really are* rather than someone we're *trying* to be, with all the *weariness* and *heavy burden* that accompanies it (Eccl 2:11, 17; 1 Tim 6:6).

David not only prepared the way for Jesus, especially as He hung on the Cross in our place, dying for our sins as David suffered so greatly for his sin (Ps 22); but he (David) pioneered the path to *brokenness* and the transformation from dead works to God's law written in our hearts (Is 57:15; 66:2; Rom 4:1–8; Heb 6:1; 8:10; 9:14; 10:16).

Several psalms record David's agony over his horrific betrayal of trust – that of God, his wives and children, his leaders in church, military, and government, his nation Israel, and Uriah (2 Sam 12:8–14; Ps 6, 22, 32, 38–40, 51).

Three of my favorites are Psalms 38 through 40. They describe David's progress through physical and emotional affliction by God's anger and rejection by "loved ones and friends" (38), the revelation of how *worthless*, *vain*, and *nothing* we are apart from God (39), and his breakthrough to victory in the pit of despair (40).

Psalm 38 became one of my "antidepressants" during the years God weaned me from the heavy burden of my need to feel approved and loved, even by God. I spent many, many hours over several years soaking in this psalm as I'd meditate on the reality of God's anger against the "deceitfulness" of my heart. For I'd been hiding behind the *image* of a "good pastor" who appeared to love everybody, but it was only superficial, because I didn't think they would or could change (Eccl 7:16).

As God exposed my heart in the midst of rejection from the church I pastored in Greensboro, NC, David's feeling of rejection and trusting God in the pain of it gave me immense consolation. It led me to Psalm 39, where I saw clearly the emptiness of my own heart in common with everyone else, whose approval I *thought* I needed (Eccl 9:11; Rom 3:9–23).

Eventually I experienced the same breakthrough David enjoyed in Psalm 40. My "horrible pit" was an endless sense of guilt and failure, knowing I acted like a super-spiritual "man of God" who fasted and prayed a lot, but hated this life of hard discipline and endless attempts to reach higher in what I thought God demanded of me (Eph 2:8–9).

Finally, through Romans 3–8 and Galatians 2–5, I learned what David found: "Sacrifice and offering You did not desire;

My ears You have opened. . . . I delight to do Your will, O my God, and Your law is within my heart" (Ps 40:6–8; 51:16–17; Heb 10:5–17).

What I'd tried desperately for many years to do through hard work and sacrifice, God has been doing through ripping off my religious mask and revealing *Himself* in its place. Through *knowing Him intimately*, I don't need to prove my worth to anyone, even God, because all I am and do comes from Him anyway! No wonder David found such relief, expressed in a "new song . . . praise to our God" (Ps 40:2–3; Phil 3:10; Acts 17:28; Col 1:17; Heb 12:2).

The right foundation

But there's another reason why transparency and honesty are so difficult and risky: why tell the truth when you can get what you want if you lie? However, *God* calls the shots, not the government, the police, the judge, your mother or dad, your kid, your girl or boy-friend, husband or wife, your enemy, or anybody else.

All these people are important, but God has the last word on anything and everything. He has the power to influence people, turn the heart of a judge, change your circumstances, influence your family or friend, punish your enemy, and make life easy or hard for you (Ps 33:9–11; Prv 19:21; 21:1; Is 45:7; 46:10; Lam 3:32–40; Dan 4:35; Rom 9:15; Jas 4:13–15; Dt 28).

And what He decides to do about your life hangs on one thing: whether you walk in *truth* or attempt to control the outcome of things with lies, deception, or manipulation. Because truth is based on reality. And reality is not what *you* see but what *God* sees. The real test of a person's integrity (honesty, trustworthiness) is what he or she does *when no one is looking or will ever know* (Is 50:10–11; Ps 51:6; 2 Cor 3:18; Heb 4:13).

Some employers cheat and lie, and may resent an employee who chooses integrity over profit. But we've all watched the collapse of huge companies which operated dishonestly or cut corners, and how it led to the stock market crash of 2008.

In the 1990's I read an article, I think in *Guideposts* (but can't find it), about a lawyer whom God spoke to, telling her to go to Russia and He would lead her to help the new government work out its new constitution after the collapse of Communism in the Soviet Union and its breakup.

She sold her law business and obeyed, and God opened the door in Russia for her to do as He'd said. The first thing she discovered is that they had no concept of truth. For seventy years the Soviet government had operated on lies to maintain control. No wonder it collapsed; it had no *foundation* (Ps 89:14; Prv 12:19; 20:28; Hos 4:1).

Telling the truth in court?

One of the world's greatest ironies is that some lawyers (not all, thankfully) – those trained in the laws that hold societies together – will *lie* to defend their clients, and encourage them to lie also. We've all heard lawyer jokes that reflect this. One of them goes like this: "Why are lawyers buried thirty feet down when they die? Because deep down, they're really good."

This joke tells us two things about ourselves. First, we all despise lying, even though many pay big money for lawyers to lie in court and tell their clients to swear or promise before God and the court to "tell the whole truth and nothing but the truth." Second, we all instinctively value ourselves by what we are "deep down," where character is measured not by outward results, but by integrity (Ps 24:3–5).

In 1960 my dad and our neighbor stood trial when a local business man attempted to rape our neighbor in the middle of the night. The man offered the neighbor money if she would sign a paper saying she wouldn't press charges, and asked Dad to sign as a witness. It was a trap to take the heat off himself and lay an extortion charge on both of them.

The district attorney had never lost a case. His prosecution was powerful, but he aimed at destroying Dad's character as a pastor by twisting facts and making it sound as though Dad were the rapist. And it appeared that way in the local newspaper, humiliating us children before our peers and teachers at school.

Dad's attorney, from another area, had also never lost a case, but he advised Dad to change one fact in his testimony to assure victory. Dad refused to lie, even though losing meant a ten year prison sentence, leaving five children, ages four to seventeen (me), without a parent. Mother had died six months earlier of leukemia.

I'll never forget the suspense as we waited for the jury's verdict, but hoping in the God Dad had built his confidence in. When the "not guilty" verdict was read, I was never so proud of him for not being afraid to stick to the truth. What a role model for his children, an example of how our character is passed to our children from generation to generation.

You may not be proud of your dad (or mom), but it's never too late for *you* to become *your* children's hero, once you decide *what you want them to learn by watching you* (Gen 17:7; Ex 34:7; Ps 103:17).

I met Mike (not his real name) in jail and he told me he'd been a drug addict for years and had lied his way through court after court case. Except his last one. As he waited for his turn in court, his public defender (PD) met with him to work out a deal with the state attorney. By this time Mike had become so skilled at lying that his PD actually relied on his lies to present to the state, whether he believed them or not.

But while he was over talking with the DA (district attorney), God spoke clearly to Mike's heart, leaving him completely humbled, broken, and deeply repentant for his life of sin and lies. When the PD returned to further discuss the details of the case, Mike confessed his lies and that from then on he would speak the truth, though it meant the long prison sentence his crimes deserved.

The public defender was upset! It meant he would lose the case. He argued with Mike, but to no avail. When the judge asked Mike how he pled to his many pages of charges, he answered that he was guilty of all of them and much more. The judge was taken aback and questioned him again to make sure, since he had only begun to thumb through the pages of his felonies.

Mike, still overwhelmed with God, held back his tears, not wanting to impress the judge with signs of remorse, but kept insisting he was truly guilty of every charge, and there was much more he hadn't gotten caught for.

The judge had rarely, if ever, seen anyone so transparent and willing to spend years in prison for telling the truth. Finally he decided to drop almost all the charges and give him 30 days in jail, and no probation on release. It will be three years this January, 2012, since he's been out, and I've found him to be faithful to his word and is still serving God.

Update: Soon after writing this I found Mike's integrity had crumbled and for the past year he'd been living a lie before me. It felt like the loss of a true friend with a huge barrier of betrayal between us. I understand the agony many parents and spouses go through when their children or mates live behind a thick wall of deception. Restoration is possible, but to rebuild trust is usually long and difficult.

Living the lie imprisons me in my own world of illusions and can certainly lead to "chronic paranoia and isolation." Because *deep down* I know I'm phony and that it's only a matter of time before my house of cards will collapse, reality will surface, and I'll be exposed before those who trusted me (Num 32:23; Job 20:5; Acts 5:3–10; 1 Cor 4:5).

Jesus compared one's character to the foundation of a house, saying that a person who *does* what He teaches is like one who builds his house on a rock; it will stand in violent storms. The person who hears the truth but doesn't *do* it is like one who builds on the sand; his house will collapse in the same storm (Mt 7:24–27).

Character Meter

Wouldn't it be neat if God had designed a personal, private *gauge* on our bodies that measured our character? In fact, He did – our conscience. And it does a whole lot more than reveal our character:

(1) It shows us how strong our wireless connection to Him is, like the little "bars" on a cell phone that show the strength of the signal; or like a fuel gage that tells when we're riding on "empty" and need to spend extra time with God to rebuild our faith. Yes, faith is spiritual fuel: the more faith we have, the more *power* with God we have (Mk 11:23–24; 1 Pet 1:5).

(2) So our conscience is an internal courtroom where personal guilt and other issues are dealt with as the Spirit, our attorney, guides us through the judicial process. For it involves God's eternal law, which is biblical Truth, and His Son, who paid the penalty for our breaking that law. The outcome depends on the genuineness of our hearts – whether we're "using" grace for a license to sin or to sincerely restore a damaged or broken relationship with God and people (2 Cor 7:10).

(3) A clear conscience before God means the case is closed and we're back "in tune" with Him and His strength and guidance. He can warn us of danger when we're about to take a wrong turn spiritually or financially, make an unwise decision, or marry the wrong person. He can tell us when to trust somebody, when someone is manipulating or scamming us, and when to use caution in relationships – how to "be wise as serpents and harmless as doves" (Mt 10:16; Is 30:21; Acts 11:12; 13:2–4; 16:6–7; 20:23).

My pastor has a friend who's invested quite profitably in stocks for years and has never lost a penny. His secret? He takes time, even days, to get alone and listen to God before an important investment. His wireless connection to his heavenly Stock Broker is his (human) spirit – closely related to his conscience – finely tuned to the voice of the Holy Spirit (Jn 8:9; Acts 23:1; 24:16; Rom 2:15; 9:1; 2 Cor 1:12; 1 Tim 3:9; 2 Tim 1:3; Heb 9:9, 14; 13:18; 1 Pet 2:19; 3:16, 21).

Paul told Timothy some had "suffered shipwreck" because they went against their conscience. It's like driving south in the north-bound lane. You've got to be stupid to do it, but millions do it all the time with their conscience and end up wrecked, and often blame others for it! (1 Tim 1:19).

I've done it too; it creeps up on me when I can't see that what I'm doing is sin or even wrong. That's why a clear conscience is so important, in order to hear God's Spirit telling us when we're going the wrong way even when it *seems* right. Like flying an airplane without instruments through clouds, feeling normal, when we're actually upside down and losing altitude rapidly (Prv 14:12).

Sometimes our fleshly desires override the quieter voice of our conscience or the Spirit. Like the time I resigned the church I pastored in Greensboro, N.C. God actually spoke to me through a church member who was listening to God better than I was and told me that God said I should *wait.* I waited a few *hours* instead of the months or years God probably meant. What followed was the greatest "shipwreck" in my whole life, when I almost lost my wife and family, and my life. It was a serious weakness in my character (Hab 2:3–4; 1 Cor 12:21–25).

I've been reaping the results of that mistake now for decades. But if we learn to listen, the reaping process becomes remedial – God's *remedy* for our character defect. I like to think my problem was simply not listening. But it was much deeper: deep enough to *need* these long, painful years to slowly deal with my issues – my own "prison time" (Ps 119:71, 75).

God's department of corrections

While I'm under God's correction, I'm helping inmates adjust to the same process. Many of them think, *If only I had . . . .* Their thought is that if they had only *listcned* before the *act* they got caught for, they wouldn't be in jail. I know the feeling.

But we don't reap punishment for one or two acts. Our behavior comes from our *character.* We should be *thankful* we finally got caught, because now we have *time* to see our problem and will begin to seek help from God and others. Correction of any kind is God's purifying instrument, preparing us for His coming and presence (Mal 3:3; 1 Cor 1:11–15; Heb 12; 1 Pet 1:7).

Many will continue to feed their minds with the same lies when they get out that got them in jail in the first place – music, rap, movies, magazines, books, friends, websites, and apps that glorify evil, hatred, violence, drugs, and sex. *They drown out any means of sensitizing and training their God-given conscience,* and allow themselves to "follow deceptive spirits and teachings that come from demons. These people are hypocrites and liars, and their consciences are dead" (1 Tim 4:1–2 NLT).

Wow! I hate to quote something so strong. I love these guys in jail and want to help them, not condemn them. Yet if I can help them see the incredible damage of constantly re-programming their minds with what goes on in *hell* instead of *heaven*, perhaps some will take heed. Because if they're comfortable with evil, they'd be *terrified* in the *transparency* of heaven! (Jn 8:44; Acts 13:10; 2 Cor 5:1–5, 11; 1 Jn 2:15–17; 3:8–12).

For the glory of heaven that fills the humble with life and joy is a "consuming fire" to the ungodly. It parallels the influence of believers here on earth: "To those who are perishing, we are a dreadful smell of death and doom. But to those who are being saved, we are a life-giving perfume" (2 Cor 2:16a NLT).

"Everything is pure to those whose hearts are pure. But nothing is pure to those who are corrupt and unbelieving, because their minds and consciences are corrupted. Such people claim they know God, but *they deny Him by the way they live*" (Titus 1:15–16a NLT).

These verses explain how something so pure and beautiful as sex, so priceless as loving and blessing your enemies, and so important as honoring those in authority, can be twisted into the very teaching of Satan himself. For "he has always hated the truth, because there is no truth in him. When he lies, it is consistent with his character; for he is a liar and the father of lies" (2 Pet 2:10–12; Jude 1:8; Jn 8:44 NLT).

When inmates, especially juveniles, tell me they hate the police because they lie and don't follow their own rules, I remind them that when we don't receive correction from people who *love* us, God often turns us over to be corrected or punished by those who *hate* us, including Satan (1 Cor 5:5; 2 Sam 24:1 with 1 Chr. 21:1).

God constantly used wicked nations and kings to correct his own people. Judges 2 and 3 show the pattern: When His people served and obeyed Him, He gave them godly leadership. But when they forsook Him, He "sold them" into the hands of their enemies, and for many years they would suffer great affliction until He saw their hearts change (Ex 1; 2 Kgs 18:11–12; chaps 24–25; 2 Chr 36; Jer 24–25, 27; Is 30:18–19).

Super Role-model

One of the most important role-models in my life is Dr. Ben Carson, the black pediatric neurosurgeon who became famous in 1987 when he successfully separated the German Siamese twins joined at the back of their heads.

His life influenced me for several reasons: (1) His mother taught her two sons to always do their best at everything they did. She cut their TV watching down to three weekly programs and required them to read two books and report on them – each week. Since their mother couldn't read they could have easily found ways to cheat and lie about it, but *they loved God and honored her enough to obey* (Ex 20:12; Eph 6:1–3; Col 3:20).

(2) Ben *always did more than he was required to do*, beginning with his required reading, and continuing through high school and college, medical school, and training afterward. As a result he had more knowledge and experience with the brain than anyone else in the world. (Look him up on Wikipedia or read his book, *Gifted Hands*.)

(3) He was deeply committed to God and church, and learned to trust Him at every stage of his life, encountering miraculous provision many times. When as a teen he lost his temper and almost killed one of his close friends with a knife, he got alone with his Bible and, like Jacob in Genesis 32, wrestled with God for hours until he had the assurance that God had set him free of his anger problem.

(4) He was a man of unswerving integrity. One of my favorite stories concerns his account of a final exam. Two days after the exam, notice went out that the papers had mistakenly burned, and the 150 students were asked to repeat it.

But when they began to read the new exam, they were horrified to find the questions "were incredibly difficult, if not impossible." Little by little students trickled out of the room. Ben heard one tell her friend she would tell the professor she hadn't read the notice, buying more time to study for a re-try.

After half an hour Ben was the only student left.

"Like the others, I was tempted to walk out, but I had read the notice, and I couldn't lie and say I hadn't. All the time I wrote my answers, I prayed for God to help me figure out what to put down....

"Suddenly the door of the classroom opened noisily.... As I turned, my gaze met that of the professor. . . . With her was a photographer for the *Yale Daily News* who paused and snapped my picture.

"'What's going on?' I asked.

"'A hoax,' the teacher said. 'We wanted to see who was the most honest student in the class.' she smiled again. 'And that's you.'"[1]

The glow I feel when I read this gives me a clue about how we'll feel when we hear these words from our heavenly Father: "Well done, good and faithful servant; you were faithful over a few things, I will make you ruler over many things. Enter into the joy of your lord" (Mt 25:21).

"If you are faithful in little things, you will be faithful in large ones. But if you are dishonest in little things, you won't be honest with greater responsibilities. And if you are untrustworthy about worldly wealth, who will trust you with the true riches of heaven? And if you are not faithful with other people's things, why should you be trusted with things of your own?" (Lk 16:12 NLT).

Follow the Lamb

One of the passages in the Bible that fascinates me concerns the 144,000 in Revelation 14. Regardless of whose interpretation is correct about who they are and whether the number is literal or symbolic, what impresses me is that they are "without fault before the throne of God."

And their purity relates to two simple factors: they "follow the Lamb wherever He goes," and "in their mouth was found no deceit" (14:4–5).

You cannot follow the Lamb and hide something (deceit), because He's all Light and Truth. Furthermore, living in truth might cost you some advantages up front, as it did Jesus. But "the truth shall make you free" from slavery to the flesh, public opinion, and peer pressure (Ps 36:9; 39:4–6; Jn 3:19–21; 8:32).

In Philippians 2:2–4 Paul describes the kind of attitudes on earth that most clearly reflect those in heaven: "Fulfill my joy by being like-minded, having the same love, being of one accord, of one mind. Let nothing be done through selfish ambition or conceit, but in lowliness of mind let each esteem others better than himself. Let each of you look out not only for his own interests, but also for the interests of others."

Of course this goes entirely against fallen human nature. So Paul goes on to give us the cure for our selfishness: Jesus – the ultimate Role Model! (Col 1:26–29).

"You must have the same attitude that Christ Jesus had. Though He was God, He did not think of equality with God as something to cling to. Instead, He gave up His divine privileges; He took the humble position of a slave and was born as a human being. When He appeared in human form, He humbled Himself in obedience to God and died a criminal's death on a cross" (2:5–8 NLT).

This is following the Lamb. It is "losing my life" to find His life: "Those who love their life in this world will lose it. Those who care nothing for their life in this world will keep it for eternity. Anyone who wants to be My disciple must follow Me, because My servants must be where I am. And the Father will honor anyone who serves Me" (Jn 12:25–26 NLT).

Living the lie is the opposite; it is holding on tightly to my life in this world at the cost of finding His life – the life and values that come from heaven (Mk 10:23–31).

Living the lie *gives Satan a legal right to my life*, "for he is a liar and the father of it." Since lying originates with him, then a lifestyle of lying makes me one of his children, and I'll end up spending eternity with him (Jn 8:44; see Rv 21:8).

In fact, *lying is the chief means by which he destroys us or attempts to.* He tempts us through his "delightful" illusions (lies), then slanders, accuses, and betrays us through more deceptions until we are destroyed, but only after he has *used* us to tempt, afflict, addict, or destroy others (Job 2:10; Ps 66:12; Is 51:23; Eph 6:12–13; Heb 11:35–38; 1 Pet 5:8–9; Rv 2:10).

He offers to satisfy our selfish needs with bait to trap us, saying, as through a woman seducing a man, "'Stolen water is sweet, and bread eaten in secret is pleasant.' But he does not know that the dead are there, that her guests are in the depths of hell" (Prv 9:17–18).

The antichrists of history (Nero, Hitler, Stalin, etc.) and the one to come seduce their followers "with all unrighteous deception . . . *because they did not receive the love of the truth,* that they might be saved. And for this reason God will send them strong delusion, that they should believe the lie, that they all may be condemned who did not believe the truth but *had pleasure in unrighteousness*" (2 Thes 2:10–12; 1 Jn 4:3; 2 Jn 1:7).

In other words, a liar, baited by comfort, pleasure, power, and pride, eventually falls into his own pit – deceived by others and by "the father of lies" (Jn 8:44 NLT; Gen 27; 29:25; 37:31–36; Ps 7:15; Prv 26:27; 2 Tim 3:13).

No wonder those dear inner-city people felt such overwhelming relief as they came out of darkness into the true light! A lot was at stake – in fact, two lifetimes: one here and one hereafter!

Is it worth it? You decide.

The truthful lip shall be established forever, but a lying tongue is but for a moment.

Lying lips are an abomination to the Lord, but those who deal truthfully are His delight.

I have no greater joy than to hear that my children walk in truth (Prv 12:19, 22; 3 Jn 1:4).

1. Carson, Ben, with Cecil Murphey. *Gifted Hands.* Grand Rapids: Zondervan Publishing House, 1990. 89-90 Print.

Caution Ahead

The following chapter may be the most difficult chapter in the book, at least for some. And it might well be the most important, since it involves our ultimate purpose and the reason God created us. I've worked hard *trying* to make it simple and understandable, but if you get bogged down *trying* to wade through it, either skim it or skip it, and save it for another time.

I learned to read the Bible that way – skipping what was too difficult or boring for me. And later the books of the Bible that had been the *most boring* became the *most interesting* (Leviticus and Job).

"I have seen the God-given task with which the sons of men are to be occupied. He has made everything beautiful in its time" (Eccl 3:10–11a).

CHAPTER 6

Jail, Church, a Woman

For why should you, my son, be enraptured by an immoral woman, and be embraced in the arms of a seductress? For the ways of man are before the eyes of the LORD, and He ponders all his paths.
Proverbs 6:20–21

Why do they cave in so quickly?
At one of my Bible studies in jail only two inmates showed up, but they were men who knew the Word, were obviously among the most faithful to participate in the meetings, and I assumed they were also among the stronger believers in the C-pod.

As I began to speak I casually mentioned, by way of introduction, "You know, of course, that it's a sin to sleep with a woman you're not married to." Suddenly both men went ballistic, shouting and beating the tops of their desks. One slammed his Bible shut and got up to leave, crying like a baby, and saying through his tears, "I can't take this! I can't take this!" while the other repeated loudly over and over, "I can't live without a woman." I tried desperately to calm them down and explain something – anything – but it was no use.

I believe they reacted this way because their conscience was "educated" enough to convict them of the one thing they needed *most,* but got through the "back door" instead of God's way of meeting that need "face to face" (Gen 32:30; Ps 16:8; Prv 9:17).

After more than two decades of ministry among inmates in and out of prison, I've found only a tiny fraction of the men who call themselves true born again believers can bear the thought of getting out of prison without almost immediately moving in with a woman, married or not.

Over a period of a year or two I found myself at times

humorously asking the men who come to my various jail and prison services, "What is the one thing that will bring a man down when he gets out?" They always responded in unison, "A woman!" Sometimes I'd use it as an introduction to teach on Proverbs 5, 7, or 22:14. It always got their attention and made teaching fun and relevant. But as time went on I began to realize it was too big a hurdle for most inmates and failed to touch the *real* problem.

Then one day at the Orlando prison in an act of desperation I asked them, "I want to know why so many of the very *strongest believers* in prison, the spiritual leaders, the ones you call Rev and Preacher, those who lead prayer groups and Bible studies, who can preach with fire and power, who know the Word better than I do . . . how is it that within a few months after they get out, they're right back in the old lifestyle?"

Hands went up all over. After four inmates told the same story, I felt I had my answer and told them. The rest confirmed my simple conclusion: After release, they get connected with a church and attend faithfully a few weeks. Then they miss a service or two, and then more, until they no longer attend.

The reason may be neglect through laziness, inconvenience, or the feeling of *aloneness* among people in a whole different class: people who have not failed, who are *normal*, successful, stable. All it may take is a misunderstanding or just a vague feeling of rejection, and the ex-con is "outa' there!"

Or he may be shocked at the level of worldliness in the congregation and/or the leadership, especially if in prison he prayed and studied the Word a lot. The volunteers who ministered to him there may have seemed so dedicated, as though they were a sample of the whole church.

He may try another church, and then another. The most spiritually advanced inmate I'd ever met (so I thought, after 11 years of prison ministry) tried three or four churches, saw something wrong with each one and finally opted to serve God alone at home. Within a few weeks he was back on the thing he vowed he'd never go back to because it had ruined his life for twenty-three years: crack cocaine!

Created for fellowship

Imagine a soldier who in a war zone walks away from his company thinking he can fight the enemy on his own just as well. The inmate above left the fellowship of God's family for fellowship with a woman. He felt their mutual love for God was enough, but it led to sexual immorality, guilt, spiritual weakness, and discontent on his job, which he finally quit and went back to the old life of crime and drugs.

There's not a person or being in the universe who can survive without some kind of fellowship. Failure in this area is the *number one* reason for failure in every other area. "Where there is no counsel, the people fall; but in the multitude of counselors there is safety" (Prv 11:14; also 24:6).

Believers in jail don't realize the extent to which they rely on their Christian brothers there. I'm not talking about the many hypocrites or "convenience believers" who look good in Bible studies but revert to carnal living when it's over. I'm referring to men who truly love God, who have developed a stable and faithful Christian lifestyle in jail.

To give up the comradery of a strong jailhouse support group for the suspicion and rejection they feel in many churches, whether real or imagined, especially if they're facing the same thing from their own families, is more than most ex-convicts can handle. I couldn't either. Really! No wonder the pull to old friends and the "mouth [smooth, enticing words] of an immoral woman" is so inviting! (Prv 22:14; 5:3; 7:21).

In one way it's tragic, but in another way I stand amazed at the incredible power God has built into all of us for fellowship and love. If we knew how to *channel* that power into its *true purpose*, we could be *giants* in the *spirit realm*! Does our Creator, our Provider, offer a solution to this massive problem?

Yes. The Bible is the story of God's grace, from beginning to end. If *mercy* is God's *forgiveness* and *pardon*, *grace* is His *favor*, His *ability in us* to walk the walk through the *power of His Spirit*. The New Testament is that grace revealed in its fullness through Jesus Christ (Jn 1:14, 16–17).

But in every book of the New Testament His grace leads us to *join with one another* in love, fellowship, and mutual support. It is impossible to separate mercy and grace from fellowship and relationship, because that's one of the main ways we receive grace – through the *ministry of others*.

This article is an attempt to help inmates and ex-cons understand that the fellowship he got in jail *must* be transferred to *God's family* on the outside, and that an immoral relationship with a woman comes far short of God's much better plan. But let's start from the beginning.

A woman for a man

God's six-times-repeated assessment of everything He created in Genesis one was that "it was good," and finally, "very good." But in chapter two He adds an important bit of insight: "And the Lord God said, 'It is *not good* that man should be alone; I will make him a helper comparable to him,'" or *corresponding*, *complementary* to him (2:18).

No wonder "a woman" is the main cause of failure for the average male ex-con; even *God* said, "It is *not good* that man should be alone," and created woman just for this purpose! And *co-responding* to him, she fulfilled his need for *relationship* on the *same level*.

If *relationship* (fellowship) is the grand purpose, then that relationship must be sealed with a lifetime *commitment* called marriage. If not, God's provision of a woman for a man can easily be clouded with insecurity, fear, and bitterness – the very opposite of God's intent in relationship. That explains why a woman may really be a major reason men fail when they get out of jail – without understanding why God made her (Eph 5:25–28; 1 Pet 3:7).

But God creating a woman for man was only the beginning. What God had *ultimately* in mind was relationship with man on *His* level – God's. *Eve was only the means of developing man's capacity for intimacy with God, in Whose Image we were created!* (Gen 1:26–27).

In Genesis 2:23–24 we read concerning her, "This is now bone of my bones and flesh of my flesh. . . . Therefore a man shall leave his father and mother and be joined to his wife, and they shall become one flesh." But in Ephesians 5:30–32, we find the *fulfillment*, the *final stage* of the relationship: it is *Christ's relationship* with *His Bride*, the *Church*:

"For we are members of His body, of His flesh and of His bones. 'For this reason a man shall leave his father and mother and be joined to his wife, and the two shall become one flesh.' This is a *great mystery*, but I speak concerning *Christ* and the *church."*

God not only made it *possible* to be as *intimate* with *Him*, the Creator of the Universe, as with our wives – bone of my bones and flesh of my flesh – but *desires* it for us and created us for that purpose. Plus He sent His Spirit to help us toward this goal (Jn 14:16–21; 16:7–15, 20–24; Rom 8:26).

Furthermore, He created us with a passion for intimacy so strong that a man will commit murder over it. It's interesting that men and women can become skilled in making lustful connections with each other, overcoming shyness and inferiority. Yet when it comes to relating to one another in *spiritual* things, we can be deaf and blind zombies (Prv 12:1; Mt 13:13–15).

"But if we walk in the *light* as He is in the light, we have *fellowship* with one another." "Beloved, let us love one another, for love is of God; and everyone who loves is born of God and knows God. *He who does not love does not know God*." Wow; that's pretty serious! (1 Jn 1:7a; 4:7–8a).

The ultimate marriage

God says, "Cheer up; I not only created you to love the opposite sex, but I did even better. I created you to love *everyone* with a love far deeper than sexual love. This love will fulfill your deepest desires so completely, you'll be able to rein in your physical lust and reserve it for its intended use – intimacy with your wife.

"Yet this is only *temporary*, and really, *not even essential*. For marriage is a picture of *My marriage with you*, and that takes place to a great extent through your relationship with *my people. My plan for your pleasure far exceeds yours*" (Job 36:11; Ps 16:11; 36:8; 1 Cor 2:9–10; 2 Cor 3:18).

In the Old Testament God speaks of His relationship with

Israel as a marriage. "For your Maker is your husband, the Lord of host is His name." But these deeper relationships don't appeal to us as long as we're having so much "fun" doing it *our* way. So God brings us into hard times in order to change our hearts and create *hunger* for Him (Is 54:5a; also Jer 3:1,8; 31:32; Dt 8:2–3; Jgs 3:4–9).

Hosea said God would bring Israel "into the *wilderness*" and "speak to her heart" [literal meaning] in order to *change her relationship with Him from one of Master-servant to Husband-wife.* "I will *betroth* you to Me [for marriage] forever; yes, I will betroth you to Me in righteousness and justice, in loving-kindness and mercy . . . and you shall *know the Lord*" (Hos 2:14–20).

That's awesome! God loves us so much He'll create circumstances that will *motivate* us to get intimate with Him so we can serve Him through love, not obligation: as a marriage partner, not a servant.

He has lots of methods to bring us to Him. Another is His "show and tell" lesson in the Sinai Desert after they left Egypt. He instructed Moses to build a tabernacle in the *wilderness* that He might "dwell among them." The details of its construction give us a picture diagram of God's people dwelling *in relationship with Him and one another* (Ex 25:8–40).

In Revelation 21 John saw the "New Jerusalem, coming down out of heaven from God, prepared as a *bride* adorned for her *husband*." Then he "heard a loud voice from heaven saying, 'Behold, the *tabernacle* of *God* is with *men*, and He will dwell with them, and they shall be His people. God Himself will be with them and be their God'" (vv. 2–3).

The New Testament is not only about Jesus, but about His Church. The longest recorded prayer of Jesus is His prayer that His disciples "may be one" in Him and the Father, "that the world may believe" (Jn 17:21; 13:35).

After His death and resurrection, He told His followers to go to Jerusalem and wait *together* until they are filled with "power from on high" (Lk 24:49). In Acts 2 it became a reality when through ten days of seeking God *together* "with *one accord* in *one place*," God's power exploded in their midst and sent them out to turn the world right-side-up. And "they *continued* steadfastly in the apostles' doctrine and *fellowship*, in the breaking of bread, and in prayers" (Acts 2:42).

Saved by grace for heaven? Or more?

There's a power greater than "the power of the Home Depot" with its building materials and power tools. In Romans Paul reveals the building blocks of grace, how and why it works, and that its ultimate design is to bring us together in unity (Rom 3, 5, 9). Romans 12 shows us what that unity looks like in practice, where everyone fits together in his place of ministry.

In 1 Corinthians we see what spiritual immaturity looks like: people *divided* from instead of *united* with one another (1:10–13; 3:1ff). 1 Corinthians 12 explains how that unity functions like a human body in which all the parts are dependent on one another.

In Galatians Paul radically destroys the idea of living by rules instead of faith and the power of the Spirit. He concludes his epistle by telling us to "serve one another" in love, "bear one another's burdens, and *so fulfill the law of Christ*." *Relationship* is the *whole point of the law!* "For all the law is fulfilled in one word, even in this: 'You shall love your neighbor as yourself'" (5:13–14, 17–25; 6:2).

Ephesians is an entire book on spiritual maturity that leads to dominion over Satan and his angels. And it's all about *relationship*. It begins with what God has done for us "in Christ," and that His ultimate purpose is to "gather together in *one* all things in Christ," including Jews and Gentiles – two polar opposites *in the same Body!* It's "the mystery" kept secret since creation (because Jews couldn't handle being joined with non-Jews) but is now revealed.

Why "now"? Because this new unified Body was made possible through Christ's death and the work of the Holy Spirit. *And His Church will display God's ultimate purpose and character to the whole universe!* (Rom 8:19–22; Eph 1:10, 17–23; 2:11–18; 3:1–10; 4:1–16; 5:25–32; 6:10–18).

What holds everything together?
Scientists have been searching for years, spending billions at the Large Hadron Collider in Europe, the world's biggest particle accelerator, hoping to discover what's at the bottom of everything: what makes atoms work the way they do. They even call it "the God-particle" or "the God-factor," and in July 2012 they announced they'd found it – the Higgs boson.

So now what? What can they do with this knowledge: make new atoms, creating matter out of nothing? Or will it be used ultimately for our destruction, as the mere splitting of the atom – releasing neutrons bonded together by a "strong force" – leads us to the brink of nuclear war? (Zech 14:12; 2 Pet 3:10–11).

Yet God reveals the mystery again in Colossians 1:16–18, where He says that not only did His Son *create* everything, but that the Son holds it all together – including the *strong force* behind nuclear energy. *He is the "God factor" eons before scientist Peter Higgs was born!* (v 17).

But there's more: the passage continues, saying, "And He is the head of the body, the church [once a 'guarded secret'], who is the beginning, the firstborn from the dead, that in all things He may have the preeminence [be supreme]" (v 18).

That puts us, His many-membered Body, in charge of things, with Him as our Head, of course. Which explains why the saints will *reign* with Christ over the planet. (1 Cor 6:2-3; Eph 3:10; 2 Tim 2:12; Rv 1:26; 5:10; 20:6; 22:5).

Then toward the end of the chapter (Colossians 1) Paul reveals the other side of this mystery: not only the mystery of His Church, unified through Christ rather than law (legalism), but "Christ in you [personally], the hope of glory" (Col 1:27; see Rom 8:10; 2 Cor 5:17; 13:5; Gal 4:19; Eph 3:17).

In other words, *we keep God's law through our union with Christ,* not by trying to obey rules. Understanding our union with Him and with one another is essential to God's entire plan! (Jn 15:1–5; Rom 3:19–31; 8:11; 2 Cor 3:18; Phil 2:1–8; 3:10–12).

At this point please stop and meditate on the last few paragraphs in light of Colossians 1:16–18, for it's the most important thing I've said in this entire book, and it's taking me most of my life to understand and appreciate it.

I was actually planning on deleting some of this chapter in hopes of making it less difficult and tedious. But now that I realize the *power* involved in Christ holding the whole universe together – through His Church, including *authority over the whole realm of Satan,* I ain't gonna delete nothin' in hopes you'll begin to see the sheer magnitude of what God is telling us! (And I'm about to go into orbit spiritually as I think about it!)

Sex and marriage

Understanding this mystery – Christ in you – makes unity with fellow-believers possible, despite our faults and divisive doctrines. *It gives us a legal basis for loving people while or before they change*; it makes it easy to love my wife when my faults make it difficult for her to put up with me at times.

Around the age of seventy I thought my libido was suddenly finished; I felt humiliated, not knowing what to tell my wife. And since I'm a health nut and hate drugs, I knew I'd never resort to Viagra or Cialis. But what to do?

Then, *mystery* solved: resentment! All I had to do was overlook her minor fault that had bothered me at the time, and yippee! Passion returned without "chemo-therapy"! (1 Pet 1:22).

Oops . . . I just realized many of you reading this are locked away from your wives, some perhaps for the rest of your lives. But not to worry: The paradox of this love-revelation is that when you love others with God's love, you don't need sex. Seriously! Because our needs are much deeper than physical or emotional.

Why do some men with beautiful, sexy wives sneak out with other women who, well, aren't so gorgeous? Because an "immoral woman" *seems* to meet that deeper need – unconditional love – and for which a man will often give up his home, along with his children and valuables. I've seen it many times, and so have you (Prv 5, 7).

Yet look what we have in Christ: "For in Him dwells all the fullness of the Godhead bodily; and you are complete in Him, who is the head of all principality and power." Through knowing the "width and length and depth and height" of His love, we can "be filled with all the fullness of God." Incredible! (Col 2:9–10; Eph 3:18–19).

I've talked to inmates who've also experienced this level of meaning and joy, and they agree, He meets *all* their needs; they don't even need masturbation, much less day-dreaming about sex. Remember, the goal is not sexual fulfillment, but *spiritual* fulfillment, which is infinitely better (Rom 8:35–39; 1 Cor 2:9).

Read what God says about sex, marriage, and divorce in 1 Corinthians 7, and unmarried sex in chapter 6. And remember, where He guides, He provides (Eph 3:20; 1 Tim 1:14).

Jail inmates are extremely valuable!

But back to God's wisdom in us: How is it that we – His people – will *make known* "to the principalities and powers in the heavenly places the manifold wisdom of God"? How and why are we going to demonstrate God's many-sided wisdom to the whole realm of good and bad angels, including Satan? (Eph 3:10; Job 1:8–12; 1 Pet 1:12).

Because "justice must be *seen* to be just" (a principle of jurisprudence in the free world),[1] God will use the weakest and neediest people in the world to demonstrate to all the angelic realm that all it takes to transform us "from glory to glory" is a revelation of His unconditional love in and through Christ, and *abiding/remaining* in Him (2 Cor 3:18; Gal 5:16–26; Jn 15:9; 17:23, 26; Eph 3:18; Rv 1:5).

I see inmates not as "losers," but as unique individuals with various issues God can easily solve with His wisdom. And each bit of wisdom we find as we learn to enjoy His love and how it applies to us in particular will be one of the "manifold" aspects of the wisdom God displays to these high-ranking angelic authorities (Eph 3:17–19).

That's why when I walk into jail or prison I feel as though I'm entering a gold mine filled with incredible riches of wisdom that will outlast all the material riches available on earth, and into the endless ages to come (Eph 2:8; 1 Pet 1:12).

The very fact that they fail so easily when they get out is not cause to give up on them, but pray they'll dig deeper into God's wisdom and power to break through the flesh barrier into the glory-realm of the Spirit (Gen 32:24–30; Prv 25:2; Is 6:3; Hos 12:3–5; Heb 11:6).

When I find myself slacking spiritually I don't resort to self-effort, but rather more *revelation of Christ* and *time to absorb it!* It should be as natural to be as righteous and loving as God is, if He lives in us. We don't have to discipline ourselves to sin; it's the nature of the carnal mind, just as godliness is the nature of the spiritual mind (Rom 6–8; Eph 1:17–18).

The beauty of this wisdom is that as we learn how to overcome sin through revelation of the mystery of Christ-in-us, we also get insight in how connected we are as *one Body in Christ!* (Rom 12:4–5; 1 Cor 10:17; 12–13; 12:20; Eph 2:16; 5:30; Col 3:15).

Because His church is not just a collection of people who think alike or who relate on a superficial level. It's about believers who have learned to see each other through the mercy and grace of Jesus Christ, past the weakness of the flesh (Mt 7:1–5; 2 Cor 5:16–17; Eph 1:17–23; Col 1:27).

It's about different members of the same Body of Christ who have learned to strengthen the whole Body through strengthening and encouraging one another instead of weakening the Body through mis-judging and criticizing (Rom 12:3–10; 1 Cor 12; Heb 10:25).

It's about men and women who have given up personal ambition to find their own little niche of responsibility so they can fulfill the purpose for which God created them (Num 4:19; 1 Cor 13; 2 Cor 5:15–20; Phil 3:12–14; Col 3:12–17; Ps 48, 133).

This kind of relationship and fellowship is a *mystery* and an *offense* to the flesh, but the way of Life and Wisdom to the eyes of the Spirit (Mt 16:23; Rom 9:33; 1 Cor 1:23–31; 2:9–16).

As this "building" of believers is "fitted together," it reveals a masterpiece of divine engineering, "a holy temple in the Lord . . . a dwelling place of God in the Spirit" (1 Cor 3:16; Eph 2:22).

And God displays this trophy of His wisdom and love to the angelic realm, especially to Satan and his rebel angels who tried another way than childlike trust in Abba (Daddy) Father (1 Pet 1:12; Job 1–2; Is 14:12–17; Ez 28:11–17; Rom 8:15; 2 Cor 11:3; Gal 4:6).

Our place in His Body, the Church

In Ephesians 4 Paul shows how "the whole body, joined and knit together," nourishes and builds itself up spiritually through humbly submitting to one another, "speaking the truth in love," and hearing one another as though God were speaking through each one (Eph 4:15–16; 2 Cor 5:16–17; 1 Pet 4:11).

And in chapter five he again explains how the Church is revealed through "a great *mystery*" – the fellowship of a husband and wife in marriage. And through *union with one another*, we become "members of His body, *of His flesh* and *of His bones*" (5:30).

It's the *same kind of intimacy God designed Eve to have with Adam and a husband with his wife!* Again, this mystery is *hidden from the natural man,* but it is *glory* and *awe* to those who live by the *revealed* Word (Dt 8:3; Mt 4:4; Rom 10:17; Eph 5:26).

In case you missed it, the Church, His Body, is "the *fullness* of Him who fills all in all," and that "*with all the saints*" we'll comprehend "the width and length and depth and height" of "the love of Christ which passes knowledge; that you [plural in the Greek] may be *filled with all the fullness of God.*" Incredible – the *fullness of God in us – many members as one Body in Christ!* (Eph 1:10, 22–23; 3:18–19; 4:2–4; Rom 12:5; 1 Cor 12:12).

And finally, Ephesians 6 concludes with the well-known passage about "the whole armor of God" in order to "withstand in the evil day, and having done all, to stand" (v. 13). It corresponds with Psalm 133, concerning brethren dwelling together in unity, and Psalm 134, the last of the fifteen "Psalms of Degrees."

This psalm (134) speaks of those who "by *night stand* in the *house of the Lord*" and "bless the Lord." It is symbolism for worship and spiritual warfare during which demonic strongholds are broken in order to *release and deliver others.* For the "whole armor" passage ends with "praying always . . . *for all the saints*" (Eph 6:10–18).

The *natural mind* doesn't see this high priority in prayer – how closely spiritual warfare is related to our union with and responsibility toward one another. And would you believe, the most quoted verse on temptation (1 Cor 10:13), where God promises "the way of escape, that you may be able to bear it," occurs in the context of the *wilderness* temptations, and is followed by a discussion of "the communion of the body of Christ" (Gen 44:18–45:1; 1 Kgs 8:28–49; 1 Cor 10:14–22).

It's God's *Tabernacle* in the *wilderness*, *His Church*, our *means of escape!* (Ps 27:4–6; 48:1–9; Ps. 91; Num 18:5; Mt 16:18).

Victory over temptation

No wonder Paul precedes that verse with, "Therefore let him who thinks he *stands* take heed lest he fall" (v.12). We can stand against temptation when we humbly *depend* on God; but that often depends on our relationship with our brothers and sisters in Christ and our *commitment* to them, as in marriage (Eph 4:16; 5:31–32; Rv 21:2, 9).

Our real problem, my dear brothers (and sisters), is not our need of a woman (or man), but our need for real fellowship with our true Lover, our Bridegroom, the Lord Jesus Christ. "God sets the lonely in families, he leads forth the prisoners with singing; but the rebellious live in a sun-scorched land" (Ps 68:6 NIV). This is *God's* answer to loneliness: our *true* "Helper," Christ and His Body, the Church.

Relating to others spiritually is *impossible* without *knowing* Jesus, for "in Him all things consist [hold together], and He is the head of the body, the church." He is the "prototype" of God's dwelling, His Tabernacle. He is the only One who can fulfill and spiritually guide the need of man for a woman, for all relationship and fellowship originate in *knowing Him* (Col 1:17–18; Eph 4:11–16; Phil 3:7–10; 1 Jn 1:1–4; 4:7–8).

If you're in prison or jail, use the "time" to soak in His Presence and Word daily by the hour, until He transforms your mind, sets you free on the inside, and invites you with His "Bride" to the "banqueting house," a *preview of "the marriage supper of the Lamb."* You can enjoy "heaven on earth" even in *prison!* (Dt 11:19–21; Song 2:4; Rv 19:9).

If you're not locked up, find time daily to get alone with God and His Word, because without it you'll find it *impossible* to avoid *stumbling* over the many offenses among God's family members. All we are is a "Treasure in *earthen* vessels," and many times the rough clay pots hide the Treasure (Christ) in various degrees, causing misunderstanding, pain, and anger (Mt 11:6; Rom 9:30–33; Heb 12:22–29; Jude 1:24; 2 Cor 4:7).

It's the believer's greatest challenge. Satan uses these "offenses" as *bait* for his trap, to pull us back into sin. If we *understand* "his devices," we can avoid those traps, humble ourselves, and experience more grace to "grow up in all things into Him who is the head – Christ – from whom the whole body, joined and knit together by what every joint supplies, according to the effective working by which every part does its share . . . for the edifying of itself in love" (Eph 4:15–16).

Now that's a love affair that will last forever! If those two guys in the C-pod only knew, how happy they'd be – even without a woman!

1. Arthur C. Custance, *The Seed of the Woman* (Brockville, Ontario: Doorway Publications, 1980) P. 403 Also available Online: http://custance.org/Library/SOTW/Index.htm (accessed July 5, 2014)

CHAPTER 7

God's Correction Department: Plan A

Poverty and shame will come to him who disdains [hates] correction, but he who regards [receives] a rebuke will be honored. Proverbs 13:18

How to tell if you're insane

You've been out of jail long enough to find a church. At last you're free and right where God wants you, doing what you'd been taught in jail about the importance of accountability, and that life is all about relationship. And God's family, His Church, "the pillar and ground of truth," is His authorized "support group" and training school to maintain your walk with Him. You intend to develop responsibility, exercise your gifts, and grow to maturity.

It feels so good after years of being herded like an animal with no rights and little respect. Now you're going to prove to your family and the world that you *have* changed, that you *don't* have "jailhouse religion," and that God *has* done a permanent work in you that will last because of His grace! (Phil 1:6).

Well . . . you do feel uncomfortable around such *normal* people. They have no idea what you've been through. They live in an entirely different world. Their problems are so minor compared to yours. It's been so easy for them – loved by family and friends, respected by the community.

They've never had to worry about a warrant, about suspicious cops, about those still nagging temptations and flashbacks to euphoric highs followed by depressing lows, near ODs, withdrawals or attempts to. Those bitter arguments and fights, screaming and cursing, shouting threats, somebody calling 911, door-slamming and burning rubber. And then back in jail for the 15th time . . . or 50th!

They'll never know and I hope they don't ever know everything, because there's no way they could understand, you think. No way!

But you're going to make it this time because you really got to know the Word and you stuck it out with the prayer groups and Bible studies in jail. You're not what you used to be. You're a *new man in Christ*; old things *have* passed away this time. You're out to stay!

The AA definition of insanity is doing the same thing over and over and expecting different results. When a man leaves jail and goes back to an ungodly lifestyle and expects different results this time, he's morally and spiritually insane. I've heard inmates tell me they stayed clean and out of trouble for x number of years and then took *one* drink and now they're back.

The most obvious way to change one's lifestyle and stay clean is to get involved in the right "support group": find a church and stay there. I see *the regular fellowship of believers as God's primary authorized correction department*. But if it's that important, why is it so difficult? Why does God allow so many offenses and reasons to give up and quit?

Offenses: Satan's bait, God's tool

Though Jesus warned of serious consequences to those who caused offenses, he told His disciples that "offenses *must* come." The word *offense* or *stumbling stone* is in the Greek, *skandalon* (Strong's #4625), a snare or trap (Mt 18:7; Lk 17:1).

Why would Jesus condemn those who cause people to stumble, and yet say these offenses *must come*, these traps must be set? My answer has three parts.

(1) *Offenses cull out or remove the insincere, half-hearted, or hypocrites*. In His parable of the sower, the Word-seed sown on the hard wayside soil and eaten by birds (demons, distractions) pictures those whose *hearts are too hard*; they really don't care or don't care enough. And the Word sown on stony ground illustrates one who at first "receives it with joy" but in "tribulation or persecution" he "stumbles" (is offended, *skandalizo*, verb form of *skandalon*) (Mt 13:10–23).

The extreme training of Navy Seals or Special Forces develops those who endure and eliminates those who don't. Should God's army, His "overcomers" be less prepared? (Jn 16:33; Rom 12:21; 1 Jn 2:13–14; 4:4; Rv 2:7, 11, etc, 12, 21; 21:7).

(2) *God uses offenses to chastise or refine the believer.* He used Satan to refine Job and crucify Jesus, wicked nations to chastise Israel, a "messenger of Satan" to keep Paul humble, and Jewish and Roman persecution to mature the Church. But when they have served their purpose, God punishes or destroys them (Job 1–2; 30; 42; Lk 13:32; Jn 14:30; 1 Cor 2:8; Heb 2:10; 5:8–9; Dt 28; Jude 3; Is 13:9–22; 14:4–6; Jer 25:9, 12; 2 Cor 12:7; Mt 5:11; 13:39–43; Acts 8:1; 14:22; Rv 20:10–14).

(3) *Offenses act like a filter to block the "natural man" from attempting to "receive the things of the Spirit of God,* for they are foolishness to him; nor can he know them, because they are *spiritually* discerned" (1 Cor 2:14).

While offenses cull out the hypocrites, they also weed out the fleshly thinking in the believer so that he *must* get beyond mind-wandering and human logic and focus with the eyes of the Spirit. Otherwise he too, will stumble with the hypocrites. Jesus taught in parables to blind his hearers from what their hearts were not willing to accept (Mt 13:14–17).

For "eye has not seen, nor ear heard, nor have entered into the heart of man the things which God has prepared for those who love Him. But God has *revealed* them to us *through His Spirit*" (1 Cor 2:9–10).

Offenses are like hurdles that *demand a higher level of spiritual energy* to overcome lazy thinking and put a demand on our spirit-man to leap into the realm of the heavenlies and maintain our "walk in the Spirit," our life of abiding in Christ. Thus offenses become valuable training tools to develop spiritual muscle and maturity (Prv 25:2–3; Rom 8:1, 3; Gal 5:16, 25; Eph 1:17–23; 4:23–24; 6:11–18; Jn 15:1f; 1 Jn 3:6, 9; 5:18).

No wonder God "lays in Zion," among His own people, "a stumbling stone and a rock of offense . . . as a trap and a snare." He wants us to grow up – tried and tested, "without spot or wrinkle"! (Is 8:14; Rom 9:32–33; Mt 13:13–15, 21, 39–43; Eph 5:27).

Separating wheat from chaff (hull)

A Christian inmate told the class one day about two weeks before his release date: "I've been in jail 55 times. But this time something has changed in me and I *know* I'm not coming back!" We all clapped. A few weeks after his release he was back. With a sense of resignation he sighed, "The distractions out there are unbelievable. I guess I do better in jail."

Many inmates adapt so well to jail routine it's like living in a space station without the normal stress the rest of us experience on the "ground." The astronauts there use special exercise equipment to keep their bones and muscles from deteriorating. Whatever inmates deal with in jail are multiplied many times on the outside, and if they stumble over the common complaints most inmates stumble over, they'll hardly make it outside (Prv 3:11; 24:10; Jer 12:5; Heb 12:3–4; 1 Pet 4:12).

There's plenty to grumble about in jail: tasteless food, ridiculous rules, harsh correctional officers, unfair judges, public defenders who don't seem concerned, corruption in the system, spiteful or thieving roomies or dorm-mates, angry phone calls with family, time it takes to get a response from most departments, can't get my property, no reading glasses, phone-blocks, no-contact orders, on and on.

Everything is about *attitude*. But those who learn to handle with a Christ-like attitude the many offenses in jail have a winning chance they'll make it on the outside. They make good use of the "exercise equipment" provided (Ps 66:12; Jer 12:5).

A man-trap

If we intend to mature, we need to know how to deal with the pride in our hearts that makes us so sensitive to offenses. And by pride I simply mean too much confidence in self rather than total, childlike dependence on God *and His family* and His Word (Mt 11:25; 18:3; Lk 10:21; 18:16).

The most common *skandalon* male inmates face when they get out is a woman: "And I find more bitter than death the woman whose heart is *snares* and *nets*, whose hands are *fetters*. *He who pleases God* shall escape from her, but the sinner shall be *trapped* by her." "The mouth of an immoral woman is a deep pit; he who is abhorred by the Lord will fall there" (Eccl 7:26; Prv 22:14).

Why is it her *mouth* and not her *body* that traps a man? "For the *lips* of an immoral woman drip honey, and her *mouth* is smoother than oil; but in the end she is bitter as wormwood, sharp as a two-edged sword" (Prv 5:3–4).

The reason is *ego!* Pride destroyed Lucifer and led Adam and Eve to the bait he used to trap them: "You will be like God!" "Everyone proud in heart is an *abomination* [utterly detestable] to the Lord." "Pride goes before destruction, and a haughty spirit before a fall" (Gen 3:5; Ez 28:17; Is 14:12–14; Prv 16:5a, 16; also 18:12).

To those who humble themselves, offenses and chastening become correction, training, and discipline. To those who hold on to their pride, these offenses become "snares and nets . . . fetters" (chains) – another form of jail *outside* (or inside) jail (Jas 4:10; 1 Pet 5:5–6; Heb. 12:5ff).

"The ear that hears the rebukes [corrections] of life will abide among the wise. He who disdains [doesn't like] instruction despises his own soul, but he who heeds [pays careful attention to] rebuke [criticism and chastening] gets understanding." "But he who hates correction is stupid" (Prv 15:31–32; 12:1b).

Proverbs five begins with a plea for understanding and wisdom, which protect a man from the immoral woman. When she nearly destroys him, he'll say, when he comes to his senses, "How I have hated instruction, and my heart *despised correction!* I have not obeyed the voice of my teachers, nor inclined my ear to those who instructed me! I was on the verge of total ruin, in the midst of the assembly and congregation" (5:12–14).

"For the commandment is a lamp, and the law a light; reproofs of instruction are the way of life, to keep you from the evil woman, from the *flattering tongue* of a seductress" (Prv 6:23–24).

God's department of corrections

What does the *assembly* and *congregation* have to do with a woman and chastening? Because the *right* woman we were created for or to be is the *Bride of Christ*, the Church (2 Cor 11:2; Eph 5:31–32; Rv 19:7–8; 21:2, 9).

"Drink water from your own cistern, and running water from your own well. . . . Let her breasts satisfy you at all times; and always be enraptured with her love." Why do I need to be told to find satisfaction with my wife and not "strangers . . . an immoral woman . . . a seductress"? Isn't my wife enough to meet my needs? (5:15, 19b).

Yes, but no: What I really want is someone to tickle my ego, my pride, to respect me and make me feel like a man. "Stolen water is sweet," says the "foolish woman" (tempting me) "and bread eaten in secret is pleasant. But he does not know that the dead are there, and that *her guests are in the depths of hell* " (Prv 9:17–18).

The real message in Proverbs 5 goes deeper than a wife and an immoral woman. *This chapter contains the mystery of relationship and fellowship – the foundation for everything in life* (Ps 133; Eph 3:9–10).

And the "immoral woman" might simply be friends and relationships that *make me feel good about myself rather than help me see my real condition.* I don't realize their flattery "spreads a net for [my] feet," a *trap* that *imprisons* me in the web of self-deception and more of the same pride that led to the fall of man. No wonder it's so hard to give up old friends and hangouts, even when we know they are slowly destroying us! (Prv 29:5; 1 Cor 15:33).

The wife who knows my weaknesses and *offends* me through her "rebukes" is, in light of Proverbs 5, like a local body of believers, a church or support group, when they've gotten to know me well enough to see through me and help me see myself. These are God's "plan A" for our correction (Eph 4–5).

They might reject me or back away when they know who I *really* am. And their rejection can push me away and into the arms of another woman or a group of friends who accept me "just as I am," as God accepts me, *so I think.*

But all I've done is run away from the God who chastens, scourges, corrects, and rebukes whom He *loves.* "Faithful are the wounds of a friend, but the kisses of an enemy are deceitful"

(Prv 3:11–12; 27:6; Heb 12:5–12; Rv 3:19).

"With her enticing speech she caused him to yield, with her flattering lips she seduced him. Immediately he went after her, as an ox goes to the slaughter, or as a fool to the correction of the stocks, till an arrow struck his liver. As a bird hastens to the snare, He did not know it would cost his life" (Prv 7:21–23).

Many of us know Revelation 3:20, where Jesus stands knocking on the door of our hearts waiting to be invited in for fellowship and spiritual nourishment. But the verse just before it says, "As many as I love, I rebuke and chasten. Therefore be zealous and repent" (v.19).

Fellowship and intimacy with God are impossible without allowing Him to deal with the secret motives of our heart. And for that, He most commonly uses His Family. *If we can humble ourselves and take it from them without running away from the heat, it will save us from having to deal with it on a more deadly level – jail, hospital, or "total ruin"* (1 Cor 11:28–32).

"And you mourn at last, when your flesh and body are consumed, and say: 'How I have *hated instruction*, and my heart *despised correction*! I have not obeyed the voice of my teachers, nor inclined my ear to those who instructed me! I was on the verge of total ruin, in the midst of the assembly and congregation'" (Prv 5:11–14).

What makes a hard heart?

One of the easiest things to do in jail is learn the Bible. But head-knowledge and even revelation of the Word do not necessarily lead to a tender heart, and, in fact, may do exactly the opposite!

The Jews of Jesus' time knew the scriptures well, but it hardened instead of softened their hearts. As a result they were offended and stumbled over the Messiah they'd been expecting thousands of years (Mt 13:15; Rom 9:32–33; 10:21; 11:9).

If all an inmate has when he gets out of jail is Bible knowledge, he may have more pride when he comes out than when he went in. But it's now a *religious pride much more difficult to detect than worldly pride because it seems so godly* (1 Cor 8:1; Phil 3:4–10).

I talked with a returned inmate recently who was one of the strongest spiritually I'd ever met in prison. His dedication to God and his example before prison staff and fellow inmates impressed me. In fact, God gave him a word of wisdom to correct me, which he handed me in a letter, and it was right on target.

When he got out and continued with the job he'd gotten in Work Release, his fellow employees asked him why he was the only one who got along so well with a hard-headed boss nobody liked. This opened the door for him to witness of his faith in Christ.

But his superior spiritual knowledge became a trap of Satan. For he found the level of spiritual life in every church he tried was so low he felt out of place. He finally decided to serve God alone in the little cottage he'd rented within eyesight of the job he loved (Eccl 7:16; 1 Cor 12:14–26).

But now without the humbling and encouragement from God's family he didn't realize he needed – *even from weak, carnal believers*, he fell into disagreement with his boss and suddenly quit his job. Then he lost his home and went to a half-way house, then left that and moved in with a woman addicted to drugs and alcohol. It wasn't long before he too fell back into his old lifestyle and they both ended up back in jail.

But he's still teachable, and now has a deeper understanding of how deceitful the heart is and *why* we need one another in the Body of Christ. And he has more years in prison to get to know God, hopefully in a different way than He knew Him before (Rom 12:3ff; Eph 4:1–16).

Two kinds: rejected and rejecters

The above inmate is an example of those I call spiritually strong. When they get out of jail, their re-entry into the Body of Christ outside jail can be very difficult, as seen above, because they tend to reject the very believers they should be praying for.

The strong should not expect to be pampered or nourished by church leaders, for God has called us, along with them, to nourish and care for others. Who am I to think I've got to be fed and pleased in God's House? "We then who are strong ought to bear with the weaknesses of the weak, and not to please ourselves" (Rom 15:1, margin; see 1 Cor 13:11).

But most believing inmates who emerge from the corrections department are the weaker type. They've piddled away most of their "time" on everything *but* spiritual things. Their devotional life, if any, is no more than the popular *Daily Bread.* They assume God's family is there to strengthen them, not *offend* them! What a surprise awaits them *if* they bother to find a church.

Many in jail don't bother to attend the church services offered by the chaplain or volunteers, even though they may participate in prayer circles among inmates. This is a good indication they won't be interested in church on the outside unless they already have a family connection with a home church. And they certainly won't find an inmate prayer circle out there to attend.

No wonder so many are unprepared for the wide variety of devices and schemes Satan has planned to *trap* them in short order as soon as they are "free" (2 Cor 2:11; Eph 6:11).

Many large churches have one or more support groups led, in some cases, by ex-cons and ex-addicts. If you endure through all the abuses and offenses, you too can be such a leader.

Another of my friends from the Work Release center did become a support-group leader, with his wife, at a large church. But he got too busy in ministry, apparently, and lost his wife through divorce. *Both* had been in crime together, and both ministered together when they got out: the perfect ministry couple who'd "been there and done that." But they fell victim to one of Satan's devices: the same one that almost destroyed me years ago – outrunning God's grace and presence while *working* for Him (Ps 131; Song 1:6; Rv 2:2–5).

Crawling down the aisle

If I sound like an expert on this subject it's not because I'm strong in this area, but because I'm weak. I switched churches three times as a pastor and four times as a member before I finally realized it was *my* problem, not theirs; there's no perfect church or pastor.

To accept this as reality can be a great blessing. In the 1970s I pastored a small church in Greensboro, NC. Half the congregation resented my style because they saw right through my intellectual arrogance: I thought my Bible knowledge set me apart as spiritually superior (1 Cor 8:1).

After about five years they couldn't handle it anymore and the visiting evangelist (traveling preacher), feeling the same way about me, talked them into leaving the church. So one Sunday morning their leaders stood up in the middle of the service and resigned.

I was thrilled! Now the church would finally start growing! But after a year the church hadn't added a single member, despite my hard work. And then the splinter group came and met me, telling me God has sent them back. But they first wanted me to give them a chance to tell me what I was doing wrong. I agreed, curious, of course, and we decided I'd sit in the pew during an open session at the church while they took turns telling me what they thought.

My wife stayed home that evening, not wanting to deal with what they might say; she'd suffered a physical breakdown years earlier through stress trying to relate to these folks. Only two other people attended: our most faithful couple, David and Marilyn Sutphin, who now pastor a thriving church in North Carolina.

Five of these leaders, four of them women, took turns behind the pulpit and for two hours told me what I was doing wrong. How I wish I'd recorded it, for I can't remember anything they said except that I preached too much on "victory." It took me decades to grasp what they meant. In my youth I couldn't see what was wrong with preaching such a positive message. But what it must have sounded like to them was, *Stop your grumbling; be victorious like me!*

When they finished I piously invited them to pray for me. One of them pronounced judgment on me if I didn't repent. I thanked them and went home, confident they'd proven they had a bad attitude compared to how "humbly" I'd handled it. I'd thoroughly studied Watchman Nee, the most popular "deeper life" writer in the 1970s, and felt I'd modeled his teaching on "brokenness" to perfection. Certainly God was proud of me!

That Saturday morning, my closest friend in the area, Bob Ellis, had just finished completely rebuilding my 1971 VW "bus" engine and brought it over for me to test-drive it with him. As we rode down Highway 150 he suddenly blurted out, "Vic, why are you trying to change these people? It takes three generations to change deep cultural roots and you're trying to mold them into your worship and teaching style overnight!"

I was shocked, but kept quiet and determined to go home and "pray through" to see if it was God or the devil who spoke through him, because he'd known nothing about the meeting that Wednesday. As I sought God, deep conviction gripped me until I ended up on the floor, writhing in agony as God began ripping out of me, as it were, clots of deeply buried roots of pride. After an hour or two, I rose up feeling clean and free!

Sunday morning I announced that from now on I would allow *Christ* to be the Head of the church, not I. They thought I had some psychological trick up my sleeve, not believing me (they told me later) until I told them I'd already called the evangelist we'd had the year before (who'd advised them to leave) to come back and hold a "revival" (a series of meetings).

When I said that, the lady who'd prophesied judgment over me stood up and quietly said, "I think we should praise the Lord." And the whole congregation stood and began worshiping the way I'd been trying to "train them" for the past six years: spontaneous worship that sounds like a symphony orchestra. With no help from me at the organ and not playing a note!

When the evangelist came, I expected him to preach as he'd preached the year before – scolding me and belittling all I represented – "learnin' and education" – and building the people up to high heaven as they shouted victory. But this time I knew I deserved it and wanted God to reduce me to dust – completely! So I decided to crawl up the aisle on my hands and knees at the right moment and lay before his feet and ask him to pray for me. Excuse me if it seems weird, but that's how desperate I was.

But as I listened, horrors: he was slicing *them* to the dust regarding their attitudes and unbelief, and built me up and up before them. Now I felt sorry for them as my need to humble myself changed to compassion for these dear people. He continued to "work them over" the entire week. It was the last time they asked to have him back for revival, and from then on we had "honeymoon" days of glory and love, like heaven on earth (Dt 11:21).

This experience, which took place around the time God delivered me from depression (chapter 1), illustrates the value of allowing God to use His church to humble us, or we're open season for the temptations our ego and lust invite (Prv 5:1–14).

Unfortunately, with success often comes over-confidence. During such a time, I hit a roadblock, and taking advantage of my newfound "freedom from the law," I resigned the church instead of profiting from the lessons I'd learned. *If only*. . . .

Which is why I understand inmates and *their* regrets. The one consolation I get from my failures is that the vast majority of people in the world are not in the comfort-zone of "success." But, like me, they are struggling with the consequences of not living up to what they should have "known better" and done. And to understand their pain is an essential aspect of our purpose as "a kingdom of priests" (Ez 3:15; Phil 3:13; Heb 2:14–18; 5:1–3; Ex 19:5–6; 1 Pet 2:9; Rev 1:6).

The Treasure, not the vessel

I came to a conclusion long ago, but too often forget it, that men and women of God must admit or own up to our weaknesses and character flaws for two reasons: First, "we have this treasure in earthen vessels, that the excellence of the power may be of God and not of us." And second, which only explains the first, our limitations and defects keep us humble, reminding us we're no different than anyone else. So God gets the glory for whatever grace He manifests through us (2 Cor 4:7).

"For you see your calling, brethren, that not many wise according to the flesh, not many mighty, not many noble, are called. But God has chosen the foolish things of the world to put to shame the wise, and God has chosen the weak things of the world to put to shame the things which are mighty; and the base things of the world and the things which are despised God has chosen, and the things which are not, to bring to nothing the things that are, that no flesh should glory in His presence" (1 Cor 1:26–29).

How ironic that we criticize gifted ministers for their weaknesses, not realizing that's why God uses them! Paul writes that love "bears all things, believes all things, hopes all things, endures all things." John tells us, "He who does not love *does not know God*, for God is love" (1 Jn 4:8; Cor. 13:7).

When I stumble over an offense in the church, instead of blaming someone, I realize *I don't know God deeply enough yet.* As a result offenses have come to serve another extremely valuable purpose – drawing me closer to God (Mt 5:6; Rom 3:19).

How to detect a trap

A dear brother I've known from jail and prison for many years knows the Word as well as I do; his prayers and testimonies are tender, compassionate, and moving. But he's a regular client at the facility.

He explained his latest failure – family problems and bitter arguments that drove him into discouragement and out of the house back to his street friends who gave him the comfort he so needed. He hadn't even committed a crime but happened to be with one of these friends who had drugs hidden under the seat he was sitting on when the cops pulled them over.

He admitted his church family had reached out to him and tried desperately to encourage him and pull him back. But apparently something in his heart was too hurt to respond.

Putting myself in his jail sneakers, I tried to imagine what he could do differently in jail that would prepare him to deal better with rejection and abuse when he gets out. All I can think of is Proverbs 8:13, "The fear of the Lord is to hate evil; pride and arrogance and the evil way and the perverse mouth I hate."

The verse contains two critical elements: First, hating evil even when it's disguised as "friends." I must *beg* God for a sensitivity to detect sin disguised as comfort and pleasure until I can sniff it out like a DEA (Drug Enforcement Administration) dog and run the other way.

And second, I need to realize that *my own* arrogance, pride, and a sharp tongue are my *real* enemies, and *the abuse and rejection I get from family or anybody else are my best friends – a sign God dearly loves me!* He loves me enough to keep dealing with my pride. Because *humility* is my best protection from the lies of Satan! (Is 57:15; 66:2; Ps 34:18; 138:6; 1 Pet 4:1–2; 5:5).

When I'm "armed" with this twofold understanding – a "shield of faith," offenses create for me an attitude of brokenness and comfort from the "God of all comfort," and that which Satan meant to bring me down, instead brings me closer to God (2 Cor 1:4–6; Eph 6:16; 1 Pet 4:1–2).

This may be the answer to the inmate who'd been in jail fifty-five times. He's back now, after six years, having served more jail – and *prison* – time. But he said his mother passed away, and now he's left with absolutely nobody to fall back on for help. Yet it's left him with the most incredible freedom he's ever felt in his life, he said. For he now feels *entirely* dependent on God alone and realizes this is what he's needed all along. He's got it right in theory: time will tell if he *continues* to rely totally on Him (Is 30:18–19; 50:10–11; Col 1:23).

Most young people in juvenile detention center hate the police. So I tell them, "If you don't receive correction from people who love you – parents, family, teachers, church leaders (plan A) – you'll end up having to take it from people who may *not* love you (plan B)." I'm always impressed by the silence of those who love to argue when I finally tell them this.

But even in plan B, *God* loves us just as much and says that if we "endure chastening," it "yields the peaceable fruit of righteousness to those who have been trained by it." Think: spiritual weight lifting in the *real* world, training for heavenly Olympics! "Endure hardship as a good soldier of Jesus Christ." (2 Tim 2:3b; Heb 12:7, 11).

"If you have run with the footmen and they have wearied you, then how can you contend with horses? And if in the land of peace, in which you trusted, they wearied you, then how will you do in the floodplain of the Jordan?" (Jer 12:5).

CHAPTER 8

From Insanity to Responsibility: You Can Make It without Hustling

A faithful man will abound with blessings, but he who hastens to be rich will not go unpunished . . . . A man with an evil eye hastens after riches, and does not consider that poverty will come upon him. Proverbs 28:20, 22

Too hard to change?

Not long ago Jim (not his real name), a Christian inmate in one of my jail Bible studies, looked me in the eye and asked, "What am I to do when my family is hungry, my baby has no milk or diapers, and we're about to be thrown into the streets? I can't find a job because of my background, and in two hours I can make a few connections and pay the rent and buy groceries."

Alcoholic Anonymous defines insanity as doing the same thing and expecting different results. As difficult as Jim's situation is, I realized that *repeated* quick-fix solutions to urgent problems that don't deal with the *cause* truly are a form of spiritual insanity. Yet it's hard to blame people under pressure for taking what seems like the only way out when that's the only way they've ever known.

How true it is that "we don't change until the pain of *not changing* becomes worse than the pain of changing." But consider two important facts about this "insane" view:

(1) The pain of not changing will affect far more than my temporary situation and health; it usually affects everybody around me, greatly increasing *their* pain, and may end up destroying my future and any potential I had.

(2) The pain of changing may not really be painful at all. The *Good News* is that God has already prepared the way for us through Jesus Christ, who took our pain in advance, loves us beyond our wildest dreams, has the most awesome plans for us;

and His Holy Spirit is here to work with and in us to do His will, changing us from the inside out.

Why then would anybody be "crazy" enough to continue on this insane treadmill when Jesus said His "burden is light," He "has blessed us with every spiritual blessing in the heavenly places in Christ," and through Him wants to "freely give us all things"? (Mt 11:30; Eph 1:3; Rom 8:32; 1 Cor 2:9).

There is one simple reason: all these blessings are hidden behind a *veil*, our flesh; we see with our *natural* instead of our *spiritual* eyes (1 Cor 2:7–14; 2 Cor 3:14–18; Heb 10:20).

Paul wrote that our eyes, ears, or heart can't imagine "the things which God has prepared for those who love Him. But God has revealed them to us *through His Spirit*." "But the natural man does not receive the things of the Spirit of God, for they are foolishness to him; nor can he know them, because they are *spiritually* discerned" (1 Cor 2:9–10a, 14).

It sounds great, but how do I pull these spiritual blessings out of the invisible, heavenly realm into my flesh and blood world where I can pay my rent and feed my family?

The real question is how badly do I want this "walk in the Spirit" where God's blessings abound, and what am I willing to pay? Yet if it's "freely given," why is there a "price"?

Use it or lose it

Jim Stovall wrote a small book, *The Ultimate Gift*,[1] in which a billionaire, Red Stevens, felt he had failed his children by giving them too much too soon without the advantage of their having learned through hard work and personal responsibility. At the end of his life he realized none of them had the maturity or wisdom to take over his businesses and organizations. So he selected Jason, the grandson whose father had died in a plane crash, to be the heir of his vast fortune. But since this pampered playboy had never worked a day in his life, he would have to submit to a plan that would develop his sense of responsibility over a one year period, one month at a time.

Each month the now deceased Stevens, on a videotape recorded before his death and with the help of his living business-partner, Hamilton, handed Jason another assignment.

Each was designed to teach him responsibility through some service-related project aimed at pulling him out of his childish self-centered world to help him feel the needs of others. If he failed even with a bad attitude, the whole plan would be canceled and Jason would receive no inheritance at all.

The first month had him on a hard-labor project at the crack of dawn for thirty days, which, like shock therapy, jolted him out of lalaland and tested him to the limit. But each month his attitude slowly improved until by the end of the year Jason looked through the eyes of someone who lived to meet the needs of others, not himself. In the final video, Stevens congratulated him and handed him, through Hamilton, ownership of assets worth two billion dollars.

I have never seen a more perfect parallel to the parables Jesus gave in Matthew 25 and Luke 19. There He compares the Kingdom of God to "a man traveling to a far country, who called his own servants and delivered his goods to them. And to one he gave five talents, to another two, and to another one, to each according to his own ability" (Mt 25:14–30; Lk 19:12–27).

In Luke each servant was given ten *minas*. A *mina* is a unit or weight of money, like the *talent* in Matthew 25. These parables teach the meaning of *stewardship*. A *steward* is one entrusted with the responsibility of something given or loaned to him by someone else. Every believer was given *"grace* . . . according to the measure of Christ's gift," and "a measure of *faith*," along with the "gift of righteousness" from the moment he received Christ (Eph 4:7; Rom 5:17; 12:3).

Then it continues with the stewardship of our families, our gifts, abilities, opportunities, our work, how we relate to people around us including friends and enemies, church relationships, our bodies (health and moral integrity), even our disadvantages and sinful past, which can become a *testimony* to God's grace. And most important, the key to it all – our *time* (Ps 90:12; Eph 5:16, 25ff; 6:4; Rom 12:3ff; 1 Cor 6:15ff; 1 Tim 1:12–16).

God will reward us according to how we develop and increase the measure of grace and faith He has given each of us as we apply it to these other areas of responsibility. In the above parables, the servant who failed to put his money to use and multiply it was cast into "outer darkness," where "there will be weeping and gnashing of teeth" (Mt 25:30).

Why did the servant fail to develop his stewardship and incur such harsh punishment? He was "afraid" because he saw his master as a "hard man." But God saw *him* as "wicked and lazy" because *he failed to take advantage of the favor his master had shown in the gift given him.* God calls it *grace,* because it's given to us – a gift – whether we deserve it or not (Eph 2:8).

In other words, God gives us a kick-start (faith and grace) as newborn believers, and all we have to do is *develop* it by *using* it. Those who do nothing with it not only miss out on God's blessings, but will be punished for their neglect and *failure to learn the true character of our merciful God* (Heb 12:15–17).

"Take My yoke upon you and learn from Me. . . . For My yoke is easy and My burden is light," Jesus said. It's not "hard." The yoke in this case was a wooden bar curved over the necks of two oxen connected to a cart or plowing instrument, enabling them to plow together. A young ox might be yoked to an older one to learn from him. In the same way a Jewish young man would yoke himself to a rabbi to learn from him through instruction and discipline (Mt 11:29–30; Heb 12:11).

What's at stake

Let's take Jim facing eviction, or similar problems with many inmates when they get out of jail with no job, no money, no place to stay, and nobody to help them get started. Will he learn the hard way or the easy way? Learning the hard way is doing what he's used to doing – hustling (drug-dealing) on the streets. But that's crazy (insane) because he'll either end up in jail or in hell, and might bring some or all of his family with him, and no telling how many others! (Mt 18:6; Lk 17:1–2; Rom 14:7).

Sometimes it helps to look at the worst that could happen if he chooses the right (easy) way: He's thrown out of his home with his family and ends up sleeping in the woods. It's dangerous, his wife and kids are crying and hungry, and he has no money and "knows" nobody will ever hire him.

The key is to *attract* this God who claims to be "merciful and gracious," whose "yoke is easy and . . . light," and who is *angered by our unbelief and laziness. Which means He actually intends to help him, maybe miraculously, and the only thing that stops Him is his unbelief and failure to get started!* (Ex 34:6; Num 11:1; 14:11–12; Mt 11:30; Heb 3:7–12).

But believing a God he can't see in this nightmare could be virtually impossible. It all depends on how he has prepared. "A prudent person foresees danger and takes precautions. The simpleton goes blindly on and suffers the consequences" (Prv 22:3 NLT).

What has he done with his measure of faith and grace since he received Christ? Did he strengthen or weaken it? Did he fill his days in jail complaining, gambling, hustling, goofing off, reading junk novels or porn, and trying to beat the system? (Gal 6:7–8).

On the outside did he listen to music and rap that built his faith or weaken it? What kind of TV programs and movies did he watch? How about the Internet and his phone? Did he hang with his old homeboys, exposing himself to temptation by their lifestyle? Or did he find a church home where the encouragement of the Word through godly people and involvement with their activities and ministries strengthened his measure of faith and grace? (Heb 3:12–13; 10:25).

Did he build his faith by feeding on the Word, spending time daily talking to God and learning to hear His voice? Did he encourage others, including his wife and children, with what he learned in this "quiet time" with His Creator? (Dt 11:18–21).

God gives us many opportunities to *develop* our walk with Him. But we may let it lie dormant, like the man who buried his gift, or like Stephen's children who never learned the responsible use of what they had been "freely given" (Mt 10:8; 1 Cor 2:12).

Jason *saw* the evidence of what lay ahead – his grandfather's riches, the video explaining it, and the counsel and warning of Hamilton every month. But Jim may see *no evidence* of any great inheritance to come, though it's all around him – unless he takes *responsibility* and *seeks* to find it. Jeremiah wrote that if you seek God with all your heart you will find Him and He will "bring you back from your captivity" (Jer 29:13–14; 33:3).

I don't have cable TV – only a small indoor antenna; yet in my small hometown I can pick up at least seven English-speaking Christian channels (six or seven more in Spanish), with preaching, clean movies with good moral values, inspiring personal testimonies, talk shows about amazing things God has done and is doing now, and news with Christian commentary.

At least half a dozen good churches lie within a half-hour's walk from my home. I can spend money on pot, beer, and cigarettes, dirty movies, gangster rap, and drugs, or I can buy Christian rap and CDs, download the whole Bible to an MP3 player (free), and listen to it while I work. Plus get a huge Bible computer program *free* off the Internet. Or get all the above with many Bible helps, word studies, and translations free through various apps on a smartphone.

These opportunities regularly remind me that I have an inheritance awaiting me, not by a rich uncle nor a mere two billion dollars, which would be useless when I leave this world. Heaven's values are beyond comprehension in earthly terms, and God longs to train us through the above opportunities, learning by trial and error, and how to enrich the lives of others through what we learn (Eph 1:14–18; Pet 1:4–5).

Some day I and millions with me will receive our inheritance – when we're mature enough to handle the endless "trillions" and no longer limited by old age, human weakness, or carnal mindedness! (Prv 3:14–15; 8:10–19).

The fear of the Lord

I heard of, but never saw, a program on TV (*Fear Factor*) where contestants did disgusting things – like eat roaches – if they thought the prize money was worth it. The Bible describes life as a contest where those who compete successfully receive a prize that's out of this world, of biblical proportions! But one "factor" keeps too many from even trying: no *fear of God;* He's not worth the risk or the challenge (1 Cor 9:24–27; 2 Tim 2:5).

The fear of the Lord is the key to wisdom, which is worth more than "all the things one may desire," because wisdom is knowing when and what to do with what you have. If you have a lot of money without wisdom, you'll lose it or it will ruin you, as it does most lottery winners. If you have wisdom without money, you'll end up having all the money you need for the wisdom you have (Dt 8; Prv 8; 9:10; 2 Cor 9:6ff).

The fear of the Lord is "the beginning of" or the basis for true wisdom because it's an attitude that pulls God into the situation, for all wisdom originates with Him. Imagine having Jesus – through the Holy Spirit – as your business partner, your intimate Friend and Counselor, and your big Brother! (Jn 14:17, 26; 16:13).

The fear of the Lord has two parts: First, *taking God seriously.* In "Christian" America, we've taken *grace* to mean *freedom from the pressure of God's law.* For many, the "sinner's prayer" only means a free ticket to heaven, they *think.*

In 2006 I "felt led" to write an article on the basic points of a Christian lifestyle. It's especially for those who have no clue what the Bible says, but also for those who have opened the door to demonic invasion by walking in ways that *oppose* God (Gal 6:7–8; Eph 5:1–17).

Seven Guidelines to See if I'm Serious about God or Am I Just Kidding Myself (chapter 12) is about agreeing with God's Word in regard to (1) what we allow into our minds, (2) the kind of friends we hang with, (3) our attitude toward sex and marriage, (4) regular fellowship with other believers (church), (5) whether we accept or avoid correction (denial), (6) our attitude toward others (resentment), and (7) surrendering the "weight that slows us down, especially the sin that so easily trips us up" (Heb 12:1 NLT).

These basic biblical values open our lives to God's *grace* when we take them seriously, but keep Him at a distance – and Satan close – when we don't. It's the *fear of God* factor, *and the beginning of a walk in wisdom and knowing God* (Prv 8:13; 9:10).

Jesus frequently related the kingdom of God to counting the cost of being His *disciple,* which means one who is *taught* and *trained* through taking His *yoke* or *cross.* The only reason the cost might include money or giving up something is when these things take our attention away from Him and His wisdom (Lk 9:23; 14:26f; 21:36; Mk 10:17ff; Jn 12:24–26; Rv 14:1–5).

His yoke, including the above seven points, is easy when we stay in fellowship with Him, because He gives us the wisdom to use the gifts He has given us. Otherwise He might seem like "an hard man" with unjust demands when we're not connected to the strength and wisdom available through His Spirit (Mt 11:29–30).

The second part I see in the *fear of the Lord,* besides taking God seriously, is humbling oneself. "God resists the proud, but gives grace to the humble." *That simple verse holds the key to success or failure,* period. Yet I find so many won't risk humbling themselves before people when if the prize were high enough, they might make a fool of themselves on TV before millions (Jas 4:6; 1 Pet 5:5).

In fact this key will unlock any door in which God's grace is needed. Jesus said the church at Philadelphia had "an open door, and no one can shut it," because they had (humbly) endured under persecution and did not deny His Name.

This was the only church of the seven listed in Revelation two and three ready to be kept "from the hour of trial which shall come upon the whole world, to test those who dwell on the earth." The church at Smyrna was almost ready, *also through persecution* (Rv 2:8–11; 3:7–10; Lk 12:34–37; 1 Thes 5:2–9).

Try *God's* way

If Jim has prepared himself through true repentance and a change in lifestyle, and has taken advantage of the stewardships available to him for his spiritual development, the nightmare of eviction with his family can actually be like a final exam leading to promotion in many ways. Fear of failure will give way to the fear of the Lord, which now places *Him* in charge! (Ps 25:14; 33:18; 34:7).

If he can humble himself in the midst of confusion and condemnation, his ears will be open for God to give him the wisdom he now needs. Instead of drowning himself in alcohol or drugs or risking another arrest followed by longer jail-time, he encourages his family (in the woods) with hopes of a God-given solution, maybe even that day or the next or the next, but to *keep believing!* (Mt 6:25–34; 11:23–26; Lk 12:22–32; Phil 4:6).

His children are now watching their daddy do something he's never done: taking responsibility in one of the toughest situations he's ever faced. When their tears dry, they will begin to admire and learn from their new hero, and the *testing of his faith* will only add to his *testimony* when God comes through! (1 Pet 1:7).

First he might find a shelter for his wife and kids, like Salvation Army or a "rescue mission." Churches offer leads and ideas, and some have food banks and certain days for feeding the homeless. The jail in our county hands out a list of dozens of "resources" for all kinds of possible "open doors." Calling 211 also offers leads and resources.

Meanwhile he will inspire his wife and children with the adventure of camping, the prospect of God coming through in some way, and the once-in-a-lifetime opportunity to experience what many millions go through in a lot worse circumstances – sleeping on sewage and vermin-infested streets (Calcutta, India), living in garbage dumps (Mexico City, Manilla, etc.), children living in big sewer pipes under streets, or long forgotten inmates in dangerous and filthy prisons in developing countries. And women and children working as sex slaves – often tortured and beaten, all over the world . . . even America!

While looking for a job, he'll pick up aluminum cans and metal and walk or ride a bike several miles to the recycler, all the while thanking and praising God. He is not afraid of menial and humble work for another meal for his family (2 Thes 3:10).

(At one of the places where I've been remodeling a home, I watch Alfonzo, a Jamaican, ride past me every hour or so with a huge plastic bag full of recycled material on the basket of his bicycle. He collects it from the trash bins people set out for the garbage trucks. He makes a decent living doing this.)

Now God at last has something to work with in Brother Jim – his humble trust and availability: he's out in the field where he and God can make a *grace*-connection together. The decision to commit it to God and take that first step was the hardest, but it put God in the driver's seat and guaranteed ultimate victory (Prv 10:4–5; 12:1; 13:4; 26:13; Eph 4:28; Heb 6:11).

Some, of course, will scoff at this, saying it's out of touch with reality. The inmates at the jail thought it was great and came up with more ideas. One said he got out of prison years ago with no job or place to stay. He found a rescue mission which gave him a start and he worked his way up (legally) to take over someone's mortgage payments on a home within three years. The next week at the state prison another inmate told me a similar story: The last time he and his wife got out of prison, they quickly began searching out leads for food and places to stay, and found many open doors. Within three years they were buying their own three bedroom home.

David Koch in his 545 page book, *Slaying the Dragon* (see endnote in chapter 2, part 1) tells of his experience getting out of prison with nothing and no prospects for a job, but armed with two attitudes that eventually made him a millionaire with a long list of awards, titles, and accomplishments. Those two attitudes were *total honesty and working hard to do his absolute best at whatever he was asked to do.* And that meant starting at the bottom mowing grass and cleaning airplanes and the hangers.

He defines the "dragon" as the set of negative attitudes (victim mentality, blame displacement, sense of entitlement, laziness, resentment toward "the system" or anyone else, refusal to pursue further education) a released inmate must "slay" in his attempt to successfully reintegrate into mainstream society.

I've heard such success stories from many inmates over the years. Why, then, do so many of them end up back in jail or prison (to tell me about it) after seeing God supply their needs so quickly and miraculously? The answer is found in Deuteronomy eight. Verses two and three show that God had only one purpose for the *chastening* in the "great and terrible wilderness" (jail): in the humbling, they would discover the true condition of their hearts – how impossible it is to obey His laws and do His will without living "by every word that proceeds from the mouth of the Lord" (Dt 1:19; 8:15).

In jail some eventually discover what it means to "abide" in Christ, "the true vine," to live daily by dependence on His Word. And when they get out they discover the power of *grace* that flows from this new lifestyle: "If you abide in Me, and My words abide in you, you will ask what you desire, and it shall be done for you." This explains the quick and often phenomenal success these ex-cons experience after release. God really is true to His Word and honors humble faith in Him (Jn 15:1–7).

But Deuteronomy eight goes on to warn that when you have "eaten and are full and have built beautiful houses and dwell in them" because of the Lord's blessing, that "when your heart is lifted up, and you forget the Lord your God who brought you out of the land of Egypt, from the house of bondage. . . . Then you say in your heart, 'My power and the might of my hand have gained me this wealth. . . . Then it shall be, if you by any means forget the Lord your God, and follow other gods . . . I testify against you this day that you shall surely perish" (8:10–19; also Dt 28; Lev 26).

And so the same grace that opened those doors, mercifully leads them back for more "correction." "For whom the Lord loves He chastens, and scourges every son whom He receives." I see them on their return visit, a little more broken and humble, having learned the way Israel and most of us learn (Heb 12:6).

Hope for the humble

My favorite story in the Bible is where the woman from "the region of Tyre and Sidon" came to Jesus begging Him to heal her *severely* demon-possessed daughter (Mt 15:21–28).

This story shows me how effective God's chastening can be when fully received, and thus why God *seems* to deny our desperate cries through what I call *abject humiliation* – the lowest kind, miserable, despised, disgraced. He completely ignored the poor woman's cries until the disciples couldn't take it anymore and asked Jesus to do something. Then he told them He was only sent to the Jews, still ignoring her, and with a racial slur!

Most of us would have walked away in disgust, which explains why many of us don't get answers. But, amazingly, this woman got even closer and "*worshiped* Him, saying, 'Lord, Help me.'" This certainly should have opened His heart. But instead he added insult to injury: "It is not good to take the children's bread and throw it to the little dogs."

What are *we* willing to go through for a big enough prize? When a father goes back to the streets and breaks the law for his family, what kind of *insanity* does that set before them? What is he teaching his children? (Jn 13:15; Phil 3:17; 2 Thes 3:9; 1 Tim 4:12; 1 Pet 2:21).

"I gotta do what I gotta do," or "Can't let my youngins go hungry." All because they don't *know* the God they sang about in jail services. *They have not prepared their hearts* (2 Chr 12:14; Prv 22:3; 24:10; Jer 12:5; Dan 11:32).

This dear woman must have gone through years of agony over her deranged daughter and probably stayed busy day and night trying to keep this wild child under control. She simply could not take no for an answer. And somehow she understood the incredible *Prize who stood before her holding the key that would change her life and that of her daughter forever!* (Jn 11:40).

Her answer to His humiliating, discriminatory, degrading, discouraging, insult? "Yes, Lord, yet even the little dogs eat the crumbs which fall from their masters' table." Suddenly . . . Jesus broke the deadlock and declared, "O woman, great is your faith! Let it be to you as you desire." "And her daughter was healed from that very hour."

Jesus saw her faith at the beginning, but knew it was not yet ready to pull the answer out of the heavenlies, the spirit realm, and destroy the power of those demons – *the legal right they had through fallen human nature, ignorant of God's ways* (Ps 16:8–11; 25:1–15; Col 2:9–15; Heb 3:10).

So He wisely and carefully *discipled* her through a refining process *under the yoke* which purged out every hindrance from human, natural (carnal) thinking, *until there was nothing left but complete childlike trust* (Lam 3:29–32; Mt 18:3–4; Heb 11:6).

What is God waiting for?

Isaiah 30:18 shows us that although God wants to give us grace, He can't because we still don't see Him truly "exalted." We still hold on to something *within ourselves.* So He must *wait* until our pride and self-trust melt and we rely completely on Him, like that woman (Ps 37:1f; Lk 17:5–10; Phil 3:3; 2 Cor 12:9; Heb 12:1–2).

Isaiah 50:10 speaks of one who is obedient and accountable to his spiritual leader, but who "walks in darkness, without a ray of light." All God asks is that he "trust in the Lord and rely on [his] God" (NLT). It's *the* formula for allowing God to *reduce us to the humility that will release the power of faith through grace* (Mk 11:23–25; Rom 4:16; Jas 4:6–7; 1 Pet 5:5–6).

Verse 11, however, warns that if we light our *own* fire (to see, escape, or "medicate" ourselves to avoid dealing with the problem) in fear and impatience, without waiting for true faith and wisdom, we'll end up in worse darkness or "great torment" (Jer 48:11–12, 29; Hab 2:1–4; Mt 23:12; Lk 20:18; 2 Cor 5:11; Jude 1:23).

Isaiah 42 describes a situation where someone finds himself in such darkness, he's virtually *blind*, yet keeps hanging on and trusting God, though God seems a million miles away. But suddenly, when all hope seems lost, God stirs Himself up "like a man of war," and destroys every enemy – every obstacle in the way – and leads the blind *waiting* one to victory. It's long been one of my favorite verses, enabling me to endure many trials when I saw no solution in sight:

"I will bring the blind by a way they did not know; I will lead them in paths they have not known. I will make darkness light before them, and crooked places straight. These things I will do for them, and not forsake them" (Is 42:16; also Ps 22, 38, 88, Lam 3:1–42 – five of my favorite "anti-depressants," besides Job 3. Because they give us God's view of our darkness).

Then Isaiah goes on to describe the kind of attitude and lifestyle that should be normal for any believer who expects to live in the provision and grace of a giving, loving God:

"Hear, you deaf; and look, you blind, that you may see. Who is blind but My servant, or deaf as My messenger whom I send? Who is blind as he who is perfect, and blind as the LORD's servant? Seeing many things, but you do not observe; opening the ears, but he does not hear" (42:18–20; other translations miss the point, implying that Israel was spiritually blind. But I agree with the more accurate NKJV and KJV. See Ps 38:13–14 for confirmation of this truth).

In other words, don't pay attention (be blind) to the wrong set of facts, which will lead to discouragement, depression, and doing the wrong thing. Because if you keep your eyes on Jesus, He'll not only bring you through, he'll give you a testimony that will bless and encourage others (Heb 11:1; 12:2).

"For His anger is but for a moment, His favor is for life; weeping may endure for a night, but joy comes in the morning" (Ps 30:5; also Ps 46:5).

While you are waiting for the morning, *do* what you can do with what's available to you; because, like Jason's inheritance, God will use it as your training for greater responsibility . . . and rewards. *Your best days are still ahead!*

1. Stoval, Jim, *The Ultimate Gift,* Mechanicsburg, PA: Executive Books, 2006. Print.

SECTION THREE

IT'S YOUR CHOICE

(Life or death)

I call heaven and earth to witness against you today, that I have set before you life and death, the blessing and the curse. So choose life in order that you may live, you and your descendants.
Deuteronomy 30:19

CHAPTER 9

Five Reasons to Seek God

Seek righteousness, seek humility. It may be that you will be hidden in the day of the Lord's anger.
Zephaniah 2:3b

1. **Life is a vapor – here today, gone tomorrow**
I have only one real fear. It is of a horror worse than rejection by family and friends, torture and near-starvation in a vermin-infested enemy concentration camp for the rest of my life, and slowly dying with a painful disease. Combined.

That is to wake up at the end of my life aware I've been successful in my career, but, though "born again" and ready for heaven, am unprepared for the words, "Well done, good and faithful servant." Or to face God in eternity knowing I never fully laid "hold of that for which Christ Jesus had laid hold of me," and to view what I could have been and done had I been completely obedient. In that moment every cost of discipleship on earth will have faded in insignificance and unbearable regret (Mt 25:21; Lk 14:26–35; Phil 3:12).

I clearly remember sitting at my desk at school, marking off each day on my homemade calendar, trying so hard to visualize myself in cap and gown, diploma in hand. The year was 1957–8. I was in tenth grade and those final two and a half years stretched out forever.

Now precious memories are fast-forward videos of graying hair, wrinkling skin, and grandchildren quickly growing into adults, soon to have their own children. In a few flying moments we'll stand on the other side of time with the fulfilled or neglected opportunities we had in what then will appear as a flitting microsecond of life on planet earth (Job 14:1–2; Ps 39:5, 11; 90:9–12; 144:4; Jas 4:14).

2. **My weakness**

The ministry of Christ and the Acts of the Apostles "show and tell" what should be the normal Christian life. We were created to soar higher than eagles, to be as much at home "in the Spirit" as in the kitchen or at our job. We are God's hands on earth, building with Spirit-led tools of the Incarnation (God in flesh) a bridge to heaven. We are destined to share authority with the King of Kings, judging the world, even angels! and displaying God's wisdom to angelic rulers, probably both bad and good, in the spirit world (1 Cor 6:3; Eph 3:10; Col 1:16--18; Rv 2:26–27).

Yet strangely, God uses our weakness rather than our strength. *But only when we turn to Him in faith, thanksgiving, and worship!* (Ps 8:2; 149:1–9; 2 Cor 12:9–10; 13:4).

Chris Panos was a hard-to-live-with alcoholic whose wife asked God to either take him or save him. God got his attention through a horrible accident and called him to the ministry. (God doesn't have to *cause* harm to us; all He does is remove a small portion of His protection.) For years he smuggled Bibles into countries closed to the gospel and avoided arrest by his sensitive ear to the Spirit's instructions on what to say and where to go (Is 30:21; Rom 8:14).

Since then he has preached to crowds of a hundred thousand, followed by hundreds of miracles – deaf ears and blind eyes opened, cripples healed, demon-possessed set free. And far from being intimidated by religious terrorists or the secret police who attempt to assassinate or arrest him, he intimidates *them* by taking dominion over them in the spirit realm – a sample of our future role as co-regents (reigning) with Christ.[1]

I must confess with Isaiah, "Woe is me! for I am undone; because I am a man of unclean lips." God touched his lips, then used him to declare and move events in world history thousands of years ahead of his time. On one occasion following his prophetic word, an angel killed 185,000 Assyrian troops encamped against Jerusalem (Is 6:5ff; 37:33–36; 2 Kgs 19:35).

If the victory and power of the above saints came through their yielding to the power of God in their known weakness, then perhaps my only problem is not realizing the extent of my weakness and more fully submitting myself to God and renewing my mind through His Word (Ps 1; Rom 12:2; Col 3:1; Jas 4:4–8; 1 Pet 5:5–6).

I love doing Bible study in jail or prison. I see these inmates, not as failures, but as more available to God's strength than I am because their needs are deeper than mine, and God will transform their weakness into His strength! I'm convinced my whole purpose in life, that for which God has allowed every hardship and learning experience, is to do my best to teach these men how to trust a God they can't see to work in them a supernatural strength beyond their own ability. "For with God nothing will be impossible" (Lk 1:37; see Gen 18:11; Jer 32:17, 27; Mk 10:27; 2 Cor 12:5–10; Heb 11).

The whole secret of the ministry and power of Jesus and the apostles is that they learned to trust, not in their own ability or strength, "but in God who raises the dead" (2 Cor 1:9; see 4:14).

3. **Relationships**

What a privilege to have known the Lord when He walked on earth with twelve "uneducated and untrained" disciples, listening, dialoging, eating together. I can't think of anything so priceless – the personal, tangible, presence of Jesus, God in flesh (Acts 4:13; 1 Jn 1:1).

Yet He told them, "It is to your *advantage* that I go away; for if I do not go away, the Helper will not come to you." Is it possible we have an even greater opportunity? (Jn 16:7; see 14:12).

Yes! God has again placed Himself within flesh, imparting His Nature through gifts and ministries by the Spirit, "till we all come . . . to a perfect man, to the measure of the stature of the fullness of Christ." The same Christ who walked the dusty roads of Galilee and Judea is still present, greatly desiring our fellowship, longing to develop His nature in us and minister through us to those who don't know Him (Eph 4:13; Col 1:27–29).

Whatever our future as "joint heirs with Christ," ruling (*shepherding*, Greek *poimaino*) the nations "with a rod of iron," it will involve the compassion, understanding, and wisdom we learn during our brief training period encased in these humble bodies, "subjected to futility" and "sown in weakness" (Rom 8:20; 1 Cor 15:43; Phil 3:21; Rv 2:27).

Oh, the limitations and the frustrations of laboring together with fellow weaklings in this limited phase of the Kingdom of God! I can hardly blame the many who'd rather stay away from church and enjoy friends who make them feel accepted than endure the misunderstanding and offenses of God's children. One day they may understand the mystery of the glory they could have enjoyed and the love they could have shared in this priceless experience . . . when the opportunity is lost, forever (1 Cor 1:11; 3:3; 2 Cor 5:16–17; Eph 4:22–32; Col 1:27–29; Mt 25).

4. **Hurting people**

Families like those in the old TV series, *My Three Sons, Father Knows Best,* and *The Waltons,* are nearing extinction, even in prosperous America. Economic pressure, stress, and loss of moral values are churning out dysfunctional "families" faster than the government or churches can care for them. Men leave their "babies' mommas" for newer models and avoid responsibility, leaving so many single-mom families, it's become a tax burden on the responsible and a headache for those working on our nation's deficit. For the health of our nation is a product of the condition of our families (Mal 4:6).

One of the fastest growing criminal activities is human sex-slavery, even in "the land of the free." Not to mention the hopelessness, poverty, undernourishment, and suffering in much or most of the rest of the world.

Is Christ still the Answer? A thousand times yes! But His Answer is in *us, because we are His Body, His hands, feet, eyes, ears, and heart.* It amazes me that God has entrusted humans, just like the ones hurting – *especially* like the one hurting – to *understand their pain* and bring deliverance through the Gospel. We are the "sons of God" for whom "the earnest expectation of the creation eagerly waits" (Rom 8:19; 1 Cor 12:12–28; Eph 4:15–16; Heb 5:2).

And for the task He has given us so much armor and weapons, we can *rest* (and must!) while we fight. It begins with

"Stand . . . praying," an easy assignment for those who seek *Him* (Mt 6:33; Eph 6:10–18; Heb 4).

5. **Judgment**

Terrorism in the name of religion is creeping over the planet like a dark cloud. Nations are polarizing toward another holocaust, if not Armageddon. In 2011 Jonathan Cahn wrote a best-seller, *The Harbinger*, followed by a video, *The Isaiah 9:10 Judgment,* pointing out nine ways America responded to 9-11 which, incredibly, parallel Israel's response to God's unheeded warning before total disaster struck (Is 9:10–11; Zeph 3:8–13; Mt 24:7; Lk 17:27–29; 21:34–35; 1 Thes 5:1–7; 2 Pet 3:3–7; Rv 6).

Jesus criticized the religious leaders of his day for not discerning "the signs of the times." He warned them of their own coming destruction because "you did not know the time of your visitation." God singled out the tribe of Issachar for their "understanding of the times, to know what Israel ought to do" (1 Chr 12:32; Mt 16:3; Lk 19:44; Heb 12:25–29).

To disciples who wondered when the end would come, Jesus concluded his "future shock" lecture with these words: "Watch therefore, and pray always that you may be counted worthy to escape all these things that will come to pass, and to stand before the Son of Man" (Lk 21:36).

"Woe to the army who is serious about the battle only when the enemy is at its threshold. Training, supplies and strategies must be worked out months and years in advance or the battle is lost the moment it begins. Complacency leaves us unprepared for unforeseen challenges."[2]

Yet no matter how terrible the earthly judgments, it will never compare with one moment's exposure to "the judgment seat of Christ." Paul knew what it was to "groan, earnestly desiring to be clothed with our habitation which is from heaven, if indeed, having been clothed, we shall not be found naked." Can you imagine the joy of those so dressed, outfitted for eternity? (Rom 14:10; 2 Cor 5:2–3).

They will be those who on earth redeemed the time, exchanged their weakness for His power, understood the infinite value of relationship and the mystery of God's Treasure in earthen vessels, participated in the ministry of redemption, and rightly discerned the times in which they lived. They fought the good fight, they finished the race, they kept the faith. They moved the spirit-world and changed eternity. "Well done, good and faithful servant. . . . Enter into the joy of your Lord" (Mat 25:21; 2 Cor 4:7; 5:17–20; 2 Tim 4:7).

In "no time at all" I hope, by His grace and *only* by His grace, to hear those words. Will you?

1. Panos, Chris. *God's Spy* (North Brunswick, NJ: Bridge-Logos, 1998. Print).
2. Jacobson, Wayne. "Gethsemane: a Battle Won, a Battle Lost," *Charisma Magazine*, April 1984.

CHAPTER 10

Four Methods God Uses to Get Our Attention

"A great number of people fail in life, not because they aren't talented, called or qualified, but because they simply get distracted. . . . I'm convinced that real prophets have more than just vision – they know how to ignore the distractions the rest of us can't. They never let go of their calling. They know how to focus."[1]

In the parable of the sower, the *stony* soil relates to the condition of one's heart whereby offenses cause the person to give up and quit. And the soil with *thorns* speaks of those who "are choked with cares, riches, and pleasures of life, and bring no fruit to maturity" (Lk 8:11–15).

While Jesus visited Mary and Martha, Mary "sat at Jesus' feet and heard His word." But Martha, "distracted with much serving," complained that her sister Mary had not been helping her. Jesus answered, "Martha, Martha, you are worried and troubled about many things. But one thing is needed, and Mary has chosen that good part, which will not be taken away from her" (Lk 10:38–42).

God draws us to Himself through His Spirit, but the Holy Spirit is compared to a dove in His gentleness; He never forces anyone. Instead He uses four methods to get our attention and wean us away from the "many things" that cause us to "bring no fruit to maturity" (Lk 8:14).

1. The example and influence of godly people

Virtually everybody who comes to God comes through the influence or example of another person. *The greatest mistake anyone could make is to avoid the influence of people who know God. The greatest benefit anyone could ever receive, a million times better than winning the lottery, is to be exposed regularly to the influence and wisdom of spiritual leaders and believers* (Prv 1:1ff, 3:13ff; 8:10ff; 1 Cor 12:12ff; Eph. 4:11ff).

In some places this opportunity is rare or forbidden by law. A Bible cover and t-shirt are available with the words, "This book is illegal in 52 countries."

"In some of these nations it is illegal to own a Bible, to share your faith in Christ, change your faith or teach your children about Jesus. Those who boldly follow Christ – in spite of government edict or radical opposition – can face harassment, arrest, torture and even death. Yet Christians continue to meet for worship and to witness for Christ, and the church in restricted nations is growing." *The Voice of the Martyrs* lists the fifty two countries on their website: http://www.prisoncralert.com/vom pw_persecution.htm (current as of July 2016).

I often feel apologetic, even guilty, that my life is so easy compared to the home-lives of most jail inmates. But what makes it easy is that I surround myself with godly influences, which anybody can do at any time, especially in America where we still have freedom of religion and churches are everywhere.

A lot has to do with my family background, but that is also a choice. Two of my siblings decided they didn't need God or His people. One died at 26, probably high on marijuana, and the other at 46, through alcohol abuse: *both caused by associating with the wrong people and influences.* (Hello!) "Do not be deceived: 'Evil company corrupts good habits'" (1 Cor 15:33).

The choices I made without consulting my mentors, thinking I didn't need counseling on such matters, cost me dearly, and for which I'm still paying – a life of "hard labor," long after retirement years! Knowing it's *God* correcting my issues is what makes *His* yoke "easy," however, and shoveling dirt (literally) is my favorite work – a heart-warming workout! (Job 14:14; 19:21; Prv 11:24; 15:22; 24:6; Mt 11:28–30; Heb 12:5ff).

As a teen I dreamed of what a wonderful father I'd be someday, but as our four kids grew into teens, I'd gotten too busy to be the dad I should have been: too *distracted* to feel their needs and pain and the love they needed in place of my sometimes overly restrictive discipline of them. I'd failed to apply what God had taught me about freedom (from Romans and Galatians).

However, since *church* was so much a part of our lives, God used a different church mentor for each of our two boys, and close *church* friends to influence our two daughters. And they all survived without drugs or sex and married godly mates, and their many children are growing up *in church – with their parents!* (Eph 4:14–15).

They *are far better at parenting than I was, having learned by those who influenced them and by my many mistakes!* All four are role models to me, especially on the *time* I should have spent *more* with them but always said, "tomorrow." When *tomorrow* finally came, they were gone (Ps 90:9–12; Prv 22:6; Eph 6:4).

It might be "impossible" for some to let go of the people destroying them from the inside out, "but each one is tempted when he is drawn away by his *own* desires and enticed." *What we really want deep down, we pursue until we finally get it – whether of God, the flesh, or the devil!* (Jas 1:14; Rom 1:17–32).

2. His goodness and mercy in the face of our failures

There's a six minute video of a skit I've shown at the jail quite often because the guys love it: a mime performed on a stage before a church audience. It graphically illustrates the idea behind taking the Kingdom by violence and force when we've come to the end of our "fun" (Jer 29:13; Mt 11:12; Lk 13:24; 16:16; 21:36).

The group is *Lifehouse*, and the name of their song in the background is *Everything*. It's on *Youtube:* Type "lifehouse, everything, skit." Many churches have done this skit, but our favorite is the one that pictures a Jesus with a wide purple sash over a white robe and a girl with a black top and jeans.

It starts with this teenage girl enjoying fellowship with Jesus until various tempters come along and lure her away – love (infatuation), money, alcohol, fashion, followed by emptiness and guilt – cutting herself. She tries to get back to Jesus but they push her back. Satan offers her a pistol and she holds it to her head. Suddenly she throws it down and lunges toward Jesus, and the fight is on as she struggles desperately to reach Him, who during the whole time has been reaching out to her.

In the background lightning crisscrosses a black sky; it's spiritual warfare, but she can't break through them and falls again and again, trying. When it looks hopeless, suddenly Jesus steps in and stands behind her, holding back her now *enemies* as they strain to grab her (Gen 32:6–31; Hos 12:3–4).

The girl is free, but unaware of the battle behind her. Then suddenly Jesus flings these wicked ones back, sending them crashing to the ground, totally defeated. Then He picks up the girl, brushes her off, and, like the prodigal son's father, resumes the beautiful fellowship they once had (Lk 15:11–24).

Jesus never violates our freedom to choose, but waits until our *heart really* wants Him. Then "You shall weep no more. He will be very gracious to you at the sound of your cry; when He hears it, He will answer you" (Is 30:19).

This verse begins with, "For the people shall dwell in Zion at Jerusalem." Zion and Jerusalem are symbolic of God's family, His church. As long as we think we can make it alone, God usually delays answering our prayers, which verse 18 explains – "Therefore will the Lord wait, that He may be gracious unto you" (Gal 4:26; Heb 12:22–23).

His grace quite often comes *through the ministry of His family, the members of His Body, the Church*, of which every believer is a member, but many don't see the need to remain in regular fellowship with them. Yet how else can we "grow up in all things into Him who is the head – Christ – from whom the whole body, joined and knit together by what every joint [*you!* not *pot*] supplies, according to the effective working by which every part [you] does its share, causes growth of the body for the edifying of itself in love"? (Eph 4:15–16; 1 Cor 12:12–27; Heb 10:25; 1 Kgs 8:28–54; Ps 27:4–6).

3. **God uses affliction to drive us to Him**

If the influence of godly people is the *pull* of God's motivation system, the hardships God allows, often from what others put us through, is the *push* of it (Ps 119:67, 71, 75; 129:2; Rom 8:35–39).

Many inmates, especially juveniles, "hate the police." My answer is that all through the Bible God uses the *worst* people, the *most wicked,* to correct us. If some cops are mean and angry, consider the people they deal with every day. I know most of you reading this are not in the following category, though you may have been at one time. But it should help you understand a cop's view:

Imagine having a job like an animal control officer where you round up and cage, not stray dogs, but *people made in God's image,* who now make a living stealing, lying, destroying the lives of others, rove in gangs with guns and knives, who think only of themselves, and spread their poison everywhere. They feel "cool" while they listen to music filled with lust, hatred, and violence. *And hate and blame those God uses in His desperate attempt to stop them on their path to hell and lead them to His love.* It's enough to make even a good cop angry and mean. Or quit before he gets shot! (Lev 20:9; Num 16; Deut 21:20–21; 27:16; Prv 30:11, 17; 20:20; Mat 15:4–6).

To control and correct this social cancer that *will nearly destroy the earth,* and it's getting closer, God uses both good *and bad,* not only cops, but the *wicked* in general, including Satan! Occasionally *God Himself* consumes them instantly when they reach a point of no return, as with Aaron's two sons and Ananias and Sapphira, who didn't fear God or thought they could outsmart Him (Lev 10; Acts 5:1–11).

"For we know Him who said, 'Vengeance is mine, I will repay' says the Lord. And again, 'The Lord will judge His people. It is a fearful thing to fall into the hands of the living God.'" "Knowing, therefore, the terror of the Lord, we persuade men" (Heb 10:30–31; 12:25–29; 2 Cor 5:11a; Gen 38:7, 10; 1 Sam 2:25; 15:23; 2 Sam 12:9–12).

When I speak to my incarcerated friends (I love you guys!) about God using the police for correction, they bring up the fact that the cops lie and betray them. Somehow they don't get it: God tried to correct them *gently* through people who loved them, but they wouldn't listen (Jer 26:13; 35:15; Hab 1:6–12).

Furthermore, God will judge and punish the wicked He uses to correct us if they don't repent – *after* He uses them to break us. And we don't *receive* the correction until we recognize that *God is dealing with us through them,* which is why He expects us to *submit* to them, no matter how badly they treat us. *Because through them we submit to God!* (Read Rom 13:1–7; Eph 5:21; Titus 3:1; 1 Pet 2:13–17; 2 Pet 2:10–11; Jgs 1:8.)

I too, have struggled with anger over those God has used to keep *me* hungry for Him, people whose lies, betrayal, and thefts have kept me up half the night to seek God for grace to forgive, pray for them, and genuinely minister to them when I see them in jail. And to "joyfully [accept] the plundering of [my] goods, knowing that [we] have a better and an enduring possession for [ourselves] in heaven" (Heb 10:24).

Read the following Bible passages to see how God actually *empowers* our *enemies* to turn our hearts when we drift away from Him and on to the devil's turf. Satan will laugh while he destroys us if we don't come (or return) to the One who gave His life for us and wants to give us "every good and perfect gift" (Jas 1:17). See Lev 26:17; Dt 28:25; Jgs 2:14; 3:8; 12; 4:2, etc; 2 Sam 12:10–11; 1 Kgs 11:14, 23; 22:7–38; 2 Kgs 13:3; 2 Chr 21:12–18; 24:24; 28:5; 33:11; 36:17; Prv 1:23–33; Is 10:5–6; Jer 24:8–10; 25:9; 27:6; 28:14; 43:10; 51:20–23; Hab 1:6–12.

"And do not fear those who kill the body but cannot kill the soul. But rather fear Him who is able to destroy both soul and body in hell" (Mt 10:28; see Jude 1:23).

4. **God uses His law to drive us to Him**

His holy law serves a dual purpose. First, it protects us like the directions on how to use dynamite without blowing ourselves up. Obeying the Ten Commandments will keep us close to God (first four commandments), and teach us respect for others (the last six) (Ex 20; Deut 5).

Only problem: Keeping them will basically keep you out of jail, depriving you of all that fellowship, almost free room and board, enough time to listen to God, and no stress over decisions. Except when they give you a choice between a trial or an offer of *more* time and fellowship!

Plus, obeying God's commandments will most likely result in you being stuck with the *same mate the rest of your life* when you could be trying out new models who make you feel young and important and still needed.

However, I've read the instructions on how to handle "dynamite." It boils down to simple bookkeeping: Buy fun on credit now and pay later with *huge* interest. Or invest in God now and enjoy increasing returns on it now and for eternity! Besides, relationship with the same person for life gets *more meaningful* as the years go by, as we mature in understanding and wisdom (Prv 5, 7; Eph 5:25–33).

Someone said, "Life is a battleground, not a playground; if you make it a playground, you'll lose the battle" (1 Tim 6:12; 2 Tim 4:7; Deut 8:11–20).

The second but *main* purpose of the law is to reveal our hearts. Despite our good intentions, something deep inside us won't let us consistently keep God's law no matter how hard we try. "For I delight in the law of God according to the inward man. But I see another law in my members, warring against the law of my mind, and bringing me into captivity to the law of sin which is in my members" (Rom 7:22–23; 3:10–20; Gal 5:17; Dt 8:2–3).

Only those who take God and His law and Word *seriously*, or get sick and tired of the pay-back sin causes, will experience the next verses: *"O wretched man that I am! Who will deliver me from this body of death? I thank God – through Jesus Christ our Lord."* It's like the girl in the *Lifehouse-Everything* skit, when she's had *enough* and now knows *for sure* there's only *One Way* that satisfies: Jesus! (Rom 7:24–25a).

There's a story on many websites called *Take the Son.* It tells of a wealthy man who loved art and had a collection of rare and valuable paintings. But his son died in the Viet Nam War while saving the life of a young soldier, an artist, who painted a picture of his friend who'd saved him. When he returned to the states, he looked up the friend's father and gave him the painting of his deceased son.

When the father died, his collection of paintings went up for auction. The first to be sold was the painting of the son. But nobody wanted it and some impatiently interrupted the auctioneer: "We didn't come to see this painting. We came to see the Van Goghs, the Rembrants. Get on with the real bids!" Finally the gardener of the deceased man made a $10 bid, all he could afford; it was accepted and the auction closed.

The crowd was shocked. "What about the paintings?" The auctioneer explained that the will stipulated only the painting of the son would be sold. "Whoever bought that painting *would inherit the entire estate, including the paintings*."

And that's how it is. If we get the Son, we get everything else – all the love we need to meet the needs of others, along with the power of the Holy Spirit to do what God has called us to do. Otherwise we get *nothing* but a few short years of empty "fun," and then the horror of eternal separation from God and the "friends" who helped us get there: "outer darkness . . . weeping and gnashing of teeth" (Mat 8:12; 13:42; 13:50; 22:12–13; 24:51; 25:30; Lk 13:28; 2 Pet 2:17; Jude 1:13).

But it's *your* choice. God attempts to *influence* us by these four ways: the influence of godly people, His goodness and mercy, His "rod of correction," and His laws and commandments. But He will never force us. Don't put it off until it's too late! (Mt 7:21–23; Lk 13:25–28).

The sinner's prayer is words by which you put your complete trust in Jesus, whose death substituted for the death we deserve for our sins. He's our link to God. Read these verses: Jn 1:12; 3:15–16, 36; 6:40, 47; 7:37–38; 11:25–26; 17:3; 20:31; Rom 5:1–22; 10:9–10; Gal 3:22, 26; Eph 2:8; 1 Tim 2:5–6; 1 Jn 5:10–13.

If you need help, read, then pray the following prayer if you can really pray it from your heart; you may change or add words to meet your own need. Then carefully study Romans, chapters three to eight for more understanding to allow what God has done in Christ for you to sink in and give you a strong foundation for faith.

Dear Lord, I truly, deeply *repent* of my lust, my selfishness, my hatred, my love of sin, of neglecting You and the people You sent to get my attention. I'm truly sorry, not because I'm in trouble, but because I *know* I turned a deaf ear to Your voice when You called me. I'm so sorry (2 Cor 7:9–10).

I know I deserve hell when I die and "hell" before I die, but I humbly cry out as a little child for your mercy. I understand Your Son Jesus suffered torture and the cruelest death on the cross as payment in full for my rebellion and sin in order to grant me the mercy and forgiveness I don't deserve, along with the grace to empower me to live above sin and temptation (1 Cor 10:12–14).

When I fail, help me not to cave in and give up, but *get* up again and keep trusting You to redeem my mistakes and heal the wounds of those I hurt. Help me to completely forgive those who hurt me, and please give them grace to forgive me for hurting them. For I know it's only through continuous fellowship with You that I'll change (Prv 24:16; Jn 15; 2 Cor 3:18; 1 Jn 1:6–9; 2:1–18).

And for this reason, I also ask that you wean me from every ungodly influence that has kept me in sin and bondage, from the wicked music and media I've listened to and watched to the friends who led me away from You. Give me a passion for Your Word and draw me to your family, including the grace to endure the offenses they might unintentionally or intentionally throw at me. Help me pray for them instead of criticizing them, knowing how much You forgive me! (Mk 11:25–26; Col 3:13).

Father, I know I can do absolutely *nothing* on my own, but through the power of Your Spirit and Word I can eventually do anything You expect of me (Jn 15:5; Phil 4:13).

One last thing, Lord: If I stray again, I give you permission to do whatever it takes to get me back on track so I'll keep You number One in my life, above everything else. I mean this with all my heart. Thank You so much! (Heb 12:5–15).

Your child ________________________________ date____________.

1. Cooke, Phil, "In a World of Disruption," *Charisma Magazine,* March 2011, 32

CHAPTER 11

Why Would a Loving God Send Anyone to Hell?

And do not fear those who kill the body but cannot kill the soul. But rather fear Him who is able to destroy both soul and body in hell. Matthew 10:28

Is hell for real?

Sometimes I find myself almost wishing God would leave us alone and just let us be nice to one another without having to worry about hell. Why does He have to put this dark cloud over our heads? There's so much more to life than thinking about a "fire that shall never be quenched" where even "good" people will go simply because they did not commit their lives to Jesus Christ. It sounds so disgusting, so gross!

Many years ago I thought I'd solved the problem by proving to myself that the personal God of the Bible doesn't exist and that God was some sort of Force that harmonized everything in nature and existed in all religions. I spent several years trying to get it all down pat, relieved I didn't have to worry about hell or the Christians who believed this fairy tale they "obviously didn't believe or they would live and act differently."

But my research finally convinced me the Bible is God's inspired Word and the evidence for the resurrection of Christ is solid. With that settled I had to deal with the problem of hell.

Art Katz, a former atheist, spoke all over the world to intellectuals and university students. Once when a smart-aleck student challenged him with the question of the existence of hell, Katz felt unusually inspired with this answer:

"Sir, I have always had a devout respect for words. . . . Words are not to be bandied about lightly. They are powerful things and can be holy or profane. They can bring life or can cripple or kill.

"There is another, about whom we read in the Scriptures, who had a profound reverence for words – Jesus Himself. He it is Who said that we shall be accountable for every idle word we speak. He never spoke one word idly, and there is not another person in all the Scriptures who has spoken more prolifically about hell than He. He is the One Who spoke of 'wailing and gnashing of teeth,' 'casting into outer darkness,' 'the lake of fire,' 'torment,' and 'the fire that shall not be quenched.' Sir, it behooves you to hear His statements about hell lest you find yourself, more quickly than you think, to be standing before Him, your knees turning to jelly, with your foolish question which you've asked to embarrass His servant played back in your hearing much too late for you to use it."[1]

That arrogant young man shrank in stunned silence, as all of us will when we stand before "the Judge of all the earth" unless we've prepared (Mt 5:22; Mk 9:42–48; Lk 12:5; 16:19–31; Rv 20:14-15; 21:8).

Is God unfair?

My biggest question about hell was how God could punish people with such torture when all of us are mere products of our background. It seemed out of character with a God of love and perfect justice.

But as I continued to study the Bible I eventually saw the answer in several passages. Paul wrote, "For since the creation of the world His invisible attributes are clearly seen, being understood by the things that are made, even His eternal power and Godhead, so that they are without excuse" (Rom 1:20).

Every microscopic cell in plants, animals, and humans is a city of thousands of molecular machines, each made up of as many as a thousand atoms, all busily carrying out detailed instructions to build and maintain that organism. They get their instructions from DNA, a genetic code that fills, with variation sequencing, roughly a hundred thousand printed pages (200 gigabytes).[2] In each cell! And *trillions* of cells in humans! (Ps 104:24; 111:2; 139:14; Job 5:9; Rv 15:3).

With advances in scientific discoveries, many scientists now recognize that the conditions that permit life to exist on planet earth are so incredibly and delicately balanced throughout the *entire universe* that a Designer seems to be the only logical explanation. And it makes less sense to believe matter and energy always existed than that a personal Designer always did. Or as some evolutionists admit, it takes more faith to believe this all came from nothing than to believe God created it. And it should be obvious that whatever "designer" created beings with *personality* would also have *personality* (Ps 139).

Next, Paul writes that all of us have an inner sense of right and wrong and will be judged by how we responded to it – our conscience. This is how those who don't know God's biblical law will be judged (Rom 2:11–16).

Jesus taught that those who knew God's will but didn't do it "shall be severely punished" but those who didn't know, yet sinned, "will be punished only lightly." For "when someone has been given much, much will be required in return" (Mt 11:20–24; Lk 12:47–48 NLT).

He said of the Jews who rejected Him, "They would not be guilty [of denying Me] if I had not come and spoken to them. But now they have no excuse for their sin. . . . If I hadn't done such miraculous signs among them that no one else could do, they would not be guilty." Their exposure to the Truth now witnessed against them for refusing it (Jn 15:22, 24a NLT; also 9:41).

Peter said regarding those who turn away from God that "it would have been better for them not to have known the way of righteousness, than having known it, to turn from the holy commandment delivered to them" (2 Pet 2:21).

Can we assume, then, that people who don't know any better are "off the hook," without *any* guilt? No, because *no one* is *completely* ignorant. As Paul said, there is enough truth revealed in nature and in our conscience to hold *all* of us accountable to God. And we'll be judged by *how we responded to it* "in the day when God will judge the secrets of men by Jesus Christ" (Rom 1:16).

I've seen written on a jail cell wall, *Only God can judge me.* What awaits those who resent man's faulty judgment when they stand before a God who *lays bare the deep and darkest secrets of our hearts?* (Ps 33:13–15; 44:21; 90:8; 139:11–12; Prv 15:3, 5:11; Jer 17:10; Jn 2:24; Rom 1:18; 1 Cor 4:5; Heb 4:13; Rv 2:23).

What I don't know won't hurt me?

Some feel it's better to leave people alone and not tell them about Jesus; what they already know is enough. But knowing truth doesn't help us walk in it and too often stirs up resistance against it. We need a "Higher Power" – *the Spirit of Life in Christ Jesus* (Rom 7; 5, 8–11; 8:2; 1 Cor 15:56).

Some years ago (early 2000s) at a summer "camp meeting" at Elim Bible Institute (Lima, NY), I heard an American missionary to India tell this story: As he stood on the bank of the Ganges River in India passing out Gospel "tracts" (pamphlets), a young Indian woman came out of the river and received one of his tracts, then stood there, dripping wet, while she read. When she finished reading it, she suddenly doubled over in pain, and wailed in loud and deep anguish, "Why didn't you give me this before I went into the river with my baby? I have just thrown him in to his death" (as a sacrifice to the Hindu goddess Ganga, the Ganges River).

Behind this tragic story is the need for every human being to find inner peace. The various world religions build their teachings around whatever method seems right: through "enlightenment" (Zen, my favorite before I found the true Light), the occult (witchcraft, Satanism, psychic mysticism), "transcendental meditation," good works, self-discipline, self-inflicted pain and privation, or animal or human sacrifice.

The ultimate sacrifice occurs when one takes his own life, hoping to atone for his guilt. I have reason to believe an acquaintance of mine burned himself alive in a last ditch effort to find relief from the pain of his past and present guilt (I'd tried to minister to him). I can understand, since that was the root of my own severe suicidal self-hatred for so many years.

Religions based on keeping high standards, laws, and statutes, even if they did come from God Himself, actually create a "veil," hiding us from God's presence, when in our ignorance we fail to find and maintain an intimate relationship with God Himself through Jesus Christ. For only the Lawgiver is able – and longs to be – the Living Law inside us through His Spirit (Rom 3:19–20; 2 Cor 3; Gal 5:16–23).

I've heard more than one version of the following account from Africa. A missionary had just finished explaining the message of the Gospel of Christ to an aged African leader of his village. The man was overwhelmed, awed, and thrilled to hear this amazing story of forgiveness, redeeming his life from the curses of sin, Satan, and witchcraft, and released into glorious liberty and joy through the Sacrifice of Jesus Christ.

Then he asked the missionary how long he had known of this "new" truth? When the missionary said he'd known it most of his life – for at least thirty years, the African's joy turned to horror, to realize his people had been deprived of this powerful reality that would have transformed his entire village *long ago*, freeing them from decades of spiritual darkness and its many chains of violence and bondage to demons and superstition.

EE Taow

In 1983 Mark Zook and his wife with their children were sent by New Tribes Missions (now Ethnos 360) to a village of 310 Mouk people in Papua, New Guinea (near Australia) who had never heard the Gospel. A society based on deceit and demonic sorcery, bound in superstition and fear, they lived in dread of death and without hope in life.

After learning their language and setting it to writing, he began to teach them the Gospel message, starting with creation, the fall, and God's restoration of man through the sacrifice of a lamb. The Mouk immediately grasped the significance of blood sacrifice since it was so prevalent in their primitive religious practices. So perceptive was their insight that several men predicted that when God told Abraham to sacrifice his son, Isaac, He would provide a lamb as a substitute for Isaac. Mark spent three months, twice daily, covering the whole Bible story.

When he finished with the death and resurrection of Jesus, he explained the significance of God's mercy to forgive and cleanse past sins through this final Sacrifice as God's Lamb. As the reality sank in, the people began to stand up and proclaim their faith in Him. Then they rejoiced, hugging one another and dancing, jumping up and down as they embraced, shouting EE Taow, "It is true, good, very true!" For two and a half hours!

With more training, they ended up, not only teaching their neighboring villages, who had been their enemies, even in sorcery, but went as missionaries to other language groups.

In some villages after a period of rejoicing, they went into deep wailing and weeping as they thought of their relatives and friends who had died before hearing such liberating truth. Their witchcraft, deceit, and murder stopped, wife-beating ended, and men spent time to be with their wives and children. They made up their own Christian songs to worship, and used some of our hymn-tunes with their own Christian words.

This is one of many examples of entire cultures and subcultures transformed in the same way, and some of their stories have also been made into popular movies, such as *Peace Child,* and *End of the Spear. EE Taow* is available on Youtube.

Ultimate Separation

While God does judge those who never heard with perfect justice and considers every minute factor that makes up our character, all of us, even in the most "developed" countries, are so bent toward selfishness and sin that we're like the drivers cruising toward the Interstate 40 bridge over the Arkansas River at Webbers Falls, Oklahoma, in May of 2002. A 500 foot section of the bridge had collapsed when a barge hit its pillars.

Two fishermen watched as people plunged their vehicles into the river to their deaths. They knew they had to do something. They got their boat to shore, ran up to the highway, and shot a flare at the next oncoming semi-truck. The driver was enraged when he saw that glaring orange fire-ball crash into his windshield, causing him to nearly jackknife his truck to a stop. Until he got out and saw how close he was to almost certain death.[3]

But the strongest message that hell exists is that God sent His Son to die an excruciating death to set us free from sin. We don't have the capacity to understand His agony as he prayed in the garden that God would remove this cup of suffering if possible (Ps 22; Is 53; Mt 26:39, 42; Heb 2:9–18; 5:7–9).

God sent an angel to strengthen Him. "And being in agony, He prayed more earnestly. Then His sweat became like great drops of blood falling down to the ground." All in anticipation of the horror He faced the next day when on the cross He took on Himself the sins of the whole world, past, present, and future. *If God takes our sin that seriously, how much more should we!* (Lk 22:42–44).

In 1978 I experienced about one minute of total separation from God. Through disobedience, I ended up feeling as though everybody, and finally God, had abandoned me. The horror was so intense it would have been a relief to jump into a raging fire to escape that bottomless dark pit of infinitely hopeless aloneness (Mt 8:12; 13:42, 50; 25:30; 2 Pet 2:17; Jude 1:13).

I'd never realized how dependent we are on our connectedness with people, which also explains how messed up we get when we're not connected to our Source – God. Since then I've had a profound respect for what God warns us about – a separation from Him with no further remedy (Col 1:16–18; Heb 2:15; Job 33:18, 22, 24, 28, 30; Ps 40:2).

It also gave me insight into the question of whether hell fire is literal or spiritual. Scientists now suspect that the physical world may be a hologram, the projected *image* of a deeper, more substantial, *invisible* reality (Heb 11:3).

I believe that what people who have returned from hell describe as literal fire is what they saw in the *time-space* dimension. But what it is in the real world is *horrible beyond description.* Who can describe eternal and infinite separation from God? We don't know because even the worst sinners experience His grace every day without realizing it (Mt 5:45).

I've also experienced heavenly glory a few times, and everything the Bible describes about heaven – golden streets, gates of pearl, etc. – falls far short of its ecstasy. In those experiences I become willing to endure any hardship, even for eternity, just for the privilege of knowing Christ in that level of glory (Rv 21:10–27; 2 Cor 4:17–18; Phil 3:10).

Is hell really eternal?

Which brings me to the second thing that always bothered me

about hell: Any kind of suffering for *eternity* seems way out of proportion to a few decades of even the worst sinning. Eternity is *forever!*

I finally solved this problem through Deuteronomy 29:29 – "The *secret* things belong to the Lord our God, but those things which are *revealed* belong to us." Eternity, like quantum physics, is impossible for us to grasp because we live in the time/space dimension. For me to judge God regarding eternity is to delve into "secret things" that have not been revealed to us.

So, counting on God's reputation for truth, I take His Word for what He says, without the *dangerous risk* of second-guessing words like *everlasting, forever, eternal,* and *never be quenched.* Why question something Jesus obviously knew more about than we do, which accounts for His strong and severe warnings, and those of His apostles? Isn't "the fear of the Lord" the beginning of knowledge and wisdom? (Ps 1:7; 9:10; Mt 18:8; 25:41; Mk 9:43; 2 Th 1:9; 2 Pet 2:17; Jude 1:7, 13).

"For what profit is it to a man if he gains the whole world, and loses his own soul? Or what will a man give in exchange for his soul?" "If your right eye causes you to sin, pluck it out and cast it from you. . . . And if your right hand causes you to sin, cut it off and cast it from you; for it is more profitable for you that one of your members perish, than for your whole body to be cast into hell" (Mt 16:26; see Lk 12:16–21; Mt 5:29–30).

The last word God gives us about hell is terrifying: "And anyone not found written in the Book of Life was cast into the lake of fire." Who? "But the cowardly, unbelieving, abominable, murderers, sexually immoral, sorcerers, idolaters, and all liars shall have their part in the *lake which burns with fire and brimstone*, which is the second death" (Rv 20:15; 21:8).

No wonder Jesus did what He did and said what He said. He is "not willing that any should perish but that all should come to repentance" (2 Pet 3:9).

Have people seen hell?

Many people have died and come back from heaven or hell to tell or write about it. One amazing account is of a Nigerian pastor who had been dead three days and in the mortuary, and had been escorted to heaven and hell by an angel. It's been documented on a video by missionary Reinhard Bonnke.

The fact that people attempt to disprove it on the Web only confirms what Jesus said in response to the "rich man" in hell who begged Lazarus to send someone to warn his five brothers: "If they do not hear Moses and the prophets, neither will they be persuaded though one rise from the dead" (Lk 16:31).

My conclusion is that if the greatest missionary in the world with crowds numbering up to 1.5 million is willing to put his name, reputation, and ministry behind it, I believe it. After all, Jesus raised another Lazarus from the dead after he'd been dead *four* days (Jn 11).

At 3 o'clock one morning Bill Wiese, through a vision, dropped into hell. He describes his experience in his book, *23 Minutes in Hell* and answers questions in his second book, *23 Questions About Hell.* [4]

I heard him give his testimony at a local meeting and respect him as a man of integrity with no other agenda than to report what God showed him. His mother, Emma, is a cherished friend of ours and speaks highly of her son, a successful real estate agent who built his business on integrity and transparency, and is now full time in ministry around the world and on many talk shows. He has been cross-examined by many, and God gives him wisdom to "turn many to righteousness" and silence many of his inquisitors (Dan 12:3; Mt 22:46).

Why should "good people" go to hell?

I especially like Bill's answer to the question about God not allowing a good person into heaven just because he's good. The first part of his answer is that heaven is based on *relationship.* It is God's *home* for those who *know Him*, who belong to His family (Mt 7:23; 25:12; Phil 3:10).

The second part is that our idea of good falls far short of God's. Only His Son met the standard of perfect righteousness *for us*, and we qualify only through relationship with Him. Furthermore, one's "goodness" is often carefully hidden behind layers of pride and "culture" (Jer 17:9; Jn 2:25; Heb 4:12–13).

C. S. Lewis wrote a book called *The Great Divorce* about a

group of people on the outskirts of hell given the opportunity to visit the outskirts of heaven and progress into heaven if they chose to. First, the sheer *density* of even a leaf or blade of grass there was painful to these unfulfilled, insecure people, who appeared as *ghosts* in a realm of *solid reality.* No doubt Lewis was thinking of Psalm 39:5–6: "Certainly every man at his best state is but vapor. Surely every man walks about like a shadow" – our condition without God (Ps 62:9; Rom 3:9–18).

For on earth the values of the "kingdom of heaven" are lived through *faith,* which gives *substance* (*substan*-tiation) and *solidity* to our beings in the *real* world where faith speaks and apprehends the *loving* and *giving* atmosphere of heavenly glory. Incidentally, the Hebrew word for glory, *kabod,* comes from *kabad* (#H3513), "to be heavy, weighty" (Mt 5–7; Mk 11:23–24; Rom 4:17; 2 Cor 4:11–18; Heb 11:1ff).

Vain carnal mindedness – materialism and especially *unforgiveness and resentment* – kept these grumbling visitors from desiring, understanding, or enduring the searing brightness of heaven (Mk 6:21–23; 11:25–26).

Their former friends and family members in heaven tried unsuccessfully to change their thinking and allow Love to swallow up their bitterness and shallow thinking, but to no avail. They felt more comfortable, or rather less terrified, in the bleak, gloomy, and dismal emptiness of hell's outskirts than the piercing and penetrating brilliance of heaven's glory and Light-revealing transparency (Lu 8:17; 11:34–36; 12:3; Jn 1:4–9; 8:12; 11:10; 3:19–21; 12:35–36, 46).

I've noticed the same thing in jail. Some are really *connected* with what's going on spiritually and relationally in a Bible study, while to others it means little more than another "program" (Mt 11:25–27; 13:13–17; Heb 5:11).

Why change?

Change is a lifetime process because our masks are closely tied to our *identity,* which in turn is tied to the *acceptance* we get from people. Nobody can survive for long without it, for acceptance is the basis of fellowship and relationship (love).

This explains why "success" and good behavior don't

ultimately satisfy. Because deep down we *know* these outward things mask or hide our inner need to be accepted *as we really are*, not because of what we do or what we have or what we *appear* to be because of our education, job, personality, connections, etc.

Being "good" works great for most of us as long as our basic needs are met. *But let these needs get interrupted, and our goodness wears thin.* Under enough pressure it can turn to anger or rage . . . and more! And if our *identity* tells us we're not that type, we repress it until it becomes depression and resentment, which often lead to physical illness, chemical addiction, and even death.

The Bible is God's story (*His*-tory) about how He looked for people who would allow Him to slowly and patiently tear off their masks without their cracking up or giving up. This is why *relationship* with Him is so essential, in spite of the pain.

The book of Job is a microscopic look at one man who loved God, but whose relationship with God was *disguised* by hard religious work. God wanted to bring him to the *joy* of *intimate relationship just as he was,* without all the effort, good reputation, and false sense of performance-based security connected with it.

Job's identity was so deeply rooted in his good deeds and personal integrity that God allowed Satan to take everything – wealth, children, health, and reputation. And that was only the beginning. Falsely accused by friends and apparently rejected and abandoned by God, he lost all sense of meaning to life, a sample of the beginning of what eternal separation from God is. No wonder he couldn't shake his fear of "the pit" (Job 1–3; 9:31; 33:18, 22, 24, 28, 30; 42:6).

At this point, or long before, people turn to alcohol, drugs, or suicide. Job wanted to die and loathed the day of his birth (ch 3). But he had one thing that brought him through that "dark night of the soul" when God chooses to wean us of all human props that cling to our fallen identity in order to purify and strengthen our spirit-connection to Him.

He had *hope*. Hope is not the same as faith. Faith is a deep heart-conviction, the *substance* of things *hoped* for, *before* it materializes in the visible world. Hope is the same as *wait* in at least a half dozen Hebrew and Greek words used in more than fifty Old and New Testament verses. It's the expectation, the anticipation, that God will eventually come through as He did for Job and many others listed in the "Hall of Faith"– Hebrews 11 (Job 14:14; 19:25–26; 23:8–12; Ps 62:5; Lam 3:21–26).

Those who say religion is a crutch are right, for it's the first crutch God attempts to obliterate (destroy) as we allow His Word to strip us "naked and open to the eyes of Him to whom we must give account." Once God revealed His *unconditional* love and power in the face of Job's nakedness, he repented "in dust and ashes," and then was able to pray – from his *heart* – for the very people who had so viciously attacked and abused him verbally. Before his stripping, he'd resented them deeply; in fact, he had *despised* them (Heb 4:13; 2 Cor 5:1–5; Job 30, 42).

Moses is another man God "emptied" of his self-importance and *appearance* of success. It took forty years, but then God used him to patiently endure persecution and abuse from a whole nation for the next forty years (Ex 1–5; Num 11–16).

Many of David's psalms are poetic expressions of that profound change from outward insecurity based on *appearance*, to the deep-level joy of knowing who you *really* are through relationship with God. The life and trials of David are, like Job, an enlightening study into how God transfers us from the superficial to the real, from the temporal to the eternal (1 & 2 Sam; Ps 32, 38–40, 51; 66:10–12; Lk 16:15).

The Old Testament is full of these character studies and the words these men and women spoke and the people and nations they influenced. Yet, they present the same *mystery* which kept me from understanding God and the Bible for so long – they all had human weaknesses serious enough to make one wonder how God could ever use them, if indeed He existed at all (1 Cor 4:8–13; 2 Cor 4:7; 12:9–10; 13:4).

Surface relationships or heart-to-heart?

As a matter of fact, Jesus said the Kingdom of God is a mystery, filled with enough *offenses* and *stumbling stones* to discourage anyone not desperately serious about finding truth. Why is it that way? (Mt 18:7; Lk 17:1; Rom 9:33; 1 Cor 1:23).

Because just under the surface, the layers of our pride, self-consciousness, and fears, lies the gold, a thing I call *heart*. It is the capacity to *understand*. It is what God (through Solomon) meant by saying "the heart of *kings* is *unsearchable*," comparable to the height of the heavens and depth of the earth (Pr 25:3).

It is that which reaches out and *takes hold* of another human being *heart-to-heart*, the inner mystical *connection* for which we were created in God's image. For God made us primarily for fellowship (Eph 1:10, 22–23; 2:21–22; 3:17–19; Col 1:17–18; Ps 48:1f; 50:1-3; 132–133; Rv 21:9–26).

"Inasmuch then as the children have partaken of flesh and blood, He Himself likewise shared in the same." He did it to set us free from our slavery, relate to *us* heart-to-heart, and take our sin-nature and human weakness before His Father as our Mediator and Intercessor (Heb 2:14–18; 4:11–16; 5:2).

This is what the New Testament is all about – explaining the "width and length and depth and height" of this *amazing grace*, that we may "know the love of Christ which passes knowledge," and "be filled with all the fullness of God" (Eph 3:18–19).

No marriage in heaven?

My oldest daughter gave me permission to print one of her blog entries regarding her daughter's question about heaven:

> As Anna and I snuggled in for a recent "Bible time" together, we read the passage in Matthew 22 in which Jesus told the Sadducees there would be no marriage in Heaven.
>
> "No marriage in Heaven?!" My almost-thirteen-year-old gasped, then sat beside me gaping in disbelief. I could read her mind. Already looking forward to the dating years, I'll bet she was praying right then and there that Jesus wouldn't come back for a very long time.
>
> Sensing her disappointment, I explained that most of us are mistaken about Heaven. We picture ourselves strumming harps as we float along on fluffy clouds in and out of private mansions. That would get dull after a few

thousand years. If Heaven is merely a pain-free, glorified extension of this present existence, I'm disappointed.

But this is what I told Anna: "Heaven is a literal place, to be sure. There are untold pleasures to be enjoyed with all the five senses and more. But beyond that, Heaven is as much about *being* as it is *doing*, since *the essence of life is relationship*.

"Heaven – or eternal life – is the ultimate experience in relationship. Complete transparency characterizes the community of Heaven. We will experience each other with an intimacy that far surpasses the physical intimacy lovers share on earth.

"Someone explained that in Heaven, when you meet a person for the first time, you see them from the inside out, as opposed to the earthly working your way in. You immediately see (sense, feel, know, realize) one's true self (character, personality) the instant you meet him or her. And better still, you love and appreciate what you see!

"It's as if the person who once rubbed you the wrong way has been completely emptied of every trace of annoyance, and the positive aspects of that personality have been condensed and magnified to make up the entire individual, so that we will understand each other as the unique person he or she was always meant to be. And we'll have an eternity to discover people as if for the first time, one at a time, and to enjoy them forever. It makes me giddy just thinking about it. And that's just the people part!

"Greater still, we'll be experiencing God – the pure essence of love. People who have momentarily died, gone to Heaven and come back, all tell of an incredible feeling of being enveloped in a love that warmed them beyond what human language can express.

"Hell is the exact opposite. . . . It is the absence of the presence of God. Here on earth, the worst infidels are still able to call on God, for He is here.

"Not so in Hell. It is a place of utter abandonment – a loneliness unlike any ever experienced on earth. Some people joke and say, 'At least I'll be in good company in

Hell – we'll party!' That won't be the case.

"Hell is a place where God respects one's wishes and allows them the fullest experience of what they always wanted on earth. So those that lived for themselves will get just that – they will have their 'selves' all to themselves.

"Randy Alcorn writes of an individual who found himself in Hell and soon heard a blood-curdling scream, thought to be a demon. He realized it was his own scream; the thing he loved too much to ever deny now turned on him to torment him for eternity.

"As will all those things some choose to hold on to – hate, fear, greed, envy, and so on. They are the only company one has in Hell. They become all consuming giants now feeding on the one who used to feed on them.

"Aren't you glad we can choose Heaven? The Bible says that Hell is reserved for Satan and his angels. God never meant for any human to go there, and He did the ultimate in giving us a way out. Just ask Jesus about that" [Jn 3:16; Rom 10:9–10].

C.S Lewis wrote, "All day long we are, in some degree, helping each other to one or other of these destinations [heaven or hell]. It is in the light of these overwhelming possibilities . . . that we should conduct all our dealings with one another, all friendships, all loves, all play, all politics."[5]

1. Katz, Aaron (Art), with Phil Chomak. *Reality, the Hope of Glory.* Pineville, N.C.: MorningStar Publications, 1990. 123–124.
2. https://medium.com/precision-medicine/how-big-is-the-human-genome-e90caa3409b0
3. I heard Ryan Dobson, James Dobson's son, tell this true story on a *Focus on the Family* radio program. See the news article at http://www.gendisasters.com/oklahoma/18589/webbers-falls-ok-interstate-bridge-collapse-may-2002 (accessed Dec 7, 2016)
4. Wiese, Bill. *23 Questions About Hell.* Lake Mary, FL: Charisma House, 2010. 15.
5. Lewis, C.S. *The Weight of Glory.* Poole, UK: The CS Lewis Company Ltd./ HarperCollins UK. 28–29.

CHAPTER 12

Seven Guidelines to See if I'm Serious about God or Am I Just Kidding Myself

Work hard to show the results of your salvation, obeying God with deep reverence and fear. For God is working in you, giving you the desire and the power to do what pleases Him.
Philippians 2:12b–13 NLT

What is faith?

A "Christian" inmate wanted desperately to speak with a "chaplain" about his many problems. Through tears he told me all the bad things that had happened to him; everything that could go wrong had gone wrong. My eyes teared up as I felt his pain. I didn't know what to tell him.

Then I began questioning him about his lifestyle. In a moment I saw his problem. Everything he did or didn't do pushed God away. He literally provided a comfortable home for demonic powers of darkness. Yet he seemed unaware he was doing anything wrong.

Many get mad at God, feeling He let them down when they needed Him, not realizing that when we live in opposition to God, even our prayers are disgusting to Him (see Prv 28:9). He not only keeps His distance from us but invites our enemies to afflict us. Yikes! (Lev 26:14–45; Deut 28:15–68; Judg 3:7–8, 12; 4:1–2; Prv 6:16–19; 15:8, 29; 16:5; 21:27; Is 1:10–15; Jer 25:8–11; Amos 5:21–22; Jas 4:6; 1 Pet 5:5 and hundreds more).

Salvation is based on *genuine faith* in Jesus Christ: "Believe on the Lord Jesus Christ, and you will be saved"; "He who has the Son has life; he who does not have the Son of God does not have life" (Acts 16:31a; 1 Jn 5:12; see Acts 4:12; 8:37; 13:39; Jn 3:15; 6:40; 6:47; 7:38; 11:25; 11:26; 20:31; Rom 10:9–10; Gal 3:22–26; 1 Jn 5:10–11).

Believe, faith, and faithful[1] occur over five hundred times in the New Testament. But to *believe* means to enter a *relationship* of *trusting God* and His resurrection power through Jesus Christ. The "sinner's prayer" (Romans 10:9) may well be the beginning of this awesome relationship – if it's really from the heart. "For with the *heart* one believes unto righteousness, and with the mouth confession is made unto salvation" (Rom 10:10).

At the tomb of Lazarus Jesus told Martha, "I am [Myself] the Resurrection and the Life. Whoever *believes in – adheres to, trusts in and relies on – Me,* although he may die, yet he shall live. And whoever *continues to live and believes – has faith in, cleaves to and relies – on Me* shall never [actually] die at all" (Jn 11:25–26 AMP – Amplified Bible).

This explains why the *stony soil* on which the Word is sown represents those who "receive the word with joy;" but "have no root, who *believe for a while,*" but "when tribulation or persecution arises because of the word," he "stumbles" (Mt 13:20–21; Lk 8:13). The Amplified Bible "amplifies" the Greek words to bring out more of their meaning. For "he stumbles," it reads, "He is repelled and begins to distrust and desert Him Whom he ought to trust and obey, and he falls away."

Faith, to be *genuine,* will be "*tested by fire.*" "That the *genuineness of your faith,* being much more precious than gold that perishes, though it is tested by fire, may be found to praise, honor, and glory at the revelation of Jesus Christ," instead of worrying and complaining (1 Pet 1:7; Num 14; Heb 3).

He who "adheres to, trusts in and relies on" God, instead of "relying on" drugs, pot, alcohol, or a person (codependency), will (eventually) give "praise, honor, and glory" as he *continues* "looking unto Jesus, the author and finisher of our *faith*" – the "perseverance of the saints" (Rom 9:16; Eph 2:8--10; Heb 12:2).

What is repentance?

Genuine faith in God begins with true *repentance* – unless one's heart is already broken and ready to receive Christ's free gift. Many are sorry they're in trouble, but don't have "godly sorrow" that "produces *repentance* leading to salvation" (2 Cor 7:10; see Ps 51; Is 55:6–7; 66:2; Lk 15:7; Acts 3:19; Acts 16:31–31; Rom 2:4–6; 2 Pet 3:9).

The New Testament Greek word for *repentance* means a *change of mind*.[2] While some may pray a sincere prayer backed by "godly sorrow" and are saved through real faith, others might repeat the same words, but their *heart* is not really in it. They want to be saved, but not enough to *change their mind* about their *lifestyle*. Too often they become a "stumbling stone" to those who are sincerely searching for God (Mt 18:7; Lk 17:1–2; Jude 1:4; Rv 2:21).

Overcoming sin may take longer for some, which is why Paul said, "Work out your own salvation with fear and trembling; for it is God who works in you both to will and to do for His good pleasure" (same verse in *New Living Translation* at chapter title: Phil 2:12b–13).

Here's how the Amplified Bible translates it (words in brackets included): "Work out – cultivate, carry out to the goal and fully complete – your own salvation with reverence and awe and trembling [self-distrust, that is, with serious caution, tenderness of conscience, watchfulness against temptation; timidly shrinking from whatever might offend God and discredit the name of Christ]. [Not in your own strength] for it is God Who is all the while effectually at work in you – energizing and creating in you the power and desire – both to will and to work for His good pleasure *and* satisfaction *and* delight."

David committed adultery and murder; too much success lured this godly man away from the God who'd blessed him with it. Many of his psalms reveal the lengthy process he agonized through, crying, "Do not banish me from Your presence, and don't take Your Holy Spirit from me. Restore to me the joy of Your salvation, and make me willing to obey You" (Ps 51:11–12 NLT; Dt 8:10–20; 2 Sam 11–12).

Because David had "godly sorrow," his sin, instead of driving him *away* from God, drove him *to* God. Through it all he ended up with a far deeper relationship with Him than he'd had, expressed through his psalms of great suffering (in consequence of his sin) and repentance (Ps 6, 22, 32, 38–41; 51; Gal 6:7–8).

In 2006 I wrote an article on the basics of a biblical lifestyle common to those who sincerely want to grow in faith and grace.

The following seven guidelines are the result (1 Pet 2:2; Pet 3:18).

1. What do I put into my mind on a regular basis?

The input I get from TV, movies, music, rap, internet, social media, books, magazines, pictures, and video games *determines who I am.* All this input goes from the mind to the heart where it forms my character.

Some believe that what they listen to does not affect their behavior. If what I listened to or watched remained only in my *conscious* mind, that could be true. But the mind is the doorway to the heart. Everything in my mind goes into my heart, whether I want it to or not. And once there, it's beyond *my conscious* control and instead, *begins to control me.*

For it begins a slow process of incubation or fermentation, like chemicals reacting. All my desires, resentments, emotional wounds, fears, anger, envy, and attitudes toward parents, authority figures (cops), bad and good people – my whole emotional makeup *interacts* with the words and pictures that entered my mind and took root permanently in my heart (Jer 17:9; Mt 15:9).

If I listened to words that reflect God's love and forgiveness through Christ, His mercy and truth, they will bring inner healing, peace, strength, and wisdom to influence others for good (Prv 4:23; 22:5; Heb 12:15).

However, if down in my heart are messages which *reinforce* my "issues," it will eat away my character like termites slowly destroying a house. Jesus compared it to a house built on sand which collapses in a storm. I will slowly and subconsciously take on the nature of what I feed my mind with, like planted seeds which some day bear fruit in some form, whether in attitudes or acts (Eccl 11:1, 5–6; Hos 8:7; 10:12; Mt 7:24–27; Gal 6:7–9).

Behavior springs from the heart, not the mind, which explains why we can't change by trying mentally. It takes a *transformed heart,* but it *begins* with the renewing of our minds, which sows its word-seeds into the heart.

The word *transformed* in Romans 12:2 comes from the Greek word for metamorphosis.[3] It's the process through which a caterpillar, having *died* in its chrysalis, if it has eaten the right food during its lifetime, will *metamorphose* into a butterfly. (Same Greek word in Mt 17:2, *transfigured*, and 2 Cor 3:18)

This is a picture God has given us in nature of how we're *transformed* as we "feed" on Christ and His Word. The result is the *fruit of the Spirit* – love, joy, peace, patience, gentleness, goodness, faith, humility, and self-control (Mt 4:4; Jn 6:50ff; Rom 10:17; Gal 5:22).

It's how grace works: "For sin shall not have dominion [control] over you, for you are not under law [will-power] but under grace [*His* power]." "So then it is not of him who wills, nor of him who runs [self-effort], but of God who shows mercy" (Rom 6:14; 9:16).

How could anything be easier? It begins with falling in love with Jesus and His Word, and *staying* there – remaining, abiding, living *in Him*: a *lifestyle!* (Jn 15; Col 3:1–6; 1 Jn 2:15–17; Heb 12:1ff; Prv 4:23).

2. **Who are my friends? Where do I *fellowship*?**
It's easy to determine my future by the friends I hang with, including my cyber-friends. For they give me a picture of *where my heart* is, because fellowship is a *heart*-thing. It's not the same as the people I must work with at my job but don't *fellowship* with heart-to-heart. *The influence of my friends gradually makes me like them.* "Do not be so deceived and misled! Evil companionships (communion, associations) corrupt and deprave good manners and morals and character (1 Cor 15:33 AMP; Ps 1; Prv 22:24–25; Jas 4:4).

Some time ago I asked a prison inmate, "What's the one thing you regret most in your life?" After about a minute of silence, he said, "The thing I regret most is the day I smoked my first joint of marijuana." He went on to explain how it involved him with the wrong kind of friends despite his mother's warning, then led to heavier drugs, followed by criminal activity, and finally the crime that landed him in prison with a life-sentence. And in Florida there's no parole: he'll never get out unless God miraculously opens the door.

Samson is one of the great leaders of Israel in the book of Judges. God called him to "begin to deliver Israel out of the hand of the Philistines." But he hung out with them and married one against his parents' wishes. Later he spent the night with one of their prostitutes, then moved in with a Philistine girl named Delilah. She pestered him to know the secret of his supernatural strength until "he told her all his heart" (Jgs 13:5; 16:17–18).

"When Delilah saw that he had told her all his *heart*, she sent and called for the lords of the Philistines, saying, 'Come up once more, for he has told me all his heart.'"

His reign was cut short in death by "friends" who lured his *heart* away from God. Read this amazing but sad story in Judges 13 to 16. Don't let it be yours!

3. **What is my attitude toward sex and marriage?**

Marriage is the single most important unit of relationship because it is designed for the highest level of intimacy and transparency. Intimacy is based on transparency, which is to be so open and honest about myself toward another person that I become completely vulnerable, which means open to being hurt or rejected because of what I've shared of myself.

When we "cover" (love, forgive, bear with, overlook faults) each other after exposing our darkest secrets and failures, we provide each other with the highest degree of security and acceptance possible. Marriage is the *covenant* (binding agreement) designed especially for this kind of unconditional commitment to each other (Gen 2:23; Eph 5:31).

Sex is more than physical pleasure; it is the physical act of *intimate bonding* (Gen 2:24; Mt 19:5; 1 Cor 6:16). When it is used for pleasure only, outside of marriage, it violates one of the most frequent commands in the Bible, exposing me to God's corrective discipline, sooner or later. Sex for "love and commitment" is no excuse, for it sets a dangerous example, *especially if they claim to be Christians. For if even doing something perfectly lawful is wrong if it causes a weaker believer to stumble, what about a lifestyle the Bible clearly says is sin?* (Prv 5:11–13; 6:26–29; 7:21–23; Mt 18:6–7; Rom 14:7–8, 15, 21; 1 Cor 8:9–13; 10:32–33).

Ignoring God's specific command by Adam and Eve led to the fall of man. And when I do it with the "grace of God" in mind because "He knows I'm only human," I change "the grace of our God into a license for immorality" (Gen 3; Jude 1:4a NIV).

If I'm disobedient in this area, restoration begins with true *repentance* leading to a change in behavior. In cases of a long term relationship (common law marriage), but for some reason I cannot make it legal through a marriage license, especially when there are children involved belonging to both the mother and father, it is important to seek wisdom from my pastor and take whatever steps he recommends, assuming He is a genuine man of God committed to His Word (Job 31:1–4, 9–12; Prv 2:16–19; 6:23–25; 11:14; 15:22; chap 7; 22:14; Eccl 7:26; 1 Cor 6:9; 10:8; Gal 5:19; Eph 5:5; Heb 13:4; Rv 21:8).

4. **What is my relationship with God's family?**

Relationship with God is like a marriage. It's developed through relationship with His children – my fellow believers. *It's the most obvious way to test my private devotions and time with Him,* because when I'm alone I can easily adapt His Word to my own conclusions and advantages (Heb 3:12–14; 10:25).

God's plan and purpose are through *people*. To ignore His family or to give it half-hearted attention is to miss the point of being saved. For some it may be an escape plan from hell to heaven the way the Jews wanted to make Jesus King without following Him as His disciples, which means "taught ones" (Eph 3:10; Jn 6:15).

The spiritual and emotional blessings of transparency and intimacy in marriage can be experienced through a serious lifetime commitment to His Body, the Church. This means finding a local body of believers who meet regularly for worship, instruction in the Word, and fellowship (Acts 2:47; 5:14; 9:31; 11:26; 13:1; 14:23, 27; 20:28; 1 Cor 11:18; 12:28; 16:19, etc).

My spiritual growth and maturity take place through interaction with these "brothers and sisters in Christ." And according to Romans 12, 1 Corinthians 12, and Ephesians 4, it *is difficult, if not impossible, to mature spiritually without regular fellowship with them* (Eph 1:10, 22–23; 2:14–16, 21–22; 3:10, 17–19; 4:1–16; 5:30–33; 6:18).

This relationship also provides protection from demonic influence, a very real "covering" in the spirit-realm when I'm walking in love, forgiveness, and unity (Ps 27:4–6; 48:1–6; Ps 133–134; Mt 18:32–35; 2 Cor 2:10–11; Heb 12:22–29; Rv 3:7–10).

5. **What is my attitude toward the correction process?**

"My son, do not despise the chastening of the Lord, nor be discouraged when you are rebuked by Him; for whom the Lord loves He chastens, and scourges every son whom He receives" (Heb 12:5b–6).

God uses many different sources to correct us. His first line of correction is His Word in our personal devotions, and through His family, the local church. When we take time to listen to God as we study His Word and then humble ourselves to receive instruction and correction through His family, we generally spare ourselves the second line of correction – jail, *some* accidents or sicknesses (not all, but see 1 Corinthians 11:29–32), and those who abuse us, though God does not spare even the *obedient*, to test and purify our faith (Job 1–2; Ps 66:10–12; Prv 16:7; 17:10–11; 19:19, 23; Jas 1:2–3; 1 Pet 1:7).

To react with anger or resentment toward those who try to correct us, *even when it's an enemy* (whom God may use to get our attention), family member, or someone who treats us like dirt, is to miss an opportunity for the refining of our faith. It may also be a tragic failure to recognize "the chastening of the Lord" (Heb 12:5).

For "the ear that hears the rebukes of life will abide among the wise." That is, a "wise man" is sensitive to correction in ways a "fool" doesn't recognize and scoffs at or resists (Heb 12:5–11; Prv 15:31; See also Ps 32, 38, 51; Prv 15:32–33; Jer 48:11–12; Lam 3:22–42; Mt 11:28–30; Jas 4:6–10; Rv 3:19).

6. **Do I live with resentment?**

The Alcoholics Anonymous Big Book says "resentment destroys more alcoholics than anything else. From it stem all forms of spiritual disease. . . . When the spiritual malady is overcome, we straighten out mentally and physically" (p. 64).

Resentment is unforgiveness, and Jesus said if we don't forgive others, God will not forgive us (Mk 11:26). And if He doesn't forgive us, His mercy and grace can't reach us, and we're "delivered . . . to the torturers" – those "spiritual diseases" and "maladies" (Mt 18:21–35; see Prv 24:17–18; Mt 6:12–15; Lk 6:37; Rom 12:18–21; 1 Cor 13:4–7; 2 Cor 2:10–11; Col 3:13; Jas 2:12–13.)

No matter how badly I have been hurt by someone, from abandonment and rejection to sexual and physical abuse by family or someone close to me, the only way to heal inside is to *forgive*. In many cases it is humanly impossible without a miracle from God, which He will grant us as we seek Him with all our hearts (Jer 29:13; Heb 10:16; 11:6).

7. Have I surrendered what's blocking me spiritually?

There's something in us that may not be sin to others, but it is to me . . . and maybe *you*. We're afraid to let it go, because it has become a substitute for God – giving us the comfort or security God would give us on a much deeper and more permanent level. It might keep us from a genuine commitment to Him, or it may hinder us from growing spiritually or filling our potential, our calling or gift. That's why He says, "Let us strip off every weight that slows us down, especially the sin that so easily trips us up" (Heb 12:1 NLT).

Sometimes we don't even know what it is without seeking Him earnestly, especially when we're not closely connected to the Body of Christ, His Church family. And it may be a good thing, even a ministry. Or it could be a habit or a person or group we're not willing to walk away from, though we could if we really wanted to and took God seriously (Rom 6:13).

It's not that we *must* obey in this before God will forgive or help us (though sometimes it is), but we need to identify it, bring it to God, and allow Him to deal with this "stronghold" that "so easily trips us up." Then His *grace* will bring victory, sooner or later. "For sin shall not have dominion over you, for you are not under law but under grace" (Rom 6:14).

We want God to do major things in our lives – deliverance from a serious addiction, a financial impossibility or hardship, a family or relationship situation that causes stress and pain, or a physical healing. But God sees a smaller problem we don't want Him to mess with; it creates a blockage in our lifeline to God and hinders His grace from accomplishing His will more effectively in us (1 Cor 9:24–27).

One young prison inmate I remember clearly because he had so much potential to be top-of-the-line in whatever it was God had gifted him with. But he was hooked on reading novels, like an addiction. I could identify with him because it was my problem: not novels, but spiritual books. Not that reading them was wrong, but not knowing how to stop reading, spiritually absorb what I've read, and *listen* long enough to pick up on the quiet voice of the Spirit (1 Kgs 19:12–13).

It was the hardest thing I ever had to give up so I figured there's no way this young man would give up his novels when he hardly knew what God had to offer in their place. What God used to wean me from reading (besides my problem with depression and anger) was the intense hunger that came through reading about people of God who *had* surrendered everything and how powerfully God was now using them. But still it took seeking God desperately for months before I finally "counted the cost" and obeyed (Lk 14:25–35; full story in ch 1).

A few years later my "idol" this time was working too many hours on my job, leaving no time for family or God. My wife kept urging me to at least come home for supper, but I kept telling her *tomorrow*. So God in His mercy removed a tiny portion of his fatherly protection, and I fell out of the tree I was trimming, which abruptly rearranged my daily schedule – to this day! Which is how I have time to write what you're reading.

Years later my wife pinpointed another problem in me – a self-righteous form of anger I didn't even realize I had because it came out in the form of a strict command as a husband and father I felt was right. When my daughter confirmed it in agreement with her mother, I decided I would simply stop this "authoritative" behavior. But surprise! I couldn't; it was a *stronghold* only God could break in me. I took it seriously enough to seek God – praying and pleading with God for deliverance all day long as I worked on my job. For two weeks! Then, suddenly it was gone. That was in April, 1993. How well I remember. It has never come back, and my wife will attest to it.

A jail chaplain volunteer had a cigarette addiction she didn't want to give up, even though she said God had been dealing with her about it. Then one day a hard-boiled egg exploded in her lips, burning them, so she couldn't smoke while her lips were healing. She told me about it during one of our volunteer meetings, so I told her what would heal them quickly: applying mashed papaya fruit as a poultice, which I'd learned from a Filipino nurse friend. She did, and God used it to mercifully heal her lips, along with the valuable lesson learned about obedience.

Now in the digital age, especially social media, the challenge to "guard your heart with all diligence" is greater than ever, and the word "overcomer" takes on new meaning and value. For a "listening heart" is essential to knowing God and walking in obedience. I struggle with distractions also and sometimes look with envy at the *time* prison inmates have to dig deep into the wisdom and knowledge of God. *It's priceless if they'll use it* (Prv 23; 8:10–35; 1 Jn 5:4–5; Rv 2:7, 11, 17; Col 1:9).

King Saul lost his kingdom, not because he committed some wicked sin, but because he did something "good," even related to ministry, but had failed to "wait" long enough to "tune in" to God's heart and wisdom. God gave him another chance and still he disobeyed, again doing something he felt was good but not *all* God had told him to do. It's where we get the biblical phrase, "Obedience is better than sacrifice" (1 Sam 10:8; ch 13, 15; Ps 51:16–17; Mat 5:24; Lk 8:18).

The church at Ephesus worked diligently for God – a model church! But they'd gotten so busy working *for* God, they'd lost their intimacy with Him, their "first love." Jesus told them to *repent or else . . . !* (Rev 2:1-5; see Mk 12:33; Lk 12:47–48; Rom 7:22; Gal 5:13; Eph 4:17–5:14; Jas 4:17; 1 Jn 3:6, 9; 5:18).

Conclusion: What does it mean to *abide, remain* in Christ?

John makes some disturbing statements about the believer's lifestyle: "Whoever abides in Him does not sin. Whoever sins has neither seen Him nor known Him." "He who sins is of the devil, for the devil has sinned from the beginning" (1 Jn 3:6, 8a).

"Whoever has been born of God does not sin, for his seed remains in him; and he cannot sin, because he has been born of God. In this the children of God and the children of the devil are manifest: whoever does not practice righteousness is not of God, nor is he who does not love his brother" (1 Jn 3:9–10).

These verses would condemn every one of us without understanding Romans and Galatians. which clarify what "abides in Him" means. To Paul, *abiding, remaining, in Christ* is to "walk according to the Spirit" (Rom 8:1, 4) or "walk in the Spirit" (Gal 5:16, 25). Romans 3 through 8 (with Galatians 2 through 5) explains in detail what this means:

Chapter 3 explains the purpose of God's law, which for me is what Jesus taught in His "Sermon on the Mount": to reveal the horrible condition of our hearts and show us how desperately we need a personal relationship with God through Christ; because *only through Him are we able to obey* (Mt 5–7; Lk 6).

Chapter 4 shows us how to change from trying to *earn* God's favor through hard work, to *expecting* it as an act of real faith that sees and speaks of things that don't exist as though they do – because faith will make it a reality in Christ.

Chapter 5 gives us two different identities – the old one from our *natural* birth in Adam, and our new one through our *spiritual* birth in Christ (2 Cor 5:17).

Chapter 6 explains the meaning of our death in Christ's death and our resurrection with Him to a life of obedience.

Chapter 7 covers the awful conflict that wars between the flesh and spirit and how God's holy laws of righteousness produce the helplessness and "death" in us that enable us to metamorphose like a butterfly from its grave (chrysalis) into our new identity in Christ.

Chapter 8 describes that resurrection life – walking in the Spirit and the powerful benefits of allowing Him to rule in our minds and hearts. Once we truly *believe* with our *heart* that

God has raised Christ from the dead and His life is in us, our "walk" and spiritual growth now hinge on "abiding" in Him.

Abide (Greek, *meno*, #3306) means *remain, continue*. "Then Jesus said to those Jews who believed Him, 'If you *abide* (*continue*, KJV) in My word, you are My disciples indeed. And you shall know the truth, and the truth shall make you free'" (Jn 8:31–32).

Remaining/abiding in Him and walking in the Spirit is a battle of the mind, waged in Romans six, seven, and eight – through maintaining "the mind of Christ" against the distractions and discouragements of the flesh, as well as the accusations of the devil and those he uses to accuse us. It's why we need the help of our "fellow soldiers," the members of His Body, the Church (Rom 8:9–13; 1 Cor 2:16; 12:4–28; Eph 4:1–15; Heb 3:12–14; 10:25; 1 Pet 1:13; 5:8; Rv 12:10).

As I surrender myself to God in these seven areas, "the Son of Righteousness shall arise with healing in His wings" for me (Mal 4:2). Little by little (Ex 23:30), through faith and *patience* (Heb 6:12), the "law of the Spirit of Life in Christ Jesus" will make "me free from the law of sin and death" (Rom 8:2). And I'll experience the resurrection power of His *amazing grace* to deliver me "from glory to glory, even as by the Spirit of the Lord" (2 Cor 3:18).

1. Faith (Greek, *pistis*, #4102) and faithful (*pistos*, #4103) are the noun and adjective forms of the verb *pisteuo* (#4100), believe.
2. Greek, *metanoia: meta* – change; *noia* – mind
3. Greek: *meta* (#3326) – transition, change; *morphe* (#3444) – form

SECTION FOUR

He's Listening for Your Call

(Your Response)

Call to Me, and I will answer you,
and show you great and mighty things,
which you do not know.
Jeremiah 33:3

CHAPTER 13

Sample Prayers in Line with God's Will

"You ask and do not receive, because you ask amiss, that you may spend it on your pleasures." "Now this is the confidence that we have in Him, that if we ask anything according to His will, He hears us. And if we know that He hears us, whatever we ask, we know that we have the petitions that we have asked of Him.
James 4:3; 1 John 5:14–15

Prayer Regarding Lust

(Adapt to your gender.)

Dear Father, I have a problem; I have abused and perverted what You created for fellowship and bonding with a lifetime mate and the responsibility that goes with it – to love and care for her and the children our intimacy produces. I have used the beauty and glory of this physical union for my own selfish purpose, to gratify my lust. In so doing, I've shirked my responsibility as a husband and father and contributed to the emotional and spiritual destruction of the women I've used [and abused?] [and the children who have resulted?].

I've excused myself in any number of ways: by saying it's what they wanted anyway, it's my bad upbringing, and it's normal now – everybody does it, even many of the "Christians." In fact, it has become so much a part of my lifestyle, I hardly feel it's wrong anymore. The women I've used would get it and are getting it from others anyway. Which is why it's hard to feel convicted about it.

It even bothers me when I hear preachers or jail chaplains and volunteers say it's sin, especially since the Bible says that lusting after a woman in your heart is the same as committing adultery with her. So everybody's guilty (Mt 5:27–28).

Yet I know deep in my heart these are only excuses, and that true Christians nip their lustful thoughts in the bud before they grow into willful, deliberate mental pornography and sexual imagery. Because my acts of lust started there, but I let them blossom into acts of sin, leading to the lifestyle I can't quit and don't even *want* to.

But God, I don't want to go to hell. And Your Bible says that those who have sex outside their own marriage will end up in the lake of fire if they don't repent. So I ask You to please change my heart about this wickedness. Help me renew my mind so I don't think about it all the time. Show me how to give my mind a bath with Your Word so I have clean, pure thoughts. Please take away my love of the music, rap, pornography, reading, TV, movies, Internet, and conversations which contaminate my mind with sex: no wonder I'm so addicted. My mind needs a complete overhaul (Rv 21:8; Jn 15:3–4; Rom 12:2).

But I can't do it on my own. It's impossible! I go back to it again and again, deeper and deeper, like a dog eating his own vomit. But at least now I truly repent about it from my heart: I honestly *want* to be set free. I long for a pure mind, a pure heart (2 Pet 2:22).

Psalm 119 says, "How can a young man cleanse his way? By taking heed according to Your word. With my whole heart I have sought You; oh, let me not wander from Your commandments! Your word I have hidden in my heart, that I might not sin against You" (119:9–12a).

Please show me how to replace the evil words and images I've been feeding on with Your Word until my mind is renewed and clean. Teach me how to "put off" my old nature and "be renewed in the spirit of [my] mind" and "put on" my "new man which was created according to God, in true righteousness and holiness" (Rom 12:1–2; Col 3:1–10; Eph 4:22–24).

Father, I ask you to work on my whole worldly lifestyle, because it's all fleshly, given over to what I want, not what You want. Change me from being a taker to a giver, from always wanting things to go my way, to feeling the needs of others. Teach me how to be a blessing to others instead of a drain on them, *causing* conflict and demanding my rights when I should be a peacemaker, willing to turn things over to You for what I can't handle (Mt 5:9; Phil 2:3; Jas 3:16–18).

Set me free from all the addictions that feed my selfish lifestyle and cause inconvenience, irritation, frustration, or pain and sheer agony to those around me. Rebuild my conscience; make me sensitive to things that aren't good for me and those around me, and give me the power to overcome. Because without You I "can do nothing," but through You, through the power of Your Spirit and Word, I can do "all things through Christ who strengthens me" (Phil 4:13; Jn 15:4–5).

Father, I surrender my will to You, inviting You to take up residence in every area of my being, cleaning out every room, one by one, or all at once, as You give me grace. Break down my resistance, my carnal reasoning, my pride, ego, self-importance, and everything not compatible with You. I long to change from one You *resist*, from one who is an *abomination* and horribly disgusting to You, to one You draw to Yourself and speak to and use for good, not evil (Jas 4:6; 1 Pet 5:5; Prv 16:5; 2 Cor 10:5).

I know it seems impossible, but didn't You say that with You *all* things are possible? So I'm going to believe that the good work You have begun in me, You "will complete it until the day of Jesus Christ" (Phil 1:6; Mt 19:26; Mk 9:23; 10:27; Lk 1:37; 18:27).

Lord, I also realize that to depend on You means to become a part of Your family. I've been slack in this area; it has not been important to me, which explains one main reason I've become what I've become. So please give me the desire to be around Your people; give me understanding how to relate to them, how to receive from them without judging them and seeing their faults or feeling offended and angry because of the way they see me. Teach me how to deal with the huge log in my own eye before I attempt to deal with the speck of dust (or log) in someone else's (Mt 7:1–5; Eph 4).

Give me the power and discipline to get out of bed on Sunday morning and make a decision to place my body in the presence of Your people as they worship and receive Your

Word, because otherwise I'll too easily forget this prayer and all my good intentions. I know I'll drift right back into my old ways, and no telling where that will lead me next. And actually I'll need more than one church service a week; increase my desire so I'll want to be with Your people as much as possible, that I'll hang around those who influence me toward You the way I've allowed the wrong friends to influence me toward evil (1 Cor 15:33; Heb 10:25).

Well, I've asked a lot, but You are big enough. Which also means, I realize, that whom You love, You discipline and chasten. I've had a habit of running from this, of undoing any attempt of You or anyone to correct or break me. I'm so sorry, Father. This resistance is so much a part of me, I don't see how I can change. But again, what's impossible for me is easy for You. So here I am. First, give me a chance to go the easy way; give me an ear to *listen*. Then if I don't get it, speak louder, whatever it takes. Because life is too short and eternity is too long to lose it over a brief "vapor" of meaningless pleasure (Ps 39:5; Prv 15:31–33; Jas 4:14)

There. Amen – "so be it." I mean this prayer with all my heart. Do whatever it takes. My life no longer belongs to me; it belongs to You. I'm Your property, Your temple, Your home. Clean it up so You'll be comfortable to live here and proud to call me Yours, so I will no longer be a stumbling stone and an offense to others, but a blessing. That when people see me, they won't see a phony, a hypocrite, but one who is real, a genuine product of Your grace and mercy. Someone they'll want to be around for the right reasons, not the wrong.

I love You; please increase my love until I can honestly say I love and serve you with all my heart, soul, mind, and strength. Because this is how I know I'll change (Lk 10:27; 2 Cor 3:18).

Your child ________________________________ date ______

Trust in His strength, not yours: Ps 37:3–9; Prv 3:3–8; 2 Cor 3:4–5; 12:9–10; Eph 3:16; 6:10; Col 1:11; Is 40:29–31; 41:10; 45:24

God's judgment on sexual Immorality: Rom 1:28–32; 1 Cor 6:9–

10, 18; 10:8; 2 Cor 12:21; Gal 5:19–20; Eph 5:5–6; Col 3:5–6; 1 Thes 4:3–8 (2 Thes 1:8–10); Heb 12:16; 13:4; 2 Pet 2:10; Rv 2:14, 21; 9:21; 20–23; 21:8; 22:15; Prv 2:10–19; 5:1ff; 6:20ff; 7:1ff; 9:13ff; 11:6; 22:14; Eccl 7:26; Jgs 16; 1 Sam 2:22–24; 2 Sam 12:1ff; Num 25; Gen 35:22; 49:3–4 (2 Chr 5:1)

*****

Prayer regarding anger and/or depression

Sometimes when I feel overwhelmed I write out my prayer. Then I imagine God answering my prayer. I'm always amazed at how encouraged I feel when "He speaks" in this manner. So here's one for you – your prayer (change to match your need) and His answer:

Dear Father, I come to You about my depression and anger. Victor, that dude who comes as a chaplain volunteer, says there are three major causes of anger or depression: our relationship to You, God, our relation to people, and our relation to the material world – money, home, food, convenience, and so on. I add relationship with myself, but he says that still comes under one or more of those three categories.

He says some medical experts have done research to prove our brains are "hardwired for God," and when our thinking lines up with You, our body and brain chemistry balances out, like taking an antidepressant. He said he never took antidepressants during his twenty years of "severe, suicidal depression" because he found what he calls five "antidepressants" in the Bible: Job 3, Psalm 22, 38, 88, and Lamentations 3:22–41. He says they worked because these chapters described men in their "lowest pit," and they are in the Bible, right under Your nose, where You were carefully observing them, displaying them as models of patience, of trusting and waiting for Your grace.

So maybe it's true: maybe I have been angry toward You because You seem so far away, so far from helping me. It feels like I'm battling my issues alone and there's no end in sight; I feel alone, abandoned, misunderstood, and the harder I try, the behinder I get.

Why do others have it so easy and I have it so hard? Why can't I be *normal* like most everybody else? And why is it so hard to forgive those who've wronged or failed me? And why did You stand by and allow them to do it when You're supposed to be "the Good Shepherd" who "gives His life for the sheep"? (Jn 10:11).

And if I'm so wrong, why can't I seriously take responsibility for what I've done to them or to myself? And how can I help but worry about *things* – my basic needs – when I've burned so many bridges behind me and people won't give me a chance to prove myself? Yet I guess I can't really blame them, though it's hard not to.

No wonder I'm angry (or depressed)! In fact, when I think about these issues, I get too angry to pray, at least to pray effectively. Which might be why my prayers don't get through. So at least help me listen so I can find out what's wrong with me and what to do about it. Thank You.

Your wayward, discouraged, confused, frustrated, angry kid.

God's response:

My dear child: I *am* the Good Shepherd and I'm here to help you. I've always been closer to you than you can possibly imagine, and now I will give you understanding. First, I want to tell you how to open the door to fellowship with Me through faith. You hear that word often, but faith is believing and trusting with your heart what you can't see, hear, or touch physically. You are discouraged, confused, and angry for the very reason that could actually make you one of My closest friends, like Abraham, whom I called My *friend* (Heb 11:1; 2 Chr 20:7; Is 41:8; Jas 2:23).

Why was he My friend? Because I talked with him so much? No. I talked with him, true, but I talked with others who didn't hold up in the dead silence with everything caving in around them as Abraham did. Or they allowed the lure of physical pleasure to replace the fellowship of My love – *which is much easier to experience in darkness than in the comfort of earthly convenience* (Jgs 2:17; 1 Kgs 11; 2 Chr 16; Jer 7:13).

When I called him to leave Ur and go to the land of Canaan, he obeyed and built an altar to Me when he arrived. Abraham is known not only as the father of faith and as My friend, but by the altars he built. This is the first secret of faith. The altar is a place of surrender, similar to marriage vows, your commitment to Me for better or worse, even in thick darkness. It signifies your intent to obey no matter what, and willingness to *wait* for My grace to enable you to obey. Because if you're not willing, we both must wait until you are (Gen 12:7–8; 13:4, 18; Ex 19:9; 20:21; 1 Kgs 8:12; Ps 34:18; 51:17; 78:8, 37; 119:2, 10; Prv 25:2; Is 30:18; 45:15; Jer 29:13).

Even I made an altar out of the lowest pit of My life until then, in the Garden of Gethsemane, where I battled the powers of darkness in yielding My will to My Father. It was not easy because I'd become like you in order to experience your weakness.

As a result of My victory that night and the next day at the cross, My will, *My obedience is now available to you as a gift.* But it comes only through faith, and even *faith* I offer to you as My gift, the fruit of My sacrifice, My death, and confirmed by My resurrection. "For by grace you have been saved through faith, and that not of yourselves; it is the gift of God" (Eph 2:8; Lk 22:43–44; Heb 10:9–10, 16).

The second key to faith, besides your willingness, is *waiting*: True, faith is all about My Word, but it is the Word that comes from My *mouth*, like fresh insight from heaven to speak to your heart. Why is waiting so critical to faith? Because it's not merely using up time, as many do without any profit at all – years and years of pointless waiting for the wrong things.

Waiting for "the word of faith" is maintaining a sense of expectancy, knowing I speak in "thick darkness," when you're not trusting in a physical, earthly answer, but in Me alone. For if you seek Me first, I'll add everything else you need when you need it (Ex 20:21; Ps 40:1–2; Mt 6:33).

This is how Abraham became "rich in faith." Read his story in Genesis 12 to 24. There you'll read of long periods – many years – when I didn't speak to Him. One of his worst lifetime trials occurred not long after he entered Canaan in obedience to

Me. A famine threatened to ruin his livestock and livelihood, so he went down to Egypt. Years later his son Isaac also experienced famine, but I spoke, telling him to stay there; he obeyed and saw My great blessing (Gen 12, 26).

But I withheld My Word from Abraham to test his faith to the depths. There, out of fear for his life, he allowed Pharaoh to take his wife as one of his own. Still I remained silent. Most men would have caved in long before and do all the time. That's where his altars came in. Like Job, his attitude was *trust* no matter what (Gen 12–13, 15; Job 13:15).

To stand in faith, he had to trust Me when I didn't give him direction during the famine; then he went to a deeper level of trust in dealing with the consequences of his failure regarding his wife (Gen 12:11–20; Ps 40:1–8; Is 50:10–11).

The next test he also failed, when he allowed his wife, Sarah, to persuade him to have Ishmael by Hagar, Sarah's Egyptian servant girl. This would cost him thirteen more years of waiting, with the added burden of conflict between Sarah and Hagar, which continues to this day in the Middle East in their descentants.

But he came to the place where the reality of his altars became a spontaneous part of his character, when he no longer "wavered" at My promise "through unbelief." His faith was now strong enough to give Me *all* the glory, seeing he was beyond hope in his own ability; he was "fully convinced" that what I had promised" I was also "able to perform." That's when I gave him and Sarah the long awaited promise, their son Isaac. This is what it means to "overcome." It's overcoming fear and doubt and fully trusting Me in the darkness (Gen 16; Rom 4:13–22; Is 30:18; 50:10–11; Rv 2:7, 11, 17, 26; 3:5, 12, 21; 21:7).

Yet his greatest test came many years later when I asked him to offer this son as a burnt offering. He would have failed if he had not learned to trust Me in previous years. But by then he believed I would raise him from the dead, and he prepared to slay him after he'd bound him on his greatest altar of a *lifetime of altars, of surrender!* (Gen 22; Heb 11:17–19).

Not only had I prepared a ram for the sacrifice in Isaac's place, but Abraham's trust brought forth from Me the strongest confirmation of my covenant with him, guaranteeing it by an oath in which I swore by Myself. Abraham's trust in his greatest test of faith and My response to him is a testimony to my commitment to *you* in *your* deepest trials, for greater darkness demands stronger faith (Gen 22:1–19; Heb 6:13–18).

But remember, I'll give you the faith as you learn to trust Me in the silence without impatiently "lighting your own fire." You will begin to see that I do provide, as I did for Abraham. I'll give you love and wisdom in your relationships and I'll provide for your financial and physical needs (Is 50:10–11; Jn 13:34; 14:12–18; 15:7; Phil 4:19).

I long to prove Myself sufficient to you, your Alpha and Omega, the First and the Last. But I *must* do it when you learn to *trust Me in what seems impossible,* or you will never grow in strength, like a butterfly as it struggles to emerge from its tomb and thereby gains the power to fly and survive as earth's most beautiful insect (1 Cor 15:42–44; Rv 1:8).

Look at your problems as challenges which will develop and strengthen your faith. And through them you will learn to hear and understand My Word and My provision. This is how my children develop faith – through testing and trials in hardships and darkness (Lk 17:5–10; Rom 5:3–4; 8:35–37; 2 Cor 4:17–18; 12:9–10; Heb 11; Jas 1:2–4, 12; 1 Pet 1:7).

Your problems entitle you to a level of grace you would never need and receive if you had it easy. All you need is to build that heart-altar, surrendering yourself to My will. Then learn to wait (Ps 25:3, 5, 21; 27:14; 37:34; Lam 3:25–26; Is 30:18–19; 40:31).

But I must warn you about waiting. Waiting is not "killing time," but learning to be faithful in things which indicate your trust in Me in the *obvious needs around you.* For it places your mind and heart in a listening mode, directs your attention away from yourself toward the needs of others, and sensitizes your heart to hear My voice so you're not misled by a "voice" that pulls you toward selfishness (Mt 25; Mk 13:34–37; Lk 16:10–13; 19:12–17; Ps 123:1–2).

That leaves you with the problem of how to be faithful doing the right thing when you're so used to doing wrong things. But it's still a matter of *trust.* Like Abraham who failed regarding his wife two times, he kept at it as he learned to deal with his anxiety through declaring in prayer and worship what I had promised him. In this way his faith became the working model for all who followed him (Rom 4:16–20; Gal 3:6–9; Heb 11:17–19).

Dare to *trust Me, My child.* Use every failure and setback as all the more reason to trust Me, and when you feel most helpless and in that helplessness build an altar of surrender in your heart, with thanksgiving and worship, I'll come through. I'll even help you build that altar. And I'll make you, as I made Abraham, a testimony to those around you, including your family.

I AM all you need: Jesus, Yeshua – "salvation, deliverance," "Wonderful, Counselor, Mighty God, Everlasting Father, Prince of Peace." Through Me, you'll *stand!* (Ex 3:14; Is 9:6; Eph 6:10–18).

*****

Prayer for your day in court (when you're guilty)

Dear Father, I'm coming to You about my upcoming day in court. I realize I'm guilty, but my flesh wants out or with a minimum sentence, preferably without probation, if possible. I think I've learned my lesson and will be careful to avoid doing anything stupid from now on.

Of course I've said that many times before. I hate to say this, but maybe I'm not ready. Maybe I don't know what I really need. Maybe, as Jeremiah said, I don't know my own heart, and that issues are hidden deep inside me that will come up under certain pressures, temptations, and with some of my friends, that will overcome my good intentions and lead me back to the same stuff that got me here (Jer 17:9).

Maybe it boils down to this: do I want freedom, or do I want to really change no matter what? You know exactly what I need, and since I'm praying to You, I guess it's important that I pray according to Your will, because, as the Bible says, if I pray according to Your will, You are listening and will answer.

Which also means that if I do not pray according to Your will, my praying is useless (1 Jn 5:14–15).

But Your Word also says that if I abide or remain in You, and Your words abide in me, I can ask what I desire, and it will be done for me. And if I delight myself in You, You'll give me the desires of my heart (Jn 15:7; Ps 37:4).

Putting it all together means, apparently, that when my heart and Your heart get together in agreement, I'll see answers to my prayers. Like James says about asking "amiss" according to what our flesh wants, that when we pray selfishly, we should not expect an answer. Because You jealously guard us, wanting us for Yourself, to be our God, our Father, our Savior, our Source, our Deliverer (Jas 4:1–5).

Okay, deep inside I really want to change more than I want freedom, because I know I'll never be free until I'm free from my own selfish craving. So if it takes more jail time, I'm willing. If I'm not willing, then please make me willing. Because I'm tired of my sinful, me-centered lifestyle. If it's possible to really change by getting out of jail, then I gladly accept that.

But if not, then I submit to Your chastening, the discipline and correction You have allowed in order to get my attention, get me into Your Word, break my stubbornness, and teach me how to listen, not only to You, but to the needs of others, especially those I'm responsible for in any way (Gal 5:13; 6:1–2; Eph 5:25–26; 6:4; Col 3:21; 1 Pet 3:7).

I realize also that change begins right here in jail. Because I won't be any different outside than I am in here. If I don't take time in here to talk to You and listen quietly for Your voice, praying, reading, studying, and meditating in Your Word, I'm kidding myself if I think I'll do it when I get out.

And if I think I'll start going to church when I get out when I'm not faithful in jail services except when the speaker I like is there or when they're showing a movie, I'm also deceived about my own heart. Because your Word says a person who fills his needs with things other than You, including "the cares and riches and pleasures of this life," doesn't need You or your spiritual blessings. But those who are hungry and thirsty spiritually and emotionally will be nourished even with what tastes "bitter" (Prv 27:7; Is 41:17; 55:1–2; Mt 5:6; Lk 8:14).

So Lord, I confess I've been wasting a lot of time in jail with things that keep me occupied and satisfied, but not with You. I'm beginning to see now why I may not be ready for freedom. If I'm not using the time I have responsibly, what makes me think I'll change if I get my freedom? Maybe that's my whole problem: I haven't taken responsibility for my life, my time, my relationships, the opportunities I've had, the abilities You've given me, the resources I had at my disposal, and the grace You gave me when I was free to run with it for Your glory (Rom 12:3; Eph 4:7).

Well that settles it. I mean this with all my heart; please do *not* let me have what my flesh wants. Eternity is forever, and I can't afford to get my way for a few brief years that flit by in seconds on Your clock. So please, Father, You know what's best for me. Keep me here or any other correctional facility as long as You know I need to stay. Be as hard on me as You know it will take to break me and truly hold my attention until it becomes my *lifestyle* and my *heart* is really in it – in You! (Prv 15:31).

I turn the judge, the state, and my legal help over to You. If the *king's* heart is in your hand and You turn it wherever You will, then the judge and anybody who can decide the outcome of my life is also in Your hands, so I hereby give You total permission to turn them any way You choose for one single purpose: whatever it takes to accomplish Your perfect will in my life! (Prv 21:1; Mt 6:10; Phil 2:13).

Not only that, but help me, *please help me*, to begin giving You thanks and praise in everything You allow – good and bad – as a result of Your chastening and correction. Because I truly don't want to waste any more time going around the same vicious circle, repeating the same unlearned lessons until everybody knows I'm hopeless and will never change (1 Thes 5:18; Heb 13:15).

I refuse that verdict; by Your grace I *shall* change, and to prove it I'm *embracing* the cross and the yoke You have attempted to put on me as a training instrument. I thank you for correctional officers who don't treat me with the respect I think I deserve, for family members who may never understand me and no longer trust me, for the people who have rejected or abused me, for police officers and anyone else in the legal system who have hurt me in any way, physically, emotionally, legally, or through racial prejudice. Because I *know* You allow all these things to test me, break me, humble me, strengthen me spiritually, and conform me to Your Image, the way You created us (Ps 66:12; Mt 11:29; Lk 9:23).

Help me memorize and really believe Psalm 66:11 and 12: "You brought us into the net; You laid affliction on our backs. You have caused men to ride over our heads; we went through fire and through water; but You brought us out to rich fulfillment."

Help me to never again complain about jail conditions: the food, my roomies, neglect by staff in any department, including medical, property, classification, programs, visitation, chapel, public defenders, and any and everything else You allow to help me bring my flesh under the rod of Your correction and Your shepherd's staff (Ps 23; Prv 22:15; 23:13; Is 10:5).

Help me not only to not complain, but to actually get excited that You love me enough to allow these things. Don't stop until I genuinely get in the habit of responding with *joy* and even *laughter* at absolutely *everything* that used to bother me or give me a bad attitude. Because even if Satan himself is involved in trying to destroy me, my greatest weapon against him and his demons is not anxiety but praise and worship (Eph 5:20; Phil 4:6; Col 3:17; Job 1:21; Ps 34:1; 149:1–9).

Please, my faithful Father, my loving, caring Shepherd, fill me with this vision and heart until it changes my whole outlook on life: because that's my whole problem. Everything has revolved around me and what I want and what I think I deserve and my rights, so no wonder I keep ending up on the wrong side of the law and things go from bad to worse.

Wow! To think the cure could be so simple! Maybe I don't need a drug program or anger management, but if there's one that You know will truly help me, then I ask You to open the door to it. So until then, I'll honestly admit the one thing I've needed most is a change in my *attitude!* (Phil 2:5–8).

You, my Lord and King, are my consuming passion, my whole delight! I *know that I know* that from now on, I'm moving and having my being in You, regardless of what happens and where You allow me to end up. I'm no longer the wimp, trying to prop up my ego with childish masks of pride and things I say to impress others, hiding my fears and insecurity (Ps 37:4; Song 2:3; Is 58:11; Acts 17:28; Heb 4:12–13; 1 Pet 1:8).

I'm Your humble servant, Your child, heir of heavenly glory, not earthly "fools gold." I'm signing up for "Olympic training," confident You have the very best trainers lined up for me, with top-of-the-line "gym equipment." I know You'll give me the grace to endure the training and won't put on me more than I can handle (Heb 12:11–14; 1 Cor 10:12–14; Jas 1:2–4; 1 Pet 4:1–2).

Father, I love You; I feel closer to You more than ever, now that I've turned everything over to You. What a huge burden lifted! Yipee! It's a win-win for both of us – *and for everybody around me!* I can't wait to see what You're going to do next. You've got my attention!

*****

Inmate prayer when you're virtually innocent

Dear Father, it is so comforting to realize the One who holds the whole universe together, from the biggest galaxies to the tiniest part of an atom is the One who knows the exact truth in my case. As long as You know, it's enough for me (Psa 37:24; 139:1–18; Is 41:10; Col 1:16–17; Heb 1:2–3).

Lord, I'd rather be in the center of Your tender mercies and in the spotlight of Your grace even here in jail, than anywhere else without You. I feel so honored that You would count me worthy to be included among the many millions who have suffered unjustly (Acts 5:41; 1 Tim 1:4–5; 1 Pet 2:19–21; 4:12–13).

Thank You for what You did for Job when You allowed Satan to all but kill him. For his pain brought to the surface long buried attitudes he had no idea had been hidden there. When they came to the Light, You enabled him to deal with them, giving him – and us – the whole secret of Your ways: That hardship and suffering mellow us, dealing with self-righteousness, allowing us to feel the pain and human weakness of others instead of judging them wrongly. And through your dreaded total silence in our lowest pit, we learn to trust You like we never would have otherwise (Job 1–2, 33, 38–42; Prv 3:5; Ps 40:1–2; Is 50:10).

I realize now that this is how You prepare us for our purpose and destiny, equipping us to share dominion with You in the ages to come. When You seem to abandon us to affliction, injustice, and abuse when we've walked in obedience, serving You faithfully, the darkness is never meant to destroy us, but to wean us from all the other things that keep us from knowing You intimately (Phil 3:10).

I think of the betrayal of Joseph by his brothers, then by his master's wife. If he'd turned bitter, he would have lost the greatest opportunity of his life. For he turned his thirteen years of slavery and prison into a "university degree" that qualified him as the head of Egypt under Pharaoh (Gen 37–41; Ps 105:16–22).

It thrills me to know that through the betrayal, harshness, and injustice of what others put us through, You make us "more than conquerors," enabling us to handle any situation, not with fear, anger, or arrogance, but with wisdom, faith, patience, and love. Help me forgive as Joseph forgave his brothers, which enabled You to use him to transform them into real men of God (Gen 45:5; 50:20).

For there are so many around me in this jail who have the same potential, but who are full of anger and bitterness. Some need encouragement, while others need to be broken, they are so hard. And here I am, tempted to be anxious about myself, but should be willing and ready to be Your agent here however You need to use me (Ps 119:71; Prv 11:30; Lk 12:42–44; Rom 8:28).

For after the horrible injustice You exposed Joseph to, You transformed the very brother who sold him into slavery – Judah

– from a low-life who avoided responsibility and almost burned his own daughter-in-law to death for his own sin of lust. Yet, You made him into exactly the man you intended from the beginning to fulfill Your highest purpose: a representative of Your mercy and grace, a "royal priest," an example, a prototype, of Your future heirs who will rule and reign with You (Gen 37–38, 42–44).

My flesh recoils at the thought that we're made perfect through suffering. I don't like the idea and wish there were some other way. Actually, I felt there was a better way: I had this inner hunch, somehow, that I should be in church. But church was a form of suffering I didn't want – boring sermons, hypocrites, asking for money, fashion show, and no love in a place where "God is love," supposedly. And since I was free to do what I wanted to do, I opted out and did other things in place of "wasting time" in church (Eph 1:22–23; 2:21–22; 3:17–19; 4:11–16; 5:30–32; Heb 10:25).

Now I understand why suffering makes us perfect: the hardships bring these attitudes to the surface where we can see them for what they are instead of blaming everybody else for *their* attitude. But I realize affliction is not enough unless we take our issues to You, humble ourselves, see things and people from Your viewpoint through Your Word, and learn to trust the Holy Spirit for cleansing and a renewed mind (Rom 5:3–5; Heb 2:10; 5:8-9).

But that takes *time*. I didn't take time on the outside, so now, even though I've done nothing to deserve being here, You in Your mercy, have given me plenty of it. Time to finally dig deeply into Your Word, time to meditate in it, to soak in Your presence, and to actually experience changes taking place deep inside (Ps 1).

I see now what I could have gotten on the outside had I taken the opportunity and the time. But You said we should forget the past and look ahead, so I'm doing just that. It is so awesome to have my understanding enlightened so I can see my situation not as a loss, but a priceless *gain:* something I would *never* have gotten for myself without this push. Truly, whom You love, You chasten in order to purify and make whole

(Phil 3:7–15; Heb 12:5–17).

I hope I retain this knowledge deep in my heart and make it my permanent lifestyle. Because I see from scripture, especially Paul's writings, that humans need a balance of good times and hard times in order to maintain our strength and focus on You (Eccl 3:1–11; 9:11; 2 Cor 4:7–18; 12:7–10; 2 Tim 2:3).

From reading the Old Testament I notice that whenever things got too easy, your people seemed to forget You. So You'd release another enemy to afflict them and they'd turn to You. From even Moses to David and Solomon to all the kings, it seems no human has the ability to maintain a close walk with You without some kind of pressure to keep us there (Deut 8:10–20; Jgs 3–4; 2 Sam 11–12; 1 Kgs 11:1ff; 13:1ff; 2 Chr 16:7–12; 18:1; 19:2; chaps 24–27; 32:25; 35:20–25; Prv 29:23; Dan 4:30–37; Lk 14:11; 18:14; Acts 12:23; 2 Cor 12:7–10; Jas 4:6–10).

No wonder it becomes a way of life in the New Testament – persecution, beatings, prison, and in the end, martyrdom! Yet in all these things they glorified You and *gloried* in their affliction. They fully understood the deep connection between suffering and purity (Acts 14:22; Rom 8:35–39; 2 Cor 4:7–18; Heb 11; 1 Pet 4:1–4, 12–16).

I know Daniel is one of Your favorites. He walked very close to You, even though he governed right under Nebuchadnezzar of Babylon and then under Darius of Medo-Persia. And if he didn't handle things through Your guidance and wisdom, he could easily end up in a fiery furnace, as his three friends did. Yet they obviously were led by Your Spirit, for they survived unharmed and accompanied by their Friend – Your Son! When Daniel also stood up for truth, he ended up in a lions' den. I can't wait to talk to him about this experience when I get there. Heaven, that is (Ez 14:14, 20; Dan 1–5; 6; 9:23; 1 Cor 13:5–6).

So Father, I thank You a thousand times for this rare privilege. How many people get to go to jail or prison for no legal reason and experience the loss of reputation and mental abuse that follows, toughening them up on the inside like steel? Nobody would dare chose this form of training, though it's worth far more than a Harvard PhD. Because they can train the mind, but not the heart and spirit. I would never have chosen this crazy "education," much less pay several hundred thousand for it, which is probably what a Harvard doctorate costs now (Acts 5:41; 2 Tim 1:5).

To think, You have made me your true *friend* through this ordeal, like Abraham! It's more than I ever dreamed. My whole outlook toward people has changed from seeing them through the eyes of my insecurities, needs, and attempts to control and manipulate them. It has taken this experience to understand how under bondage, how miserable and anxious I was, living under the illusion that everybody else needed to change except me (Rom 2:10–20).

Now I see people as no different than I am, and how we all need encouragement and support and prayer. And the meanest ones are actually the *most* insecure. This is now my greatest challenge: To allow You to use me to penetrate some of the stony hearts around me who have deep needs inside, who may shed tears in the night or wish they could, and think – or *know* – nobody cares, or if they did, what could they do? Who wish they'd never been born, yet dread the thought of death, or even "long for death," as Job did (Job 3; Ps 88; Lam 3:1–42; 2 Cor 1:4; Heb 5:2).

Here I am – immersed right inside the neediest mission field in America. All because of Your grace. I can't thank You enough! All I ask, my Dear Father, is that You keep training and breaking me until You can use me to see major breakthroughs spiritually among those around me. Because some of them have incredible potential to be giants in the Spirit – if only they can behold Your love as You've shown me (Jn 17; Eph 3:17–19; Phil 1:6; 1 Jn 4:7–8).

So, however long You keep me here, my times are in *Your* hands, not mine, not the state's, not the devil's. I'm Yours, Your property, Your temple, Your little missionary here in the Lions' Den with Jesus. Thank You, thank You, thank You! (Job 38; Ps 22:1–22; 31:15; Prv 16:7–9; Eph 1:1–23; Phil 2:12–14).

CHAPTER 14

An open Letter to Inmates on Death Row

In 2003 on Death Row at a state correctional facility after a time of fellowship with my friend Edward (not his real name), I walked down an aisle in front of a row of barred cells eager to rap with anyone who would listen. Before that experience I had imagined that Death Row must be the greatest place in the US to minister to hurting men facing death. What a shock I received to find it was far from that.

I found four types of inmates there. First, the one so hardened against religion he despises anyone attempting to talk about it. Second are those who love to talk religion. They know the Bible in and out and can address any biblical question at length, and some are expert on other religions as well. Third are those who challenge the "system," especially the death penalty. They write letters to politicians and the media. And fourth, those who are honest with themselves and others.

I found only one to be the latter type – Edward. The rest seemed divided among the other three. So I have a brief word for you if you are honest enough to see yourself in one of these categories (or can tell me of one I missed).

1. Don't-talk-to-me-about-God type

To the first, those who despise religion, perhaps I understand you best, because I was there once. Eventually I gained enough understanding to realize the real God was far deeper and more real than I'd ever imagined, and it is this God who works relentlessly to break down our religious and other masks to get us to be real. It is why He "hides Himself" and why it's the "glory of God to hide a matter, but the glory of kings is to search out a matter" (Job 23:9; Prv 25:2; Is 8:17; 45:15).

He doesn't want us to find Him in a superficial way, even at the risk of all the apparent contradictions, offenses, and tragic, heart-breaking situations around us. These lead most of us to give up or settle for a cheap substitute (intellectualism, religion, philosophy, rebellion, reckless living, etc.) before we find Him in reality and learn to know Him intimately (Phil. 3:10).

But one thing for sure: when you find Him and get to know Him intimately, He is everything you always wanted Him to be, and satisfies every reason you rejected the phony. *How sadly ironic that many of those who despise "religion" have the potential to be the most genuine and real men and women of God around!* (1 Tim 1:13).

2. **Dr. Theology**

To the second, those who love to talk religion, I'm not sure if I have anything to say. I should understand you more than anybody because I was exactly that longer than I was an atheist, and maybe that's the reason I don't have the heart to tell you anything. I know how futile it was for even God to get past this hard exterior based on years of knowledge about God without knowing Him personally.

These are the only people Jesus severely condemned – a whole chapter (Matthew 23), not because He hated them, but because he made one last attempt to rip off their religious masks before they crucified Him.

It took my going nearly insane with depression, anger, and rage before I finally became willing to give up all my "spiritual" knowledge in order to have a one-on-One, intimate relationship with Jesus.

But because I know you have it fairly comfortable (from what I observed), you will probably never come to a place of desperation where you "seek Him with all your heart" as in Jeremiah 29:13.

Furthermore, with nothing to do but read or watch TV, I would imagine it's almost impossible to resist basking continuously in this form of sheer pleasure, this "idolatry of the mind." It certainly would be my greatest temptation, except that I've tasted of the Real Thing and hope I wouldn't settle for anything less.

Yet, who knows what God will do in your life? Nothing is impossible for Him. My only suggestion is to think about the opportunity available to you and *beg* God relentlessly to break that shell and get through to you at any cost! Your life will be heaven on earth! (Job 42:2; Jer 32:17; Mk 10:27; Lk 1:37; Eph 2:4–10).

3. **Jailhouse Politician**

To the third, the politicians and legal experts, I'm not sure what to say, because that also is a form of religion, like a drug dulling your real need for relationship. My only hope is that you will sense there is infinitely more than winning a legal or political battle, and that you'll find out true freedom has nothing to do with incarceration or laws, justice or injustice.

All the men of God in the Bible became that way through the injustices, contradictions, hatred, and abuse of mankind. One obvious case was Joseph, who was sold into slavery by his brothers, then thrown into a dungeon on a false rape charge. If he had fought "the system" politically or legally, he would be lost among the countless others who lived that lifestyle without ever finding their true purpose.

But because he refused to get sidetracked with resentment, God used him not only to save the entire Middle East during seven years of famine, but to restore his hard-headed, dysfunctional, renegade brothers into the heads of the twelve tribes of Israel (Genesis 37–45).

The apostle Paul used the Roman privilege of legal appeal, not to avoid incarceration, but to avoid assassination by the Jews who wanted to kill him. And once and probably two more times he allowed the Romans to beat him illegally without a trial (Acts 16:37; 21:31ff; 22:25–28; 23:12ff; 25:9–11; 28:17–19, 2 Cor. 11:25).

He ended up on death row, but as he wrote letters of encouragement to churches from those miserable and crude Roman prisons he never complained about his condition or the death penalty and accepted his imminent death with deep joy and anticipation (2 Cor 11:23; 2 Tim 4:6–8).

And most significantly, he never spoke disrespectfully of a single Roman official, including Caesar Nero, who ranks as one of the most perverse and wicked kings who ever lived and who finally removed Paul's head.[1] Furthermore Paul warned his readers to submit to the governing authorities because they are "appointed by God," and those who resist "will bring judgment on themselves" (Rom 13:1–7; also Titus 3:1; 1 Pet 2:13; 2 Pet 2:10–11; Jude 1:8).

No wonder Paul's example influenced "the whole palace guard" and won some "in Caesar's household" to Christ. His letters from prison (Ephesians, Philippians, Colossians, 2 Timothy, Philemon) encouraged and strengthened those on the outside who seemed to be free but in reality were bound by fear and ignorance and the inner issues stemming from them (Phil 1:13; 4:22).

If those of you gifted with intelligence and communication skills will find your real purpose in life, what a blessing you can become to those around you, and perhaps even to those of us on the outside. It was Paul's "prison epistles," especially Ephesians, Philippians, and Colossians, that are among the richest sources of understanding God's ways in the New Testament, and in some ways, the whole Bible.

4. **Mr. Open-heart**

And finally, to that rare breed of those who are still real and transparent, I plead with you to "guard your heart with all diligence, for out of it are the issues of life" (Prv 4:23).

Edward was the only one I felt was real during the time when I was there, but that may be simply because he was new and hadn't yet succumbed to the dull routine of endless time which tempts men to fill it with such empty pursuits. Will the same thing happen to him? Will he also become a Bible expert, impressing everyone around him with his wealth of scriptural truth, but empty of the genuine presence and glory of God?

Like a beautiful car no longer used for driving, but merely a museum piece for admiring. Like the fifty-year time-capsuled 1957 Plymouth they brought up from its "sealed" burial in 2007: it had rusted completely, everywhere! [2]

That must be the irony of Death Row – that in the very place where men could find ultimate Reality, especially in preparation for departure into eternity, their spiritual senses slowly leach away, leaving them only "rusted" empty shells of human beings without purpose and unprepared to meet "the Judge of all the earth" (Gen 18:25).

I hope this letter will serve to alert at least one person to this awful tragedy – a spiritual death before the physical one – and bring him to a place of determination to get real with life, with people, and with God.

Your friend, Victor

1. Nero is designated by the title "Augustus" in Acts 25:21, 25
2. (http://dailynewsdig.com/time-capsule-disaster-recovery-in-oklahoma/)

CHAPTER 15

The Time Machine: Good News for Bad Girls

I originally wrote this for juvenile girls, who pay a much bigger and earlier price for the irresponsible "use" of their delicate bodies. Guys can survive until they're old men, with babies' mamas scattered everywhere trying to raise their kids and grandkids while the dads are still going strong and laughing about their wild oats. That's why I haven't gotten around yet to writing a matching article for the boys, unless they can relate to the ones in this book.

But I trust this article will be a wake-up call to the men who participate in the breakdown of families and the mothers and children left without responsible husbands and dads. And some of you were those children whose "needs" have driven you to repeat the cycle. So you probably understand the pain – if you'll take time to *feel it!*

After reading this, if you have a daughter or know of someone else who might find help through this article, it's available on my website: *www.heartsup.org*. If she (or he) is in jail or prison, please have someone on the outside mail her a printed copy.

And now to the "bad girls" about to read this:

What you are about to read may offend you, anger you, discourage you, or depress you. But please read it all, for this is a message of hope and redemption, no matter where and in what stage your life is in now – even if you're too old and it's totally impossible for "a time machine" to give you a new beginning. For God actually specializes in restoring lost years and ruined lives, as you'll see toward the end of this article.

Too late, and now look!

Here you are, no longer a young, sexy teenager with a list of cool dudes wanting to crawl in bed with you. And you can't believe you actually wanted to get pregnant, more than once!

Those cute little tykes gave you somebody to love and live for. Plus they guaranteed you some kind of income – from the state or your boyfriend, as long as he stayed out of jail. You hoped.

What do you have now to show for what you thought was love and fun back then? You're only thirty-six, but you look fifty and feel older. A lot older.

Where are your old boyfriends now, and your babies' daddies? One's in prison, another is cheating on his nine or tenth live-in girlfriend, like he did with you. And one actually became a Christian, married his woman, and goes to church with their kids.

He tried to talk you into giving your life to Jesus, but you weren't ready yet. You've been saying that for years, but your heart is getting harder all the time.

Back then it was because you were having too much fun. Now it's because you feel you're too far gone; it's too late to change. And that nagging sense of guilt has hardened into a ball and chain around your neck making you meaner and harder to get along with than ever.

As a young teen you tried drugs and smoked cigarettes and pot because it was cool and you wanted to "fit in." Now you're addicted to prescription drugs to keep from going crazy. And you tried to quit smoking a thousand times and finally gave up, even though it's ruining your health and drains what little you get from welfare, especially since one pack now costs four times the cost of a gallon of milk, which you couldn't afford without food stamps.

Then you found out smoking destroys brain circuits and lowers your IQ. No wonder you're losing your mind! No wonder you can't do anything right anymore, like handling your bratty kids.

They fight with you just like you fought with your mom. You feel guilty when you don't bail them out of jail because you don't have the money or don't think they need to be out; but then you hate yourself and can't stand them when you do get them out.

And most of the time they don't even thank you, because they think you owe it to them for making them that way!

You tried too many times to warn them about doing what you did, but they laugh and ask why *you're* still doing such stupid stuff.

Like hanging out with one dead-beat after another, because you still can't live without feeling somebody loves or needs you – even though you know they need you only for sex and a place to stay!

Driven by shame and low self-esteem, you'll take anybody you can get, and just hope he'll help out with the bills. But that rarely happens, because half the time he's smoking weed or is on drugs or alcohol and always has his "reasons" why he can't afford to help. And you wonder if one of his "reasons" is another girlfriend he's *using*. Because you *know* him too well!

The few who do have a little income have to send child-support to someone else who's better off than you are. *If only I'd gotten pregnant by the one who's a Christian now*, you think. *He's got a good job and probably pays his bills on time, including honest child support! How'd I get so unlucky?*

Once you dreamed of living in your own home with a happy family. Now it's ridiculous to dream anymore. You'd heard that teens who get pregnant end up living in poverty, but you knew some who made out okay and thought you'd be like them.

But too many things went wrong. Now you're living in government housing. Drugs are everywhere. Somebody got shot dead a few doors away just a week ago. You alternate between fear for your life and wishing you'd get shot too. Hell couldn't be any worse.

At least you don't have to pay for your medication, but it barely keeps your STD's under control. And you live in fear of another cancer, like the one that cost you a hysterectomy.

You've got a lump in your breast but keep putting off telling the doctor either because you don't care anymore, or because you dread losing what still might attract those losers who only want that one thing.

You lived for the day you could finally be real friends with your mom, but when you couldn't pay her back for that loan for your son's lawyer, she hasn't spoken to you since. And he's back in jail on another charge, and now *you* won't speak to *him* even though he's all mushy and gushy about asking you to forgive him. As if you haven't heard that line before.

And you watch helplessly while your girls do exactly the same stuff you did and take your warnings as nagging and screaming, accusing you of driving them out of the house and blaming you when they get into trouble! Unless they're sweet-talking you to get them out of it.

The state "programs" they've been to give you a little relief for a few months, but when they're back home, they act even more arrogant. They're getting out of control, but what can you say when you act the same way toward them?

And now the oldest is bringing her drug-addict boyfriend home with her, expecting you to feed him and let him stay! And you think he might have AIDS or hepatitis, but it might be the drugs. Which means she must be into drugs too, and no-telling what else!

No wonder things have been disappearing around the house lately and you never seem to have the money you thought you had, what little it is.

When it can't get any worse, it does! Your baby girl is pregnant and thinks you don't know, but she can't fool you through all her lies. There's a lot of other stuff you're pretty sure is going on, but if you accuse her she'll explode, then *you'll* blow up and have her back in juvy. And more guilt.

Because you know you did the same with your mom again and again. Now you're reaping the wild oats you sowed, just like they read out of the Bible during the few Bible studies you attended in jail (Galatians 6:7–8).

How you'd give *anything* to go back to when you were young and free, this time to think like a responsible adult and make mature decisions instead of acting like the reckless, dumb teenager you were!

God, is there any hope? you ask. *Is this the way my life is going to end, only to yet end up in hell when I die?*

What would you do differently?

I'll let you think awhile: do some deep, heart-searching about the "what ifs" – what you would do differently if you had a second chance, which God longs to give you if you'll take it!

What if I had a mom and dad like some of the other kids had, parents who showed respect and love to their kids?

But no, I can't go there. First, because that's an excuse, failure to take the blame myself. And second, some of the friends who got me into trouble were from good families with a mom and dad.

So maybe it was the friends I hung with. I knew the clean-cut smart kids kept their distance from me. And no wonder, with my gutter language: F-this *and* M-F-that. *Filthy, sexual language. I just fell in with my kind – the sewage plant of the city.*

If I'd known it would mold my character into such a low-life, would I or could I have done anything about it?

Of course I would have, but how could I have ever predicted such a horrible outcome? Yet if I could have seen a clear picture, a 3-D video of what I'm going through now . . . yes, I would have done absolutely anything to change direction.

Like what? What could I have done about my bad friends? Where could I have gone to find friends who'd be good role-models for me? Mom never went to church and certainly never expected me to go.

It would have been almost impossible to suddenly leave my old friends and start going to church to find better friends. Besides, they wouldn't have accepted me.

Yet, wow, if simply choosing better friends could have changed my entire future, then, yes. I would have done whatever it took to find some church and someone in that church who would accept me and help me change.

I would have asked the pastor or youth leader or some caring woman for help. I wouldn't give up until I found somebody to be my friend who could influence me the right way and keep after me.

But there I go again, putting the responsibility on someone else. Yes, I'd have to be the one to keep after myself and never give up. That is, if I could have known how much it would change my future and save me from this hell.

Then there's another thing I would do differently. I'd change my attitude toward sex. Now I don't get pleasure out of it any more. I feel used because I am *used – a worn out, bacteria and virus-infested body for lust-driven men to find release on. Of course they deserve the sex diseases I have. I got 'em from them in the first place.*

How could anything that once seemed so beautiful and loving end up so disgusting and repulsive?

But could anything have stopped me from something all my friends were doing? Could I have stood my ground against the social pressure? Could I have said no to my boyfriends, knowing they'd simply go to another prettier girl and get what they wanted?

Never in a million years. Unless, that is, I could have seen clearly what it would lead to – a wasted body, ruined emotions, no ability to feel the deep joys of intimacy, a heart and mind filled with the torture of resentment, bitterness, hatred, anger, and depression. And broken relationships damaged beyond repair. Emptiness. O God, such lonely emptiness!

Yes, if I had a second chance, I would absolutely stand my ground, look my friends in the eye, and almost shout, No way! Go ruin somebody else's life, not mine!

Or better yet, because I know I still might cave in, remove myself entirely from their influence. At any rate, I would make sexual abstinence a huge priority, top of the list. I would carefully save my precious young feminine body for one man who would marry me and stick with me for life.

Wow! To think there are marriages still like that. Do they realize what they have? It has to be worth more than anything in the world – more than winning the lottery a thousand times over.

Yes . . . no doubt! That's what I would do if I had another chance. But there's no way that could ever happen. I forget, I'm old and beat down to a worthless rag loved by absolutely nobody – not my mother (why can't she forgive me?) or my kids (may they get what they deserve!).

But there's something else I would change that would make a major, major difference, I think. I would change the kind of music and rap I listened to. I thought it was so cool back then. It fed my lust for evil and pagan, and justified my rebellion against the police and the government and my mom and tradition.

I thought it didn't affect me at the time, but over enough time I turned into what I listened to – a hateful, evil, bitter person with a rotten attitude toward everybody good.

The very people I needed, the people who could have led me right, school teachers, church folks, even the correction I needed from law enforcement officers, I hated, until that hatred drove me away from good people right into the arms of Satan himself.

But that was not all. I fed on movies and TV programs the Christians called trash – murder, rape, horror, sex, and laced throughout with the filthy language I now speak without giving it a second thought.

When I wasn't bathing my brain in sewage, I was on my phone, contaminating my friends with my filthy mouth and feeding on their garbage and more from the Web.

No, it's not surprising I am where I'm at now. I lived – ate, slept, drank – a lifestyle more like hell than heaven. What did I expect? Duh!

But of course I dared anybody to stop me. I laughed at jail volunteers or Christian COs who quoted verses about loving not the world and renewing our mind with the Bible and Christian music.

O God . . . what I would give now to have the kind of peace and happiness I remember them having. I never dreamed my lifestyle would have betrayed me like this. I thought it was so cool back then; it made me feel important, sometimes invincible, like nothing could touch me!

Yes, if changing what I fed into my mind could have changed my attitude and outlook on life and toward others, I would have done it in a heartbeat – whatever it cost, whatever the trouble. I'd pursue a clean lifestyle with every atom of my being – if only I could have known. If only!

The rest of it – alcohol, drugs, partying all night, sex-orgies, smoking pot with my friends because we couldn't stand anybody telling us it was a "drug" and not a God-created plant for "medicine" and a mind-enhancer – it makes me sick to think I was so deceived, so lied to.

Half or more of those friends are dead now, some from drugs, some from criminal activity that backfired, literally, and some from bodies ruined by misuse and abuse – cancer, heart failure, disease.

And heartbreak. Yes, friends I'm sure who died of a broken heart – rejected by their mates, parents, children, and most of their friends.

I used to cry myself to sleep. Now I have no tears left. So pills put me to sleep, and pills help me get up and cope and deaden some of the pain. Some of it. Not all. Not all by a long shot.

A second chance? I wish. But it's no use wishing. It's too late.

The time machine

No it's not too late. In *real time* you're a teenager – young, still fairly healthy, and still capable of finding true happiness. You've made some bad choices, but it's not too late to make the good choices you wished you would have made. But you left out the main ingredient in your wish list: God's Son, Jesus Christ.

You probably couldn't change if you tried, and God knows you can't without His help. Because what He did for you through Jesus is enough to not only change your life from inside out, but fill you with joy in circumstances that would normally be depressing and hopeless (Romans 15:13; Galatians 5:20; 1 Peter 1:8; 1 John 1:4).

Of course you saw this when you compared your life with happy people. But many are happy because they live in a happy family surrounded by love. But God wants to fill you with joy right where you are so you can become a channel of His joy for others around you.

Because then your happiness is not dependent on getting what you want or being who you wish you were, but simply on knowing Jesus, who has your whole life planned out and invites you to begin to *enjoy* it (Psalm 139; Luke 12:22–32).

His love and power reach out to those who truly want to change, who are *broken* by sin and rebellion, who come to the end of themselves. Jesus told about the "prodigal son" who blew his inheritance on booze and women and ended up deserted, homeless, penniless, and starving. But it took this before he could appreciate what he'd walked away from for what he thought would be fun and pleasure (Luke 15:11–32).

God can use your failures and hopeless circumstances when they bring you to the end and you finally realize what *truth* is and what you really need, for *"the truth shall make you free"* (Jn 89:35).

And He has already prepared a "banquet" of joy and fellowship just waiting for you, like that bad son's father did for him. God sent Jesus, not just to die for you, but to go through the trials of real humanity and suffer abuse and rejection more than any human being, all for one purpose: to truly understand what you are going through so He can effectively convince His Father to give you mercy and turn your life around (Luke 14:16–24; 2 Corinthians 5:21; Philippians 2:5–8; Hebrews 2:14–18; 5:1–9).

He died as a criminal, as the worst sinner who ever lived, even though He'd never sinned. The sins He was punished for were *your* sins and mine. We've all sinned in some way, even good people (Romans 3:23; 4:25; Galatians 3:13; 1 Peter 2:24).

Sin is like driving the wrong way on a busy highway. Sin is breaking spiritual laws, which is more deadly than breaking physical laws, because you may end up in hell, not just dead (Proverbs 1:24–33; Galatians 5:16–23).

When you ask God to forgive you for going the wrong way (sin), you invite Him in and give him the driver's seat of your life. He'll not only steer you back in the right direction, He'll fill the deep emptiness that made you *want* to sin (Romans 8:1–4; Psalm 40:8; Jeremiah 31:33; Hebrews 8:10; 10:16).

The joy and pleasure you get from knowing Him makes doing the right things more fun than doing bad things. You find it's more fun to love and be kind to your worst enemies than it is to resent or hate them or try to get even with them. Because the Holy Spirit helps you *understand* them (Matthew 5:44–45; Romans 6:22; Galatians 5:22; Psalm 40:8).

Even giving up a sinful pleasure like unmarried sex can fill you with joy when you know your body belongs to God, who will take better care of it than you can, and give you better and deeper pleasure than sex. Or make married sex what it's supposed to be – the uniting of husband and wife into *one* intimate union, where the pleasure goes deeper than physical and emotional (Proverbs 5:18–19; Matthew 19:3–6; Ephesians 5:31–32).

This is how people change from being extremely wicked to awesome men and women of God with glowing, powerful testimonies. They find God's love to be far more powerful and pleasurable than anything sin offered (John 3:16; Romans 11:30–36; 1 Corinthians 2:9; 1 John 4:10).

So now you have a choice: there's a very slim chance, maybe a thousand to one, that if you continue in a sinful lifestyle you will turn to God before it's too late. But even if the odds are in your favor, you still have the rest of your life to live out the results of abusing your family, your body, your relationships, your employment history, and the record that comes up on a background check when you need a job or a place to live.

But reaping what we sowed is part of the healing and restoring process. Suffering humbles and changes us. But the sooner we repent and come to God, the more pain we save ourselves in the recovery years. Just look at what King David suffered for his sin, long after he repented and God forgave him (2 Samuel 11–19; Psalm 32, 38, 51).

Of course God gives you this joy even in your suffering, and many will come to Him only through this long, painful path.

My wife's mother is an invalid and watches Christian TV all day in our living room. When I pass through I hear anything from preaching to *The Lone Ranger* (a 1950s cowboy TV series).

But what stops me in my tracks is when I hear the testimony of a woman radiating love and beauty, who once was a prostitute and drug-addict, driven to the streets by bitterness and anger from sexual or physical abuse by a relative or mate. A wasted street tramp.

When it seemed all hope was lost, bodies ruined, brains fried, given up by professionals, and abandoned by family and friends, they fell in brokenness at the feet of Jesus and He began to restore them.

It's almost impossible to believe some of their stories when I see who they are now and how God is using them to minister to others. For they more deeply understand their pain than those who never fell (2 Corinthians 1:4).[1]

I remember one addicted mother who began dealing drugs to support her habit, then ended up in prison as an accomplice to a murder. But there she gave her life to Jesus, went on to write a book, and now has an active counseling ministry in prison. You'd think she served in the White House by the look of joy and peace on her face, even though she's deprived of her children.

Two of the most popular speakers in the world, Joyce Meyer and Beth Moore, are products of sexual abuse (Joyce) and drug addiction (Beth). They speak to the *heart* of the hurting and God is using them to restore probably millions.

And He will redeem *your* life from destruction and re-set your life on a collision course with the creative energy of the universe – Christ in *you*, the hope of *glory!* He will make you *more than a conqueror* through *Him who loves you* because of His power working in you. So don't *give up* because you've *messed up* (Romans 5:20; 6:1; Ephesians 1:6–8; 2:1–5; Colossians 1:27; 1 Timothy 1:13–16; James 1:2–4; 5:11).

Whatever you've done so far, it's not too late for your "second chance," made possible by this journey into your future: come to Jesus now while it's still easy, and let Him *make-over* your life (2 Corinthians 5:17).

Don't wait and buy a few short years of fun on credit, then begin making daily installments – pay back – for the rest of your life, and wish "for God's sake" you'd only listened, back when you were young.

Read this verse carefully: "He who did not spare His own Son, but delivered Him up for us all, how shall He not with Him also *freely give us all things*?" (Romans 8:32).

He really will. It's happened to millions; it can – it will! – happen to you.

1. Get the book, *Forever Changed: A Story of God's Transforming Power* – the "true story about how Teresa Kemp's life was destroyed by sexual abuse, drugs, alcohol, and incarceration. Hers was a life broken into pieces, a life without hope. But on July 20th, 1997, at 9:30 in the morning, Teresa had an encounter with Jesus Christ and was touched by the transforming power of God. She would never be the same again because after that day her life would be forever changed." (Available at www.breakingchainsint.org)

Chapter 16

The Blackness of Darkness Forever Don't Let It Happen to You

Fallen angels, their sin, and those who copied it

Peter and Jude use a phrase which magnifies the intense darkness of what may be the lowest part of hell. Jesus' description of hell as "outer darkness" with "weeping and gnashing of teeth" gives only a hint. But Peter and Jude deal with the very origin of evil when they compare it to "the angels who sinned" (Mt 8:12; 22:13; 25:30; 2 Pet 2:4).

What was the nature of their sin? Both Peter and Jude mention it: "And I remind you of the angels who did not stay within the limits of authority God gave them but left the place where they belonged. God has kept them securely chained in prisons of darkness, waiting for the great day of judgment." Peter adds, "cast them down to hell," using the Greek word for Tartarus; according to some, it is "the deepest abyss of Hell."[1] The common words for Hell in the N.T. are *gehenna* and *hades*. Tartarus is used only this once (Jude 1:6 NLT; 2 Pet 2:4).

Isaiah 14:12–15 gives us a clue as to the nature of their rebellion against "the limits of authority God gave them," since they followed Satan. *Envy* is feeling cheated that you don't have what someone else has. Satan was the greatest of God's created beings, but he wanted more. His quest for it is commonly known as "the five I wills of Lucifer," which describe the manner in which he attempted to go beyond the authority God had given him. His final I will was to "be like the Most High" (God). No wonder he tempted Eve with the same lie: "For God knows that in the day you eat of it your eyes will be opened, and you will be like God, knowing good and evil." The first murder (Cain of Abel) occurred also through *envy* (Ez 28:12–19; Gen 3:5; 4:3–8).

But Peter and Jude go on to describe certain people who seem to have identified with this particular class of fallen angels in their rebellion against God. Both writers name three characteristics of their rebellion: greed, lust, and they "reject [and despise] authority, and speak evil of dignitaries." Dignitaries is the translation of the Greek word for "glories," and most likely refers to angelic beings. And in the same passage Jude, referring to the fallen archangel, Satan, says, "Yet Michael the archangel, in contending with the devil, when he disputed about the body of Moses, dared not bring against him a reviling accusation, but said, 'The Lord rebuke you!'" (Jude 1:8–13; 2 Pet 2:10).

Peter and Jude name Balaam as the model for greed, and Jude adds Korah as the prime example of rebellion. His rebellion, through *envy* in Numbers 16, connects very soberly with hell and "the blackness of darkness." For God split the earth under him and the two leaders who followed him. "So they and all those with them went down alive into the pit; the earth closed over them, and they perished from among the assembly. Then all Israel who were around them fled at their cry, for they said, 'Lest the earth swallow us up also!' And a fire came out from the LORD and consumed the two hundred and fifty men who were offering incense" (Num 16:1–35).

Korah and his rebels "rejected" and "despised" Moses and Aaron, who, though they were mere men, were "appointed" and "authorized" by God. And since both Satan and Korah attacked the authority of Moses, it's obvious where Korah got his inspiration (Num 16:3; Jude 1:9).

Digging a little deeper, we find that God stands behind all human authorities, who in turn are influenced, controlled, or protected by angelic beings, whether good or bad (the bad with their demon accomplices). These also answer to God, authorized or permitted by Him, to be used for His purpose (2 Sam 24:1; cf. 1 Chr 21:1). (cf. = compare)

"Let every soul be subject to the governing authorities. For there is no authority except from God, and the authorities that exist are appointed by God. Therefore whoever resists the authority resists the ordinance of God, and those who resist will bring judgment on themselves" (Rom 13:1–2).

"Remind them to be subject to rulers and authorities, to obey, to be ready for every good work, to speak evil of no one, to be peaceable, gentle, showing all humility to all men." Not only that, but honor them and pray for them! And who was "king" when Paul and Peter wrote this? Nero, their executioner! (Tit 3:2; 1 Tim 2:2; 1 Pet 2:13–17)

Is it right or wrong to submit to evil rulers or leaders?
Why would God "appoint" evil rulers manipulated by demonic angels, then tell us to "be subject" (obedient) to them (as long as they don't make us disobey God) or we'll "bring judgment" on ourselves (from God)?

Because He is either chastising or testing us through these earthly rulers, and our *response* is what gives the invisible "rulers of darkness" operating behind them their authorization (permission, right). So that to despise the human ruler God has placed us under is to miss the whole point of why God "appointed" them in the first place.

In other words, we're not "getting the message" God is using them for, and instead, giving in to our rebellion – the very reason God is using them for our correction, and permitting or even enabling demonic power to enforce the authority of the earthly rulers they control. Which explains why many wicked rulers operated under the guidance of witchcraft, like Hitler[2] (1 Kgs 22:20–22; Ez 38:1ff).

Yet it would have been rebellion against God to rebel against Hitler's civil law, which made Germany the greatest industrial nation in Europe. And my dad was proud to be German until Hitler's secret agenda became obvious. Then it was an honor to protect and hide Jews against his tyranny and seek God for wisdom in discerning when it was right to "be subject" to Hitler and when it would otherwise lead to disobedience against God.

The apostles faced this same dilemma when threatened by the religious leaders to not preach any more in Jesus name, answering, "We ought to obey God rather than men" (Acts 5:28–29).

Rather than "despise" these anti-Christian leaders and rebel against their authority in general, they allowed the persecution and beatings to channel their pain into earnest prayer, which on two occasions, literally shook the building with God's power. And no doubt led to the conversion of the chief Jewish "terrorist," Saul, who became the apostle Paul (Acts 4:1–31; 5:40; 9:1–22; 16:18–26).

Because the real battle is not against human rulers, but the spiritual powers operating behind them. And our complaining and bitter attitudes are precisely what give them the authority to continue. "For we do not wrestle against flesh and blood, but against principalities, against powers, against the rulers of the darkness of this age, against spiritual hosts of wickedness in the heavenly places" (Eph 6:12; cf. 2 Cor 10:3–6; Num 14).

Job, a landmark "Supreme Court" case

God is using the people He redeemed from the "fall" to judge the heavenly beings who indirectly caused them (us) to sin in the beginning. That's why God allows them to test and refine us, to purify our hearts and motives so our judgment will reflect His heart and wisdom.

God is so "fair" and "just," He does not consign these evil, rebel angels to their eternal punishment without just cause, and He uses their redeemed victims to show it – a "jury of peers," as it were. "Do you not know that the saints will judge the world? And if the world will be judged by you, are you unworthy to judge the smallest matters? Do you not know that we shall judge angels? How much more, things that pertain to this life? (1 Cor 6:2–3).

But there's much more. The book of Job is a classic study in divine jurisprudence. Satan is minding his own business when God suddenly tells him, "Have you noticed My servant Job? He is the finest man in all the earth. He is blameless – a man of complete integrity. He fears God and stays away from evil." Incredible: a direct invitation to the Tempter, Deceiver, and Destroyer, to put Job through the meat grinder (Job 1:8 NLT).

Sure enough, Satan goes after him with every atom of his evil being, destroying everything he has, then attacking his health, just short of death. Because God put a limit on Satan: "Behold, he is in your hand, but spare his life" (Job 2:8).

But that was only the beginning, the first two of 42 chapters. The next 29 chapters record the intense conflict within Job as three of his closest friends accuse him of having incurred this "judgment" because of his sin. Satan is called "the accuser of our brethren, who accused them before our God day and night," so he is still at work through whom Job now calls "miserable comforters" (Rv 12:10; Zech 3:1–2; Job 16:2).

Satan and his religious helpers have no idea that they are bringing to the surface all that is still "unrefined" in Job's heart. For in chapter 29 Job laments his former days of glory, using the same number of first person pronouns (I, me, my, mine, myself) as in Romans seven (KJV and NASB), where Paul shows how God's holy law cannot make us holy, but can only reveal the "wretched" condition of our "self" (Rom 3:19; 7:12–13; Gal 3:24).

Which is what is happening to Job. For in chapter 30 he lashes out against his friends, saying their fathers don't even measure up to his former sheepdogs. Then, without interruption, he spends chapter 31 enumerating his acts of righteousness, proving indeed what God had said about him: "blameless – a man of complete integrity."

Job has not figured out yet that God is using Satan and his tools to purify him entirely of self-motivation, that his righteousness may stand in God's grace alone. Then Elihu, his fourth friend, begins to speak, pinpointing the cause of his suffering to only one problem: Job has failed to see that God is behind it all, not Job's sin, except for not recognizing God using the affliction to deal with his pride, in order to keep "back his soul from the Pit" (Job 33:17; Eph 2:8–9).

When God finally speaks, displaying His sovereign control over all creation, including the most untamable beasts, a hidden reference to Job's enemies, probably including Satan, Job is humbled completely and God is vindicated: "I have heard of You by the hearing of the ear, but now my eye sees You. Therefore I abhor myself, and repent in dust and ashes" (Job 38–41; 42:5–6).

And Satan, far from breaking the relationship between God and Job through discrediting both (see Job 1:9–11), has only justified God in condemning him to his ultimate doom in hell.

Now Job is spiritually equipped to fulfill his purpose: to pray for his "friends" with genuine love and understanding, knowing he is no different aside from God's grace. "And the LORD restored Job's losses when he prayed for his friends. Indeed the LORD gave Job twice as much as he had before" (42:7–17).

This masterpiece of God's wisdom is an example of Ephesians 3:10, "God's purpose in all this was to use the church to display His wisdom in its rich variety to all the unseen rulers and authorities in the heavenly places" (NLT).

Read Job 28, where a mine with jewels is used as a metaphor to show the mystery of where wisdom is found and what it is. Then read Proverbs 8, an entire chapter on the purpose and value of wisdom. "By me kings reign, and rulers decree justice. By me princes rule, and nobles, all the judges of the earth. I love those who love me, and those who seek me diligently will find me" (8:15–17). So God used Satan to prepare Job for spiritual rulership, which began when he prayed for his friends (1 Jn 5:16).

Spiritual warfare is a legal battle.

Colossians 1:16–18 gives us a picture of God's administrative hierarchy. I see it in three parts: verse 16 describes His invisible creation, the spiritual realm: "thrones or dominions or principalities or powers," and a hint of His purpose – "all things were created through Him and for Him"; verse 17 reveals the mystery behind the cohesive unity of the universe: "and He is before all things, and in Him all things consist [hold together]"; and verse 18 tells *how* He holds it together: "and He is the head of the body, the church, who is the beginning, the firstborn from the dead, that in all things He may have the preeminence," referring to v. 16, "through Him and for Him."

It also shows the three top levels of government under God: (1) Christ, the Head, (2) His Body, the Church, and (3) the rulers in the spirit realm – thrones, dominions, principalities, and powers. What an eye-opener! We, His people, united together in love, are the means through which Christ, our Head, exercises His administrative dominion over the planet, beginning with authority over these powerful angelic princes. It's absolutely mind-boggling.

If this is not obvious yet, read the following scriptures: Ephesians 1:18–23; 2:6; 4:3–16, which show His Church enthroned with Him "in the heavenly places far above all principality and power and might and dominion . . . . And He put all things under His feet, and gave Him to be head over all things to the church, which is His body, the fullness of Him who fills all in all" (Eph 1:20–23; cf. Mt 19:28; Lk 22:28–30; 2 Tim 2:12; Rv 2:26–27; 3:21).

In fact, Ephesians blends God's sovereign purpose in everything (1:3–14) with the authority He gives us as His Body in unity, ministering to one another (2:14–22; 3:4–12; 4:1–16), as His betrothed or married Bride (5:21–32), who exercise our authority and dominion through spiritual warfare, clothed with "the whole armor of God," which is actually the knowledge of

Christ, accomplished through faith and prayer for one another, as Job did (6:10–20; Col 1:9–11; 2 Pet 1:3).

This is God's governmental protocol, a picture of His authority through us! Especially when we take these powerful truths from Ephesians, confirmed again in Colossians 1–3, and place them in Romans 8, the chapter on our "walk according to the Spirit," which should be our *normal* daily walk.

Wicked rulers God uses for His purpose

The Bible, from Genesis to Revelation, especially Revelation, is filled with the incredible power God grants wicked rulers, for only one purpose: to break our hardness and drive us to obedience! (Mt 21:44) And when they've served their purpose He'll deal with them with incredible vengeance, described in graphic detail in many places in scripture (Is 13; Jer 50; Rv 17–18, etc.).

When He finished using Egypt's Pharaoh who hardened his heart against God and Moses, God drowned his entire army in the Red Sea (Ex 14:28). The whole event, from Israel's crossing on its dry bed to the loss of the Egyptian army in it made God and Israel famous even among other nations (Josh 2:10; 1 Sam 6:6). Read Romans 11:32–36!

"For the Scriptures say that God told Pharaoh, 'I have appointed you for the very purpose of displaying My power in you and to spread My fame throughout the earth'" (Rom 9:17 NLT).

It's shocking to see how He literally commands and empowers God's enemies to do their dastardly work, both to chastise His people, and to produce His spiritual giants who rise up and take dominion over the enemy when they've "had enough!" This is precisely how every man or woman of God in the Bible got that way – in the heat of affliction! (2 Cor 4:7–18)

Phrases like, "I will set My face against you, and you shall be defeated by your enemies. Those who hate you shall reign over you " (Lev 26:17); "He delivered them into the hands of plunderers who despoiled them" (Jdg 2:14); "the LORD strengthened Eglon king of Moab against Israel" (Jdg 3:12); "so the LORD sold them into the hand of Jabin king of Canaan" (Jdg 4:2); "now the LORD raised up an adversary against Solomon, Hadad the Edomite" (1Kgs 11:14); "the LORD has put a lying spirit in the mouth of all these prophets of yours, and the LORD has declared disaster against you" (1 Kgs 22:23); "moreover the LORD stirred up against Jehoram the spirit of the Philistines and the Arabians" (2 Chr 21:16); "the LORD brought upon them the captains of the army of the king of Assyria, who took Manasseh with hooks, bound him with bronze fetters, and carried him off to Babylon" (2 Chr 33:11).

I've never heard the following verse used except in a positive way when God's people work together in unity. But the verse actually speaks of God using Israel's *enemies* against them when they walk in disobedience: "How could one chase a thousand, and two put ten thousand to flight, unless their Rock had sold them, and the LORD had surrendered them?" (Dt 32:30). The once popular praise song, "Blow the trumpet in Zion," describes how the army of the Lord "carries out His Word." But the long passage in Joel actually describes God giving our *enemies*, prefigured by an army of locusts, supernatural power to destroy us unless we repent! "'Now, therefore,' says the LORD, 'Turn to Me with all your heart, with fasting, with weeping, and with mourning" (Joel 2).

The prophet Amos describes how God pleaded with backslidden Israel in five stages of destruction: (1) famine, hunger; (2) drought; (3) destruction of agriculture by blight, mildew, locusts; (4) plagues, war, death; (5) Sodom and Gomorrah-type destruction. And yet this was only the prelude to what was to come, since they still had not repented: "Therefore, I will bring upon you all the disasters I have announced. Prepare to meet your God in judgment, you people of Israel!" (Amos 4:6–11; 4:12 NLT)

"So He turned Himself against them as an enemy, and He fought against them." He used the most wicked world emperors to chasten His people: "Woe to Assyria, the rod of My anger and the staff in whose hand is My indignation," whom He used to completely destroy Israel, north of Judah in 722 BC (Isa 10:5). Then He repeatedly called King Nebuchadnezzar "My servant" as His means of destroying Judah and the surrounding nations. "I am raising up the Babylonians, a cruel and violent people" (Is 63:10b; Jer 25:9; 27:6; 28:14; 43:10; Hab 1:6a).

"So the LORD brought the king of Babylon against them. The Babylonians killed Judah's young men, even chasing after them into the Temple. They had no pity on the people, killing both young men and young women, the old and the infirm.

God handed all of them over to Nebuchadnezzar. . . . Then his army burned the Temple of God, tore down the walls of Jerusalem, burned all the palaces, and completely destroyed everything of value. The few who survived were taken as exiles to Babylon [605, 598, 586 BC], and they became servants to the king and his sons until the kingdom of Persia came to power (2 Chr 26:17–20 NLT; cf. 2 Kgs 25; Jer 39).

The false prophet Hananiah, who had earlier taught the people not to submit to Nebuchadnezzar against Jeremiah's warnings, died the same year according to Jeremiah's prophecy against him, because he had "taught rebellion against the LORD" (Jer 28:17–18). Judah's King Zedekiah also had ignored those warnings and even put Jeremiah in prison. So Nebuchadnezzar "made Zedekiah watch as they slaughtered his sons and all the nobles of Judah. Then they gouged out Zedekiah's eyes, bound him in bronze chains, and led him away to Babylon" (Jer 39:6–7).

Ruling wisely under the authority of another

Now Let's look at a few godly leaders whose response to God under wicked leadership has become a role model for us. First was Joseph. He was betrayed by his brothers and sold into Egyptian slavery; then he ended up with a life-sentence in a dungeon because of his obedience to God, having overcome a serious moral temptation. But God used it as testing and training for his future role as governor of Egypt under the pagan Pharaoh, whom he served faithfully. And for an even higher purpose: to chasten and transform his irresponsible brothers from their *envy* to their "assigned authority" as the leaders of the 12 tribes of Israel (Gen 37–45).

About 1200 years later Daniel was brought to Babylon among the captives from Judah by wicked Nebuchadnezzar. God used the trials and testing of Abraham, Isaac, Jacob, Joseph, Judah, Joshua, and Moses to lay the foundation for our faith. And He used Daniel and the prophets to show us our future and how to face it victoriously (Is 60:1–2; 1 Jn 5:4).

Nebuchadnezzar, noticing Daniel's wisdom, put him in authority under himself as the Pharaoh had done with Joseph. Daniel by that wisdom knew when to submit to the king's authority and when to graciously, with a humble attitude, draw the line and submit only to God, though it might cost him his life. So God used him and his three famous friends (famous because God delivered them from a blazing furnace meant to destroy them for refusing to bow to the king's golden idol) to ultimately bring this wicked despot to a shocking and humiliating repentance. And because Daniel was faithful to God and to his king, God showed *Nebuchadnezzar* the world's political future for the next 2500 years and used Daniel to interpret it for him, and for us (Dan 1–4).

But that was only the beginning. When the Persians conquered Babylon, the new (pagan) King Darius put Daniel in authority under him as Nebuchadnezzar had done. But again, when Daniel chose to obey God contrary to the new law devised by *envious* nobles, he was thrown into a den of lions, where God miraculously protected him, to the astonishment and joy of Darius, who'd hoped his God would do this. So the king had those leaders thrown to the lions, who devoured them even before they hit the ground (Dan 6).

But the best was still ahead, for Daniel and for us. To continue to walk in wisdom required that Daniel remain intimate with God to know His presence, His purpose, and His voice. And in the process he ended up interceding (praying) for his own disobedient people (the Jews of Judah still living in exile), and while he prayed the "heavens" opened up and he saw what was going on in the spirit realm: the angelic powers of darkness holding dominion over world empires, which currently was Persia, and Greece would follow (Dan 9–10).

His intercession (prayer) would open the door for the restoration of his people (Ezra 1:1ff; Dan 9:2ff), and God would reveal to Daniel in more detail the political events down to the "end times," as well as the keys to navigating through it in triumph over the enemy, until even death is destroyed and the saints "possess the kingdom forever, even forever and ever." "Those who are wise shall shine like the brightness of the firmament, and those who turn many to righteousness like the stars forever and ever" (Dan 7–12; 7:18; 12:3; 1 Cor 15:25–26; Heb 11:5–6).

Esther

The last of the godly saints who reigned with an ungodly, pagan emperor was Queen Esther. I call it an example of how the weakest person, Esther, brought down the strongest – not her King, Ahasuerus (Xerxes), but one who personified evil and Satan himself, Haman the Agagite, who secretly aspired to the Persian throne through *envy.* His treacherous aspiration was revealed when Ahasuerus wanted to honor Mordecai the Jew for saving his life from assassins. Haman, thinking he himself would be honored, suggested that a high ranking noble lead the person to be honored on one of the king's horses, dressed in royal apparel with a royal diadem or crown on his head (Est 6).

But it turned against him because he had just come to the king to suggest Mordecai be hanged on the gallows he'd just built for the purpose. Furthermore, Haman had tricked the king into a permanently binding agreement to destroy every Jew in the Persian Empire. Haman is not only a picture of the final Antichrist, but being an Amalekite, the story of Esther, the last historical book in the Old Testament, is also the account of the final destruction of Amalek in the person of Haman and his ten sons. For the Amalekites are the enemy God has singled out to be "utterly destroyed," though it will take continuous warfare for generations until it is done (Num 24:20; Dt 25:17–19; 1 Sam 15:2-3).

It is so important, I need to write a book titled, *Conquering Amalek: the Terrorist in Me.* For the Jews see Amalek in historical figures like Hitler in his attempt to destroy their race, and culminating in modern terrorists determined to destroy Israel. But my point is that God permits these arch-enemies because He's really dealing with our own disobedience since the fall. And seeing how Esther won this history-changing battle through her humble submission is a clue to our own spiritual warfare, as well as a serious warning to those who take Haman's approach of hatred toward authority, rooted in *envy.*

There are two clues to indicate Esther's secret. First, her preparation. While all the women chose what they thought would please the king when it was their turn to appear before him to see whom he would select as his queen, Esther alone left that choice up to Hegai, the king's eunuch in charge of the women. It's an example of trusting God's wisdom in our preparation, rather than complaining or manipulating things for our benefit (Est 2:12–17).

The second is her decision to lay down her life for her people, the Jews, when she took the life or death risk of appearing before the king uninvited. "If I perish, I perish" (Est

4:16), matching the heart of the "overcomers" in Revelation 12:11, "They did not love their lives to the death." You will have to read the ten chapters of Esther to see the details of this "Alfred Hitchcock" thriller.

The present kingdom of His Presence

The New Testament introduced an entirely new order of dominion with many godly men and women "ruling" among the earthly administrators of the mighty Roman Empire, though these demigods had no idea they were being "used," even as God had used the former emperors. While the apostle Paul sat in a Roman dungeon not far from Nero, an emperor famous only for his utter perversity and sadistic wickedness and who later beheaded him and crucified Peter, he, Paul, waged a war with only pen and parchment that would ultimately bring down the Empire and all others after it. It was the Stone of Nebuchadnezzar's dream that Paul would elucidate (clarify), a Kingdom so powerful that anything that stood in its way would and will be obliterated to dust (Dan 2:44–45).

The only problem, which explains why Paul waged his mightiest battles from a prison cell, is that the Stone does not discriminate between friend or enemy: only truth and love survive its onslaught. Which also explains why Paul never wrote a word of condemnation or complaint against his Roman captors, but won many over to this Kingdom hidden among them.[3] Because he knew even a wrong attitude cannot stand in its Presence, and prison has a way of bringing either the worst or the best out of us, as it did with the great apostle (1 Cor 4:9–15; 2 Cor 4:7–18; 6:4–10; 11:23–33; 12:7–12; Phil 1:13; 4:22).

Revelation, the book which details the terrifying termination of this planet's self-rule, "reveals" that Jesus Himself is that empire-smashing Stone of Daniel 2:34. It is obvious, not only through His being qualified to open the seals of judgment in chapter five, but through the words *gives* and *grants* (same word in Greek) used 15 times throughout the book by which He permits these evil powers of destruction the timed and limited means to do their work for His ultimate purpose: first to refine those needing it and willing to endure, and finally to bring retribution on those stubbornly refusing to repent, including the Antichrist, the Beast and False Prophet (Rv 9:20; 16:11; 18:11; 19:20; 20:10).

But it's literally "the prayers of all the saints" – *the spiritual warfare of Ephesians 6:12* – which, as with Daniel, give Him the legal basis to begin the process of reclaiming the dominion we lost through our "fall." Because prayer is far more than mere words. It is fellowship with the King of Kings as we learn to know Him intimately, along with His purposes and ways. And also to know His heart and desire for those under "the limits of our authority" He has assigned us to help, encourage, and intercede for. Because this is the beginning of our co-regency with Him, to continue in the ages to come (Rv 8:3–6; Jn 14:17; Phil 2:10; 1 Jn 5:20; Ps 103:7; Prv 24:11–12; 31:8–9).

So the choice is yours. You can join those who hate our political leaders because of their obvious and serious flaws, and in so doing, join the ranks of the angels whose rebellion sucked them into a black hole. Or you can do it God's way, fight the battle where the real action is taking place in the spirit realm, where humility and faith are like nuclear warfare released through prayer and love, especially for your enemies. Because some, like Saul-turned-Paul, may become spiritual giants who will end up praying for and teaching us! Which is already happening, even among former terrorists[4]

"For though we walk in the flesh, we are not waging war according to the flesh. For the weapons of our warfare are not of the flesh but have divine power to destroy strongholds. We destroy arguments and every lofty opinion raised against the knowledge of God, and take every thought captive to obey Christ, being ready to punish every disobedience, when your obedience is complete" (2 Cor 10:3–6 *English Standard Version*).

1. Strongs #G5020; also in Greek mythology, the lowest part of hell. See Tartarus in Wikipedia.

2. "Hitler and the Occult," Wikipedia

3. Josephus relates that "the empress Poppaea was favourably inclined to Christianity, that she was a worshipper of the true God," and that "Paul had converted many in Caesar's family . . . and turned the house of Christ's persecutor [Nero] into a church." https://biblehub.com/niv/philippians/4-22.htm

4. Do a Web search on "former terrorists converted to Christ."

Made in the USA
Columbia, SC
04 February 2021

32381095R00134